1001 Model Railway Questions and Answers

Patrick Stephens Limited, an imprint of Haynes Publishing, has published authoritative, quality books for enthusiasts for more than 25 years. During that time the company has established a reputation as one of the world's leading publishers of books on aviation, maritime, military, model-making, motor cycling, motoring, motor racing, railway and railway modelling subjects. Readers or authors with suggestions for books they woud like to see published are invited to write to: The Editorial Director, Patrick Stephens Limited, Sparkford, Nr Yeovil, Somerset, BA22 7JJ.

1001 Model Railway Questions and Answers

C.J. Freezer

Patrick Stephens Limited

First published in 1992
Reprinted 1994 and 1995

British Library Cataloguing in
Publication Data

A catalogue record for this book is
available from the British Library

Library of Congress catalog card
number 92-72550

Patrick Stephens Limited is an imprint of
Haynes Publishing
Sparkford, Nr Yeovil, Somerset,
BA22 7JJ.

Typeset by G&M Raunds, Northamptonshire.
Printed and bound by
Butler & Tanner Ltd, Frome and London.

10 9 8 7 6 5 4 3

CONTENTS

INTRODUCTION

When my publishers suggested this book, I had few doubts that I could find the necessary number of questions, since over the years I have had to answer considerably more than a mere thousand questions, though in many cases they were repetitive. Some technical matters turned up so often that my secretary knew the answers herself – and she didn't have any interest in the hobby! So, once we had agreed on the size of the book, it was just a matter of sitting down in front of the word-processor, sifting through old issues, searching my memory and typing in the questions. As I suspected, as soon as I had dealt with one obvious question, two or three supplemental queries sprang to mind.

I have deliberately avoided two major fields. First of all, I have eliminated all but a few product-related queries; these tend to date rapidly and within a few years are meaningless. One of those questions my first secretary knew by heart dealt with the conversion of Hornby Dublo locomotives and stock to two-rail; today, those who still have three-rail Hornby Dublo equipment cherish it. Second, I have not attempted to cover prototype detail, for vital as much of this is, I hardly felt that information on the finer points of Swindon, Derby, Crewe, Doncaster or Ashford practice is really dealing with model railways as most people see them. If you want lists of engine numbers and names, there are plenty of reference books on the market.

The book is broken into main sections with smaller groups of questions under each main heading; this should help locate your area of interest more rapidly. At times I have had to make an arbitrary decision, since some queries tend to overlap into many fields.

I have used metric measurements throughout, occasionally appending an imperial equivalent. I have also maintained the apparently illogical mixture on metric and imperial standards for scales that are ingrained in our hobby. I merely advise metric dimensions for current work; the initial proposals to metricate the hobby were made in the year I was born, 1924, metric standards for scale and gauge were generally adopted by 1930, and it's high time we finished the job.

Although I have tried to impart a good deal of practical know-how, this is not a 'how to do it' book as such; more I have tried to point a reader in what I see as the right direction. Accordingly, there is a short Bibliography appended where you will find the titles and publishers of some recent books I consider you will find of use. I make no apologies for including many of my own titles, since it has long been my practice to write books that answer the questions I have been asked time and time again.

C.J.Freezer
Hemel Hempstead
1992

PART 1
MAKING A START

The first dozen queries are intended as a little light-hearted relief before we get down to the serious business of dealing with real problems. I can assure you that every one of these questions has been put to me in the past, most of them more than once. Wherever you see 'X', simply insert the name of any product, service or individual you think fits the bill.

We then go on to detail with the various problems that need to be looked at, if not actually dealt with, before work begins in earnest on the layout. It is as well to point out that although in theory design comes before construction, many model railways evolve over a period of time. This is possible because, although the entire layout is a single model, it is made up from a large number of individual units, each of which can be a model in its own right. This provides a tremendous amount of flexibility.

Section 1:1
Before we get started . . .

1 How do I build a model railway?
Start building it! It's only child's play when you get down to basics; most of us started with a train set.

2 Will you please explain in full detail exactly how to build 'X'?
This really needs a small booklet and, what is more, such a booklet does exist. Furthermore there are a number of textbooks on the subject which you should borrow or buy. Above all, read the model magazines – you'll find plenty of constructional articles therein.

3 I do not intend to make any mistakes. Will you tell me what to do?
Certainly. Subscribe to all the magazines and buy every book on both the hobby and the prototype that you can find, make yourself comfortable and settle down for a long, satisfying read. This is known as armchair modelling and is extremely popular. You can justify it by claiming to be researching in depth before beginning anything, and you can also break the monotony by pointing out people's mistakes. Providing no one finds out you've never built anything, you can even pose as an expert.

4 I am thinking of building a model railway for my three-year-old son. What advice can you offer?
If it's really for your son, get him a set of push-along wooden trains with wooden track and give him hours of fun creating his own system. When he's older and still interested, buy him a good train set, but let him make his own mistakes. If, on the other hand, you're using him as an excuse to build a railway for yourself, be honest with your wife.

5 I think that 'X''s layout is the finest in the world and want to build one exactly like it. Can you please provide me with full working drawings?
Sorry, there aren't any! The model was built in the usual manner, except that nothing was bodged and no corners were cut to save time, effort or, come to that, necessary expense. In addition, the builder took the trouble to use his eyes and head when studying the prototype and paid meticulous attention to significant detail. Copy these methods, but don't copy the end product. Carbon copies are never quite as good as the original.

6 **How did 'X' make such a marvellous model railway?**
Mainly by hard, persistent work over a number of years. In addition, he had a master plan, an overall scheme which, whilst modified in detail as his experience grew, remained constant throughout construction. He not only studied the prototype carefully, but also selected those features he thought significant. Above all, he took pains to see that every part of the model was not only wholly congruent with the overall scheme, but that the level of craftsmanship and detail remained constant.

7 **Everybody I know agrees with me that 'X' should be done. Why hasn't someone done something about it?**
What have you and your friends done about it? Most significant developments in the hobby began with a small group of like-minded individuals who got together, worked out the details and, by building a convincing model which they then publicised as widely as they could, convinced others that it was a good idea. In a number of cases, one keen enthusiast has single-handedly influenced the development of the hobby by building a better layout and then telling others about it through the pages of the hobby magazines.

8 **Why doesn't someone make a model of 'X'?**
You're someone, aren't you? Why don't you?

9 **I am certain there is an enormous demand for 'X'. Why isn't it on the market?**
If you care to work out the full details of manufacture and then invest the necessary capital in the scheme, you can find out for yourself. Who knows, you might even be right!

10 **I saw 'X' advertised four years ago, but didn't want to buy it at the time. I now need it urgently, but the firm is no longer advertising and letters are returned marked 'Gone away'. What can I do?**
Not a lot, as the firm concerned has gone out of business. Perhaps if you'd bought their products some years ago, they'd still be around. At the very least you'd have the model. All you can do now is to put an advertisement in the Wanted columns of your favourite magazine, offering at least twice the original list price. You may be lucky!

11 **Why is 'X' no longer made? I'm sure it was very popular.**
So was the Morris Minor and the Volkswagen 'Beetle', to mention but two popular, widely available but discontinued products. All good things come to an end sometime, but if they're good enough, enthusiasts cherish them.

12 **Why was 'X' done in the first instance?**
Because it seemed a good idea at the time!

Section 1:2
Starting a model railway

13 **What is the best way to begin in the hobby?**
Find an old train set and start laying it out on a baseboard as realistically as you can. Don't worry too much about the details – aim for the broad effect at this stage. Keep the whole thing as small and simple as possible for a start, but get something running. The biggest mistake you can make at the outset is to spend too much time thinking about the hobby and not enough modelling.

Buy all the model railway magazines you can find in your nearest large newsagents. *Railway Modeller* is probably a must, if only for the advertisements. *Model Railway Journal* deals with the advanced aspects of the hobby – admire the superb photographs of equally impressive models, but take the more forceful statements with a small pinch of salt; much of the magazine is written by men who make model railways rather than operate them. *Modeller's BackTrack* is new but shows promise, while *Your Model Railway* and *Scale Trains* are patchy. For Continental models get *Continental Modeller*; for the US prototype, *Model Railroader*. Read at least some of the books listed in the Bibliography.

14 I really want to build the sort of railway one sees in the magazines and at exhibitions. How should I do this?

Start in a modest way and find out what aspects of the hobby you like best, and those you can do well. For a start you have to find out what sort of railway you want to model.

15 Is there more than one sort of railway I could model?

Even if we confine yourself to the UK, you can choose between steam age or diesel era models. You can select where to set your model – the West Country, the Highlands of Scotland, the Midlands, Wales, the South – anywhere. You can model at any period in history you like, back to the dawn of railways. You can opt for narrow gauge, or even copy one of the specialised lines – a pier railway could be quite interesting. Then there are overseas railways, offering even more choice. And that's just the start – we've not looked at scale and gauge.

16 I am bewildered by all those scale and gauge letters. What do they mean?

At this time, a headache! It's best initially not to bother about scale, and concentrate instead on gauge. This is the distance between the rails, and is denoted by a simple code. The newcomer need only look at three alternatives – OO, HO and N – since these are the ones found in the majority of model shops and High Street dealers. The others are either obsolescent or for advanced modellers and only confuse the issue. The important thing in the initial stages is to use models that are readily available in your own locality. This does restrict the initial choice, but that is not necessarily a bad thing.

17 I want to avoid making a costly mistake. Surely I should plan carefully before I make a start?

The only way that you can make a *costly* mistake is by buying a lot of equipment before you have any experience. If you start in a simple way with a small layout, you gain invaluable experience with the minimum possible outlay. Although this sounds haphazard, if you're only using the absolute minimum of equipment, and following a published plan, you can't go far wrong. You should always remember that the only man who never made a mistake, never made anything.

18 What is the minimum equipment needed?

A baseboard, enough track and points to make a simple layout, a power unit/controller, one general-purpose locomotive, a couple of coaches and a selection of wagons are enough at the outset. Later on you will need a station building and platform, and a signal box and goods shed, but these can be produced from kits or even scratchbuilt when the track is laid and in good working order. Scenery will follow later, if you find you want it – many people don't bother.

19 What do you mean by a general-purpose locomotive?

Something that is equally at home at the head of a passenger or goods train or shunting in a yard, since it is the only motive power you have. You do not need to be too fussy – almost any diesel outline locomotive will meet this requirement and, so far as steam outline models are concerned, a tank locomotive is preferable to a tender locomotive.

20 I rather fancy a large named express locomotive. Couldn't I start with this?

If that's your pleasure you can, but it does look a little out of place pulling four open wagons and a goods brake!

21 I am interested in modern traction. Should I begin with an HST?

The trouble with HSTs and, for that matter, diesel railcars is that they are integral units. You can only drive them back and forth, or simply round in circles – you can't shunt with them and you can't reform the train. Half the fun of operating a model railway is lost if this is your only form of motive power.

22 Must I restrict myself to one locomotive?

You can have as many as you can afford, but the more you put on the track, the more problems you have with control. At the outset it's a lot easier to keep the wiring as simple as possible – elaboration can follow when you've a better idea of what you want.

23 Which is the best gauge for a beginner?

If there is an existing train set in the home, this is the best start. Otherwise check what is readily available in your immediate locality, or close to your place of work, and settle for this.

24 Why do you stress availability? Surely I can get anything I need by mail order?

It is a sad fact that the further you are from your point of supply, the more problems you come up against. Using a handy retailer makes it a lot easier to get what you need when you want it, and with mail order there will inevitably be delays. Furthermore, when you buy over the counter you can easily exercise your statutory right to inspect the goods before parting with your money.

25 What is the difference between OO and HO? They look alike to me.

In actual practice the technical difference is the nominal scale of the models, 4 m or 1:76 for OO, 3.5 mm or 1:87 for HO. A more significant difference is that all commercial OO models are based on British prototypes, and that the rest of the world works in HO.

26 Can I run HO and OO gauge models on the same layout?

Certainly – both run on 16.5 mm gauge track and, with the exception of Marklin products, use 12 V dc two-rail current supply. It does, however, look better if you ensure that each train is made up from either OO or HO stock. This also helps sort out the coupling problem. Whilst some individuals sneer at the idea of mixing scales and prototypes in this manner, it is a matter of personal choice. A layout on which one can see examples of famous named trains in action, regardless of their country of origin, has a very definite purpose in the scheme of things.

27 What is meant by OO/HO scale?

This is anybody's guess. Usually it means that the manufacturer wishes to indicate that the product can be used on either OO or HO gauge layouts, but it can also mean that the model is to a somewhat nondescript scale. When applied to British kits and other items it generally implies that the nominal scale is 4 mm to the foot; if the product is imported it could meant that it is 3.5 mm scale.

28 Can I use products of different manufacturers on the same layout?

Clearly, all scenic parts and accessories are interchangeable, since we are not concerned with track or wheels. In general all OO or HO gauge models work together, the exception being Marklin products which use a non-standard system of electrification. All ready-to-run N gauge products conform to a common standard.

However, at the very outset it is best to use the products of one manufacturer for the locomotives and rolling-stock and to use one manufacturer's track, for there are small differences of interpretation which, to the inexperienced worker, could possibly create minor difficulties. Once the layout is established and in working order, you can spread your net wider.

29 How much will it cost? Some of the layouts I have read about seem to have cost four-figure sums for the locomotives and coaches alone.

The quick and easy answer is that a model railway costs as much as you can afford – at the time. Most model railways are built up over a period of years, with the various models being bought as and when the builder is in funds. In practice, most railway modellers find the main lack is time to put the models together.

30 There appear to be a lot of options. How can I decide what is best for me?

A good approach is to spend some time looking at model railways, in books, magazines and, best of all, at exhibitions, whilst making your initial steps with a small, low-cost trial layout built on a couple of relatively small baseboards which can either be stored in a large cupboard or left erected in a spare corner of the home. At the end of this process you will have a better idea of what you like and, more important still, what you can actually achieve.

31 Why do manufacturers persist in producing models to outdated standards? It has long been established that EM gauge is perfectly practical – why then are 4 mm scale models still made to run on underscale track? Alternatively, why doesn't someone produce British models to 3.5 mm scale?
Manufacturers, quite properly, attempt to keep faith with their customers and so produce new products that are compatible with their previous models. It is not for them to insist that every user should change standards which are quite acceptable to the majority. At the present time a ready-to-run EM gauge model would, in fact, be virtually unsaleable; it is unlikely that above a dozen retailers would order any since the majority of their customers couldn't use it. This doesn't mean that this cannot happen, but until there is a ready-assembled EM gauge track there will not be a big enough base to support EM ready-to-run models.

There have been no fewer than four attempts to introduce HO gauge British outline models, by Marklin, Palitoy (Jouef), Lima and Fleischmann. Each one failed to gain any real support. Lima switched to 4 mm scale and is now a major force in the British market.

32 I have seen frequent references to 'modeller's licence'. Surely the hobby isn't that regulated?
Far from being a form of regulation, 'modeller's licence' is often taken as an invitation for a free-for-all. Its proper implication is that since, in order to compress a prototype measuring hundreds of kilometres into a small space, certain compromises must be made with strict scale dimensions and prototype practices. However, these variations should be kept as small and inconspicuous as possible. Probably the best rule is the old drawing-office saw: 'If it looks right, it is right!'

Section 1:3
Where will it go?

33 I live in a three-bedroom semi-detached house, with no spare room for the railway. What should I do?
Look about you, for there are several possibilities that have been tried and tested. If the loft is usable, it offers ample room for the layout. The garage is another possibility. Failing this, you can consider a portable layout, or fit a small wall-hugging system into a living room or bedroom. There is also the possibility of building an extension or moving into the garden.

34 How can I best make use of the loft?
First, provide access, ideally a loft ladder; failing that, get a good extension ladder. Next, board the central area with 18 mm chipboard, but remember that there is less reason to board under the layout except to increase storage space. Line the underside of the roof, with additional insulation for greater comfort all round (see Plate 1).

Unless you are well versed in electrical matters, it is best to provide light and power to the loft by means of a long cable that plugs into a socket on the landing. This has the undeniable advantage that you cannot forget to disconnect power to the layout. In general, the only circuits readily available inside the loft are the low-powered lighting leads, and in all probability an experienced electrician, used to the tricky business of running additional power circuits around a house, will be needed if you want a permanent installation.

35 What about loft ventilation? Should I have a dormer window put in?
This is a possibility, but modifications to a roof are not really a DIY job and a contractor should be employed. Whilst this would be necessary should you wish to install a regular room in the loft, for a model railway a cheaper alternative is to seal off the space between two rafters with hardboard and install an extractor fan at the top (see Plate 1). This will blow air out through the eaves and promote good circulation of fresh air from the loft trap.

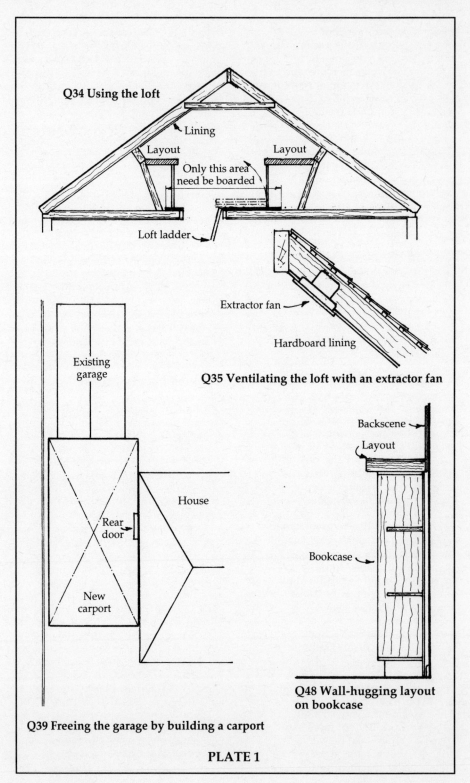

Q34 Using the loft

Lining

Layout   Layout

Only this area
need be boarded

Loft ladder

Extractor fan

Hardboard lining

Q35 Ventilating the loft with an extractor fan

Existing
garage

House

Rear
door

New
carport

Backscene

Layout

Bookcase

**Q48 Wall-hugging layout
on bookcase**

Q39 Freeing the garage by building a carport

PLATE 1

36 **Would you recommend a professional loft conversion?**
If funds permit, this is a sound scheme, but make sure you employ a reputable firm, preferably a member of a recognised Trade Association. If this course if followed, it is a good idea to have a habitable room built into the roof.

37 **I have a modern house with prefabricated roof principals. These obstruct the layout space, so can you advise me what I must do to be able to remove them?**
Unless you want to bring the roof down, do not make any alterations yourself. Professional loft conversion firms of repute are the only people who could make the alterations and it will not be a cheap job since they will have to rebuild the roof internally. It is best to accept the limitations and design the layout around the obstructions.

38 **If I use the garage, must the car stand outside?**
There are two options available to get the car inside the garage with a permanent system – a layout across the rear of the garage, lifted high enough to clear the bonnet of the car, or a narrow wall-hugging scheme leaving space to drive in. It will be necessary to allow room on the driver's side for the door to open. Both options could of course be combined in one layout. A lot depends on the internal size of the garage.

39 **I would like to use the whole of the garage, but don't like leaving the car outside. Have you any suggestions?**
If space is available, consider the possibility of a carport (see Plate 1) or, better still, a second garage. As an alternative, consider a portable layout which could be stored across the rear of the garage and erected inside for a running session, leaving the car outside overnight if need be.

40 **Is a garden shed suitable for a model railway?**
If we exclude the very smallest patterns, which are really no more than toolstores, a garden shed is a very good solution, but budget for at least twice the initial cost of the shed for the necessary

fitting out. However, check that you can erect a shed – covenants or local regulations may prevent this. It is also advisable to check the current general regulations concerning the location of a timber shed – generally it must be at least 2 m from the house and 1 m from the boundaries.

41 **What sort of fitting out is required for a garden shed?**
The basic essential is a supply of mains electricity and an all-weather path to the shed. Internal lining and insulation, whilst not absolutely essential, are desirable, whilst draught-proofing the door and fitting secondary double glazing to the window(s) is a good idea.

42 **Is it acceptable to run an extension lead from a socket in the house to provide a supply of mains electricity to a garden shed?**
The Institution of Electrical Engineers (IEE) regulations lay down very strict rules for a mains electricity supply to an outbuilding, and these do not permit a permanent connection by means of a length of flexible cable. Furthermore, a temporary lead to any equipment in the garden should be fed though a residual current device (RCD) – a quick-acting safety socket. The provision of a proper electricity supply to an outbuilding is a fairly expensive matter.

43 **Is planning permission needed for a small home extension?**
One small extension may be made to a dwelling without formal planning permission, but what constitutes small is laid down by regulations. It is sound policy to consult the Borough Surveyor's office before going beyond the preliminary planning stage, since local byelaws can affect your scheme. It is also good policy to let your neighbours know what you have in mind. Above all, check your deeds, as there may be restrictive covenants. Town planning is not exactly a minefield, more a murky area full of pitfalls. Get expert local advice.

44 **Are there any specific difficulties with home extensions for a model railway?**
Assuming the necessary finance is avail-

able, the first problem is that you need to have proper plans and a detailed specification prepared for quotations. You then have to find a reliable contractor. Certainly insist on a member of a recognised Trade Association, even if this means ignoring the lowest quotes. There will be a certain amount of upheaval, so if possible have the completion time included in the contract; it would be a good idea to have your solicitor check this important feature. Finally, don't over-extend your budget with heavy repayments – remember that you have also to pay for the model railway to go in the extension!

45 Is it possible to get a packaged home extension for a model railway?

The current trend in home extensions is almost wholly directed towards conservatories. These are basically sound as an extra room for entertainment during the warmer months, and as a general store for useful household goods for which there is no other home. They are also excellent places in which to cultivate houseplants. However, the amount of glass makes them less suitable for a model railway, since most plastics wilt when exposed to direct sunlight through glass, and there is a lot of plastic in most modern model railways.

46 Will a home extension add to the value of the house?

Despite the claims of salesmen, this is improbable unless you can add an extra bedroom to the dwelling and use this as the railway room. It is best to regard the cost of an extension solely as a way of increasing your enjoyment of your home.

47 What are the possibilities for a model railway in a small flat?

The two main options are a portable layout, that is stored away for most of the time, and a wall-hugging scheme in a living room or bedroom. Portable layouts are discussed in detail in another section.

48 What is a wall-hugging scheme?

This is a relatively narrow layout placed against the wall, often supported on bookcases or low cupboards (see Plate 1).

It can be combined with portable sections to increase the size of the model. Because it is in a living area, some form of cover should be provided for protection. In any case the model should be attractive to look at, and tidiness is not so much a virtue as a necessity.

49 I can have the use of a storeroom measuring 2 m by 1.25 m internally. What is best – to use this to store sections of a portable layout, or build a very compact permanent model railway?

Even in OO/HO there is space for a reasonable branch line layout; in N gauge or narrow gauge there is even greater scope. On the other hand, you could comfortably store a much larger portable scheme and leave space for a workshop – it would be just possible to fit in a compact permanent line with storage space for a modest portable layout beneath.

50 We have what is technically a spare bedroom, but the room is not needed for this and is currently used to store various items we don't actually need but do not wish to dispose of. Could you suggest how I can persuade my wife that it would be better used for the railway?

Begin by pointing out that most, if not all, of the stored equipment can be comfortably housed under the baseboards and that with everything neatly arranged it will be a lot easier to find the spare kettle or whatever should the need arise. If this fails, accept the inevitable and start work on a portable layout which could be stored in a bedroom, but make sure it will fit easily into it when erected. If you happen, by chance, to leave a section erected over a weekend, it is quite likely that you will be told to take it up to the spare room and never bring it down again.

Any layout in a bedroom should be on sectional baseboards so that the room can be converted back should the need arise.

Section 1:4
Scale and gauge

51 Could you explain what those letters OO, HO, etc, mean?

They refer to the gauge of the model, and hence by implication the scale, which in turn determines the size of the model. In practice, they are a convenient way of indicating the locomotives, coaches, wagons and track that are intended to work together.

52 What is meant by gauge and scale?

The gauge is the distance between the top of the rails. The scale is the proportion between the model and the prototype – the full-sized item on which the model is based. Scale can be expressed as a unit measurement on the model representing a unit – generally a foot – on the prototype, or as the ratio between the sizes. Thus OO gauge is 4 mm scale, or 1:76 scale.

53 What gauges are used in the hobby?

At the start, before 1914, there were five gauges:

0 gauge	1¼ in
1 gauge	1¾ in
2 gauge	2 in
3 gauge	2½ in
4 gauge	3½ in

They had their origins in the late 19th century in the Nuremberg toy factories and initially the models were proportioned by eye to fit on to standard mechanisms, chassis, etc, rather then built to any fixed scale. 3 and 4 gauge were rather uncommon, but became very popular with model engineers constructing live steam locomotive models. 2 gauge did not survive.

In the 1920s the two remaining gauges were redefined in metric standards:

O gauge	32 mm (7 mm scale)
1 gauge	45 mm (10 mm scale)

At the same time O gauge was roughly halved to provide a table-top system. This was indiscriminately called OO or HO (half-O) and settled down with a gauge of 16.5 mm. The correct scale is 3.5

mm but to fit the models round the early commercial mechanisms, 4 mm scale was adopted. After a while the confusion between OO and HO was resolved, with the former at 4 mm scale and the latter at 3.5 mm scale.

Two gauges were developed in the USA:

TT gauge	12 mm (2.5 mm scale)
S gauge	⅞ in (³/16 in scale)

In Britain TT was built to 3mm scale.

Experiments with 9.5 mm gauge, 2 mm scale, took place in England in the 1930s, but when a half-HO system appeared it had a gauge of 9 mm and was designated N. The scale is 1:160, except for British outline models where 1:148 scale is preferred. Marklin have produced Z gauge 6.5 mm gauge, 1:200 scale.

In Britain EM gauge, 18.2 mm, and P4 gauge, 18.83 mm, are used with 4 mm scale models by experienced modellers.

54 It all seems very complicated. Couldn't a simple system be used?

It isn't really complicated, just a little strange. Providing that we consider the gauge letters as a reasonable indication of the size of the models and their compatibility – the original purpose of the system – then we have no problems. Alternative suggestions have only proved to be more confusing. However, where precision is needed the practice of quoting both the scale and gauge (ie 4 mm scale, 16.5 mm gauge) has arisen, and this is to be recommended.

55 Why are so many odd dimensions used? For example, why is HO 3.5 mm scale and 16.5 mm gauge? Couldn't we use round figures?

The trouble really began when George Stephenson standardised the Northumberland waggonway gauge of 4²/3 ft (4 ft 8 in) to which a further half-inch was added more or less by accident. The gauge itself is therefore irrational and any measurements derived from this cannot be other than odd.

56 You say the Nuremberg toymakers worked to inch measurements. Surely they would have used metric standards?

Although Germany adopted the metric

system in the early part of the 19th century, the inch remained in popular use alongside the centimetre. The gauges are rational when quoted in imperial standards; this would not have happened had a centimetric base been used. It is as well to point out that the millimetre did not gain widespread use until well into the 20th century.

57 Why do OO and HO have the same gauge but different scales?

Again, George Stephenson is the culprit. British railways have a very small loading gauge for a standard gauge railway – most metre gauge and 3 ft 6 in gauge systems are larger. As a result a 4 mm scale model of a British locomotive or coach is about the same size as a 3.5 mm scale model of its European counterpart and appreciably smaller than a US locomotive or coach. In the early days of 16.5 mm gauge it was very difficult to fit a 3.5 mm scale body over the smallest commercial mechanisms that could be made at the time. In the 1930s only in the USA were commercial models produced to a true scale/gauge ratio. It is important here to distinguish between what a skilled modelmaker could do in a well-equipped workshop with no restrictions on the time spent in construction, and what was commercially viable for a mass-produced model that had to be sold at a reasonable price.

Whilst Continental European models are now made to 1:87 scale, 1:80 was extensively used, and in pre-war days Marklin worked to 1:76 scale (4 mm to 1 foot).

58 Which is more important, scale or gauge?

As George Stephenson emphasised, it is vital to have all tracks to the same gauge, within fairly close limits, otherwise the locomotives and rolling-stock cannot run smoothly. Remember that an out-of-scale model will work perfectly well, but if it is out of gauge it will not run. As a result, models to 3.5 mm, 4 mm and even 7 mm scale can run together on a layout laid with 16.5 mm gauge track.

59 What is the importance of scale?

Scale is of vital importance when one is scratchbuilding an accurate model, but anyone working entirely with ready-to-

run models and kits does not need to be deeply involved with this concept. The main use here is to ensure that kits are the right size, since the best of these are described by their nominal scale.

However, the importance of scale can easily be over-rated. Models are judged visually – the old drawing-office rule of thumb, 'If it looks right, it is right', is an important consideration. It is notoriously difficult to estimate dimensions by eye and therefore small differences in scale are visually acceptable. Many 2 mm scale workers are perfectly happy to use N gauge wagons, even though these are made to a scale of $2^1/_{16}$ mm to the foot.

60 Surely it is better to have a model railway that is completely to scale?

It would be were it feasible. However, the fact that the prototype railway is measured in miles or kilometres does make it rather difficult to model even a short section of railway *exactly* to scale. Even in Z gauge the majority of prototype stations would be too large to fit into a normal home. This does not of course prevent one from having scale models or locomotives, coaches and wagons on the layout.

61 Many stations are comparatively small. Isn't it possible to model one of these?

Small stations are small because they have little traffic and so, when modelled, are rather dull to operate. If you have any doubts about this, make a true scale model of St Ives, Cornwall, as it is today. It won't take a lot of time and it will provide an excellent excuse to spend a week in a delightful part of the world measuring and photographing the prototype. It will make a fine exhibition eye-stopper, particularly with automatic control of the railcars, but when you've finished building the model there will be very little more you can do with it.

62 What is meant by finescale and what has it to do with scale?

Finescale has nothing to do directly with scale, which remains, nominally, the same. It involves a deliberate choice of better-quality products, coupled with a narrower wheel profile and shallower tread. It should be coupled with a reasonably accurate scale/gauge ratio, but as many workers speak of OO finescale, this is open to question. The object is to improve the visual appearance of the complete model, but in many respects it is an attitude of mind on the part of the builder – a refusal to accept compromise, an insistence on the highest possible standards of detail and finish.

63 What is the scale/gauge ratio?

It is the relationship of the model gauge to the nominal scale. 100% is spot on, HO is 99.9% correct, OO gauge track is 87% of the correct size.

64 What is meant by nominal scale?

The nominal scale is the one specified by the builder. Being human, errors occur; furthermore, the use of commercial parts, or the need to fit the model into a given space, often involves some compromise. Using the adjective 'nominal' prevents nit-pickers from arguing the toss over the odd millimetre or so.

65 Surely it is possible to work precisely to scale?

It is often said that 'you cannot scale nature'. A 12 mm clearance on a full-sized mechanism is large – reduced to 4 mm scale it is a running fit and needs to be lubricated. The trouble arises because we say that 4 mm = 1 ft when we mean 4 mm *represents* one foot. Whatever we may say, 4 mm obstinately remains 4 mm, neither more nor less.

66 I have seen scale quoted as 4 mm to the foot, as a ratio (1:76.2) or as OO scale. Which is correct?

All are acceptable. However, the term OO scale is an American usage which is open to abuse and is frequently employed commercially to fudge the question; for example, what precisely is OO/HO *scale*? The ratio is the most useful figure for precise modelling; it is the only one that can readily be used on a pocket or desk calculator and works equally well with metric or imperial standards.

67 What is meant by metric and imperial standards?

The old foot/inch and ton/pound system is known as imperial, though today it is only a true standard in the USA. Metric standards are based on the metre, though strictly speaking current standards are ISO, one refinement being the use of units in steps of 1,000 to avoid confusion if the name of the unit is accidentally omitted. It is rather difficult to confuse millimetres with metres! The centimetre is not a standard ISO measurement, but persists in common usage.

Metric dimensions are used throughout this book except where, in quoting a prototype dimension, the original was measured in imperial standards.

68 The metric system has been used for British model railways for some time. Surely we would have been measuring in inches. How did this come about?

This occurred largely because it is much more convenient to express small dimensions in millimetres than it is to use fractions of an inch, particularly as most rules are sub-divided in octal rather than decimal sub-units. In inches, dimensions were given in 64ths or 32nds, not easy fractions to deal with, whereas in millimetres it is generally accepted that 0.5 mm is close enough for all practical purposes. It is not widely known that the model railway industry was, to all intents and purposes, the first British industry to go metric.

69 How can one calculate the exact scale of a prototype?

First convert imperial sizes to a single unit, either feet or inches, in decimal terms – ie 56.5 in, not 4 ft 8$\frac{1}{2}$ in for standard gauge. Then, using a calculator and the scale ratio, determine the scale equivalent in inches, then convert to millimetres. It is simpler in metric – it is even simpler to use a scale rule.

70 What is a scale rule?

A scale rule is a ruler with its divisions marked out to represent the equivalent size of the prototype to a chosen scale. The main use is in drawing-offices – draughtsman's scales are very accurate. Model railway scale rules are made to measure scale feet and scale metres and the majority are by no means precise, though good enough for the purpose.

71 Where can you get scale rules?

Draughtsmen's rules can be purchased from drawing-office suppliers and major stationers – W. H. Smith carries a good range of accurate metric scales. Imperial standard scale rules appear to have gone off the market. The better model shops stock model scale rules.

72 I have calculated a scale size as being 4.175 mm. How do I measure this?

Even a micrometer or vernier gauge will only measure millimetres to two decimal places, and neither instrument is much use for marking out parts. Practical tests at the National Physical Laboratory, Teddington, showed that even skilled craftsmen could not achieve a greater consistent accuracy in marking out than 0.5 mm. Accuracy of 0.005 mm (5 microns) is only possible in specialised workshops, and a good deal of production engineering is limited to 0.01 mm tolerances, which are tight enough for most purposes. Where hand work is involved, a dimensional accuracy of 0.1 mm is the practical limit, though it is possible to mate parts to 0.01 mm so long as you aren't bothered which 0.01 mm it is! In modelmaking, a quarter of a millimetre is about as close as one needs to go. Your scale dimension should be rounded to the nearest 0.1 mm, and given as 4.2 mm. If you're using a rule, then the old craftsman's term, 'a full 4 mm', is a good rendering. In other words, you set your mark just on the far side of the 4 mm division on the rule.

Section 1:5
Planning and design

73 How should I set about planning my layout?

You should begin with an idea of the sort of trains you intend to use and their length, since this determines the size of stations and other features. Remember that if any shunting is to be done, the effective length of a station is 2.5 times the length of the usual train (see Plate 2).

Next you have to decide on the type of traffic you wish to run, and then prepare a list of the special features you would

like in the layout. Having done this, you can consider, if you have not already made up your mind on this point, the prototype you should follow.

You now need to decide where it will go and how much room you have. At this point you will almost certainly have to compromise on some of your ideals, and will almost certainly discover that you can't fit all the features you would like into the layout.

74 Is it absolutely necessary to follow a specific prototype?

It is more a case of it being desirable from two aspects. By limiting models to those which one could reasonably expect to see together, the overall picture is more convincing, but of greater importance is that it narrows the area of choice down to manageable proportions. With the amount and variety of models now on offer, this is very important. It's not merely a matter of cost – if you were given all the models you would like to own, where would you put them?

75 What is the best prototype to follow?

All prototypes can produce an effective model, so in that sense no one is clearly superior to another. However, the availability of suitable models is an important factor; equally, the information available has a bearing on the choice.

76 It appears that I must choose between modelling the steam age, or using modern diesel and electric motive power. I like them both, but which is best?

You don't have to make a choice. It's your railway, and you can run anything you like on it. If anyone objects, you can ask him to leave, although it's as well to be polite; there's no need for both parties to be uncouth.

Having said that, one of the best periods for modelling the British prototype to combine all types of motive power, particularly in 4 mm scale, is what is beginning to be known as the 'green diesel' period, circa 1960. At this time most types of steam locomotive were much in evidence, working side by side with the first generation of main-line diesels. The BR Mk 1 coaches were plentiful, and worked side by side with the more recent examples of pre-nationalisation stock. The railway system was still being operated in a traditional manner, with loose-coupled wagons of innumerable patterns, a lot of branches were open and a good deal of industrial traffic remained. Best of all, it is possible to buy ready-to-run models in the correct colours! All you loose are the latest coaches and diesels, and, with the exception of the Southern Region, the older pre-Grouping classes of steam locomotive. Even so, a couple of historic locomotives were restored for enthusiasts' specials, so 'modeller's licence' would allow one to have any older engine, providing it were in its original condition.

77 What are the main difficulties of historic modelling?

The biggest problem is finding out the smaller details of railway construction and operation and, above all, avoiding anachronisms such as TV aerials on a pre-nationalisation railway, short skirts on a pre-1914 model, or crinolines on a layout set in the 1890s. These may seem very obvious faults, but I have seen all three perpetuated on layouts constructed by above-average modelmakers. Information on the general shape and form of the prototype as far back as a century ago is quite easy to locate in any well-stocked library, and quite apart from the support one will get in most clubs, there is also the Historical Model Railway Society to provide help and guidance to members.

78 What problems does one face modelling an overseas prototype?

Primarily cost, not so much for the models themselves, but on trips to the country concerned to check out the finer details. In addition, most of the information on European prototypes is in German or French, whereas books on US railroads are in English. However, the comparative nearness of the Continent makes on-the-spot research much easier. The major European systems have good support societies, and a number of specialist suppliers carry good stocks of models for HO and N gauges.

79 Is it necessary to prepare a detailed plan for a layout?

When you start any medium- to long-term project, it is a good idea to know where you intend to end up, and a track plan provides a guide to your intentions and should ensure that you get all you want into the model. The amount of detail incorporated is up to you, but you should rough in the areas you intend to devote to various features.

You should have a reasonable idea of what these features are going to be before you start, but as you draw, redraw and reject, what you can hope to incorporate should become clearer. There is, however, no need to go to the detail seen on many plans published in magazines. My own project plans usually show a good deal of scenic detail around the tracks, and this is put in for two reasons – it makes the plan more attractive, and I happen to enjoy doing it.

80 How should I prepare a plan? Are a drawing-board and tee-square a necessity?

For most people it is more convenient to work on squared paper, with each square representing the smallest convenient measurement, 1 in or 1 cm as the case may be. Set out curves with compasses and pay particular attention to the length of turnouts, diamond crossings, etc. It is a regrettable fact that many published plans are defective in this respect, showing turnouts about half their true length. Indeed, the main error on most plans is underestimating the size of the majority of features. In particular, the total length of the required train needs to be known; the easiest way of getting this right is to assemble the train from the models in your possession. It often helps to make a three-dimensional plan out of card, wood and modelling clay to gauge the effect of scenery and, in particular, the arrangement of multi-level tracks.

In any case, the small-scale plan should be regarded solely as a project. The best scale for the final plan is full size, and rather than draw things in detail, set out the actual components, or paper templates cut to the exact size, on the baseboards or even on the floor. Many modellers make simple card mock-ups of buildings and other structures (cereal packets are ideal for this) to gauge the effect before embarking on the actual model. For a multi-level scheme, it can be helpful to make card templates for the track sub-bases and offer these up to see if any modifications are needed before cutting the boards to size.

81 Where do I get sheets of paper large enough for full-sized plans?

From bargain bins of wallpaper outside decorators' suppliers; from discarded fanfold computer print-outs; and from printers with web-fed rotary presses. Felt-tip pens and marker pens produce good bold lines on rough paper.

82 How does one draw track curves full size?

A good deal can be done with a length of string, a pencil and a drawing-pin (see Plate 2). A more sophisticated approach is a long strip of wood with pre-drilled holes at one end large enough to take a pencil or felt-tipped pen, and at the other end small enough to take a pin. Several holes are needed, adjusted to the required length. A metre- or yard-stick is ideal – you don't have to set out the lengths and the holes don't stop the measure being used for its normal purpose.

83 What is the minimum radius I can use?

This depends partly on the gauge but mainly on the type of models you are using. Ready-to-run models are arranged to negotiate fairly sharp curves, but kit and scratchbuilt models need larger curves. For OO/HO, 450 mm (18 in) is the minimum; 600 mm (2 ft) is a better choice for serious work, as this will allow most kit-built locomotives to be run, whilst 1 m (3 ft 3 in) is to be preferred. For N gauge, halve these figures; for O gauge, double them. For finescale work, the larger the radius the better. There is a considerable amount of overhang on sharp-radius curves, and one side benefit of historical modelling is that with few coaches longer than 50 feet and much shorter locomotives, the effect of underscale curves is less obvious.

84 What is the steepest gradient I can use?

This depends partly on the power of

your locomotives and the length of train you intend to use. In general, 1 in 30 is regarded as the steepest gradient, with 1 in 50 or shallower where trains of more than four coaches are to be run. Gradients of 1 in 20 are only advisable on branch lines and narrow gauge systems.

85 What is meant by 1 in 30, etc?

A rise of 1 unit for every 30 units along the track. In 1 m, a 1 in 30 grade lifts the track 30 mm, and since one needs at least 60 mm to pass one OO/HO line over another, it makes sense to allow for 2 m of track to do this (see Plate 2). Remember, the track and sub-base have an appreciable thickness.

86 I am very short of space. What sort of layout do you advise?

There are three possible answers: the diorama; the portable layout; and narrow gauge. All three can be combined in a single scheme. Many modellers short of space adopt a branch line theme, though in point of fact many city termini were, and in some cases still are, remarkably compact.

87 What is a diorama?

Originally it was a model designed to be viewed from one position, giving the effect of a larger space by perspective modelling. The term is now loosely applied to small, very detailed, very realistic models, built to finescale principles. To a large extent, most small portable layouts contain some elements of diorama modelling.

88 Are there any problems in modelling narrow gauge prototypes?

The interest in narrow gauge railways has grown over the last 30 years, with the result that there are now plenty of books on the subject and there is a good deal of support for modellers, both from the trade and through specialist societies.

In the main, narrow gauge modellers rely on kits or scratchbuilding. A limited amount of 9 mm gauge narrow gauge ready-to-run stock is available, but currently the best selection of ready-to-run narrow gauge equipment is in HOm, 3.5 mm scale models of Swiss metre gauge stock running on 12 mm gauge.

Narrow gauge is a good way of working in a large scale, 7 or 16 mm to the foot, and even 1.22, whilst keeping the models small enough to fit into a reasonable space.

89 Many model railways today incorporate a good deal of scenery. Is this the right approach?

It is certainly a popular approach! If the object is to produce a visually satisfying model then some scenery is indicated, though one must always bear in mind the fact that the railway itself can be very attractive in its own right. However, we usually think of scenery as being those things situated beyond the railway boundaries – the roads, rivers, buildings and, above all, the landscape itself, with its natural or cultivated vegetation. Within this context, scenic modelling can be approached in many ways, ranging from the 'scenic corner' to the 'railway in the landscape'.

90 What exactly is a 'scenic corner'? Surely it can't be just a bit of scenery stuck in a corner of the railway?

In the 1930s it was just that, a length of fencing round the perimeter of the track, a field made by spreading green cloth over the baseboard and a couple of Brittain's best 3/8 in scale lead cows to round out the scene, even in O gauge; model farms had very prime cattle in those days. Ambitious modellers included a farmhouse roughly the scale size of a meagre cottage. Alternatively a pair of mock-Tudor semi-detached houses represented the townscape, with a tinplate Ford 8 standing proudly in the drive and a Minic London Transport bus on the road alongside, even if the layout was supposed to be set in Yorkshire – there wasn't a lot of choice in those days.

Where, as is so often the case, space is limited, the corners are often the only areas one can easily spare for landscape modelling (see Plate 2). Indeed, where it is necessary to have fairly sharp curves, judicious use of scenic features can do much to disguise this. One popular approach solution is to locate a model town over the curve – you can produce a very effective town square in the space above a 600 mm double-track curve in 4 mm scale.

91 What is meant by the 'railway in the landscape' principle?

This is a relatively modern idea where the railway only occupies the centre of a wide baseboard, which is otherwise largely given over to fields. It requires a good deal of space, but where a large room is available it is a good idea to have one part of the layout where a complete train can be seen clear of all stations. One sound approach is to model a wide valley crossed by a long viaduct – this allows much of the scenic effect to be in the vertical plane, where there is always space to spare.

92 What is the best type of plan – point-to-point or continuous run?

Providing some form of off-stage storage is provided to allow the sequence of trains to be altered so that a realistic operating schedule can be followed on the visible section of the model, either scheme is sound, but in practice all but the smallest and simplest layouts incorporate both elements, so get the best of both worlds.

93 What is an out-and-back scheme?

This is a layout comprising a terminus as its main feature, with the tracks so arranged that trains proceed out along the main line and, possibly after spending some time in storage loops, return to the terminus (see Plate 2). It requires a reasonably large room, but is ideally suited for single-handed operation, particularly if storage loops are provided to allow a realistic sequence of trains to be operated.

94 What is a dumb-bell layout?

This is a layout built around a through station with reversing loops at either end, which normally incorporate a series of storage loops (see Plate 2). This allows a train to pass through in one direction and return in the other, greatly improving the realism of operation. It can be regarded as a single-track continuous run, drawn out and squeezed together in the centre. It is also known as a 'dog-bone', both names referring to the basic form of the plan. It requires a good deal of space; a common practice is to arrange one set of loops above the other.

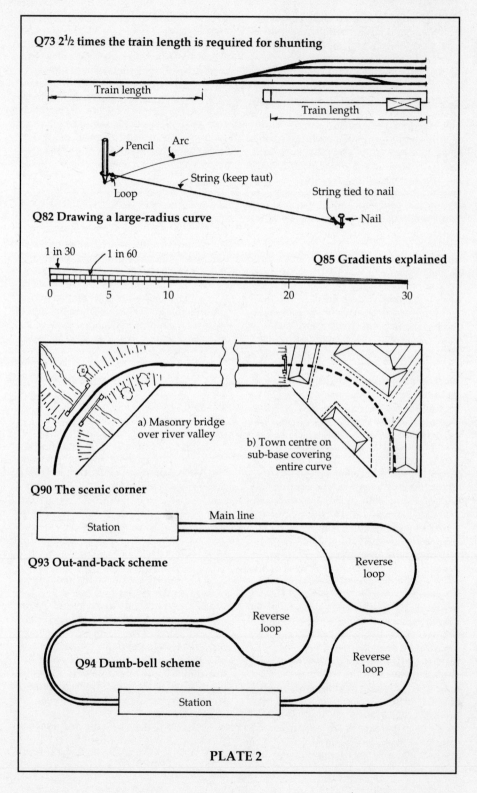

Q73 2½ times the train length is required for shunting

Train length

Train length

Pencil — Arc

String (keep taut)

Loop

String tied to nail

Nail

Q82 Drawing a large-radius curve

1 in 30   1 in 60

Q85 Gradients explained

0   5   10   20   30

a) Masonry bridge over river valley

b) Town centre on sub-base covering entire curve

Q90 The scenic corner

Station   Main line

Q93 Out-and-back scheme

Reverse loop

Reverse loop

Q94 Dumb-bell scheme

Reverse loop

Station

Reverse loop

PLATE 2

95 What is a looped eight layout?

A looped eight layout comprises a multi-level continuous circuit which loops over itself (see Plate 3). It is extremely popular since it provides some interesting scenic effects in a relatively small area.

96 What is a L-type layout?

This is terminus fiddle yard scheme fitted into the corner of a room, the name being derived from the plan view (see Plate 3). It is a very popular arrangement where space is limited and is frequently based on steam age branch-line practice; however, it is equally suited, particularly in N gauge, to main-line usage. It is also ideally suited for the younger enthusiast since it can be fitted into quite a small bedroom without any compromise of its normal function.

97 What is a fiddle yard?

A fiddle yard is a series of storage roads on which complete trains are held, to be brought out and returned in accordance with the operating schedule. The main varieties are fan, traverser, sector plate and train turntable, and they are used primarily in the terminus-fiddle yard type of layout; storage roads perform an analogous function on continuous runs.

98 What is a fan fiddle yard?

A storage yard where the roads are fed through a series of turnouts. It occupies a fair amount of length but has the advantage of being able to be remotely controlled; it can also be placed hard against a wall. It is frequently combined with a locomotive turntable at one end to allow running round (see Plate 3).

99 What is a traverser fiddle yard?

A storage yard where the tracks are mounted on a sub-base which may be moved sideways (traversed) so that the entry/exit road(s) may be aligned with any desired storage road (see Plate 3). It is necessary to set the traverser plate far enough away from the wall to permit the outermost storage road to be correctly aligned. The addition of locomotive holding roads adds to the flexibility. Most of these yards are mounted on drawer slides, since these provide a ready-made system of moving the traverser sideways in a straight line.

100 What is a sector plate fiddle yard?

A set of storage sidings mounted on a pivoted sub-base so that the entry/exit road(s) may be aligned with any desired storage road (see Plate 3). It is normal practice to reposition locomotives and/or rolling-stock by hand. It is necessary to set the sector plate far enough away from the wall to permit the outermost storage road to be correctly aligned.

101 What is a train turntable?

A set of storage sidings mounted on a centrally-pivoted sub-base so that not only may the entry/exit road(s) be aligned with any desired storage road, but also the entire unit may be turned end for end to reverse trains (see Plate 3). It requires a considerable amount of space in which to turn and may give rise to problems in the home. In many cases train turntables are only used as such in exhibition halls; in their normal sites they are used as sector plates.

102 What are train storage roads?

These are a series of hidden loops on a continuous run or reversing loop. They provide storage for complete trains, which may be brought out on to the open tracks in accordance with the operating schedule. To save space, a traverser may be employed, but this requires manual operation.

Section 1:6
Garden railways

103 Is it possible to build a model railway in the garden?

Certainly – until the Second World War a high proportion of model railways were built in the garden, as this was often the only space large enough for a decent O gauge system. When OO took over as the most popular gauge, garden railways went out of fashion but are beginning to return to limited popularity.

104 Is OO unsuitable for outdoor use?

Although this was once the case, it is no longer so. In pre-war days most coaches

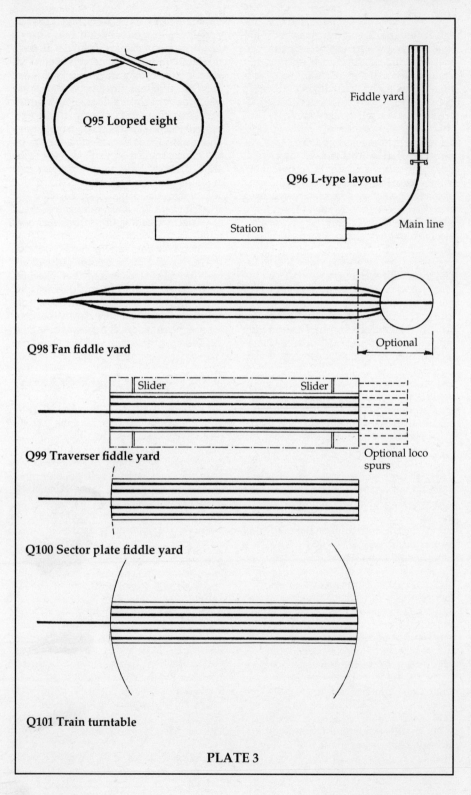

Q95 Looped eight

Fiddle yard

Q96 L-type layout

Station

Main line

Q98 Fan fiddle yard

Optional

Slider

Slider

Q99 Traverser fiddle yard

Optional loco spurs

Q100 Sector plate fiddle yard

Q101 Train turntable

PLATE 3

and wagons had lithographed paper sides, and in the early post-war days most track systems used fibre sleepers; these materials are ruined if they get wet. Modern plastic equipment stands up to practically everything the British climate can throw at it and standard plastic-based ready-assembled track with nickel silver rail has been used outdoors for many years. Indeed, even N gauge has been used out of doors, but there is really very little purpose in this since even a small garden will provide ample room for an extensive OO gauge system.

105 What sort of weather can cause trouble?

Prolonged hot sunshine will warp most plastics used for locomotives and rolling-stock, but the most important consideration is the effect of frost on ground-level tracks; this is clearly more serious where the smaller gauges are concerned. However, bad weather appears to have more effect on the operators than on the equipment.

106 What are the main hazards for the stock and track?

A good deal of routine trouble is caused by grit and leaves falling on the track, so most outdoor operators carry out a routine inspection of the entire route before a major operating session. For less formal occasions the routine is to run the train and find out where it falls off.

107 I've heard that wildlife can cause trouble. Is this so?

Cats appear to love model railways – at the slightest provocation they will sun themselves on the tracks and need to be shooed away before operation can continue. Small rodents and other burrowing creatures regard tunnels as ready-made homes, so it is essential to block these at the end of every operating session. In the main, wildlife can be a minor nuisance, but most garden operators regard animals and birds as part of the fun.

108 I understand that regular maintenance is needed. Isn't this a chore?

It depends on your attitude of mind. The real garden railway enthusiast considers that it adds to the realism of the model when the same type of work, scaled down to a comfortable size, is needed on both model and prototype.

109 Can you run a garden railway throughout the winter?

If you feel up to braving the elements, you most certainly can. However, many operators remove much of the equipment in late September or October and spend the winter months refurbishing and replacing it for reinstatement in late March.

110 Is there any problem with electrical pick-up out of doors?

Providing regular maintenance and track cleaning is undertaken, there is little difficulty, though some large-scale workers use 24 volts. This, however, is as much governed by the availability of large ex-equipment 24-volt motors as a desire to punch through dirt on the track.

111 I am having difficulty getting good electrical pick-up on my garden railway. Is there an alternative?

There is a growing interest for O gauge and larger layouts in the use of rechargeable cells to provide battery power. It should also be possible to arrange this in OO by fitting batteries in vans. Remote control is difficult, though radio control has been used with considerable success. The majority of garden railways in pre-war days relied on clockwork power, but this is no longer available.

112 What can be done with steam in the garden?

A great deal! Most people are inclined to agree that live steam is at its best out of doors, for the fumes do tend to linger indoors. Steam is mainly confined to Gauge 1 and the larger narrow gauge scales, but O gauge live steam has been shown to be perfectly feasible.

113 Can you lay tracks directly on the ground?

As a purely temporary measure, track can be laid on the ground, but for serious work it must be laid on a prepared trackbed. A shallow trough, filled with fine gravel, is probably better than concrete slabs, since it is easier to restore the correct level after frost has distorted the ground (see Plate 4).

114 I intend to construct a large-scale narrow gauge railway in my garden. A good deal of the main line will run alongside the lawn and I have a feeling that my mower will damage the track. How does one trim the grass close to a low-level garden railway?

Modern grass trimmers, which cut with a rapidly rotating nylon cord, can be used close to large-scale track without any serious problems. You will of course have to brush the clippings off the track afterwards.

115 Isn't it awkward and uncomfortable working on a model railway set at ground level?

It can be, which is why many low-level garden lines are provided with operating pits. These are basically holes in the ground about 1 m deep, with side walls, steps, some form of dry base and, most important of all, drainage. It is also possible to construct raised beds or rockeries for the layout (see Plate 4).

116 How does one construct high-level outdoor baseboards?

Much as one builds indoor baseboards, except that the only acceptable top surface is marine-grade plywood (see Plate 4). This can be used for other timber work to advantage, but well-seasoned deal, coated with preservatives, has proved adequate. Some garden operators build sectional bases which are unbolted at the start of winter and stored indoors, or even taken to exhibitions! It is essential to coat the threads of the bolts wit grease before assembly to prevent their rusting solid during the summer months.

117 How should one arrange supports for the layout, and what material is recommended for this?

Although timber has been used, the probability of rot suggests that concrete posts are better suited to the job. Another alternative is to construct dwarf pillars with standard concrete blocks or common bricks on a firm cement foundation.

118 Is scenic work possible out of doors?

Where the tracks are laid at or near ground level, the line is automatically provided with a natural landscape – alpines and heathers provide vegetation, small conifers the trees. Here the dividing line between modelling and horticulture is blurred. Pools can be bridged, and depressions spanned with concrete viaducts cast in situ. Rocky cuttings can be created as part of a rock garden. In most cases a good deal of heavy digging and barrowing of soil to other parts of the garden will be needed at the outset. It will also take several years for the plants to mature, but this is something that can be left largely to nature. Indeed, scenic garden railways require a sympathetic approach to the subject – you cannot force nature into a straitjacket without inordinate effort and not a little disappointment.

119 How does one store the locomotives and stock overnight?

A popular answer is to house the main station or stations inside garden sheds. These can also house power units and other electrical equipment, in particular block instruments, since on many garden railways the operators are out of sight and comfortable earshot of each other. Failing this it is necessary to remove them and place them in suitable storage trays for carrying indoors.

120 What is the ideal sort of garden for an outdoor railway?

One where there is a small area some 2 to 3 feet lower than the rest, with a fairly abrupt change of level. This allows part of the line to be on high-level baseboards and to run into a station or storage sidings in a shed, whilst the rest is at or near ground level. However, providing you are prepared to tackle a good deal of hard work with spade, fork and wheelbarrow at the outset, and are ready to build dwarf walls or rockeries, a sloping garden can be terraced or a flat garden built up to provide a variety of levels.

121 Is vandalism a problem on a garden railway?

It is not so much a problem – should it happen, it is a disaster! What is more, it

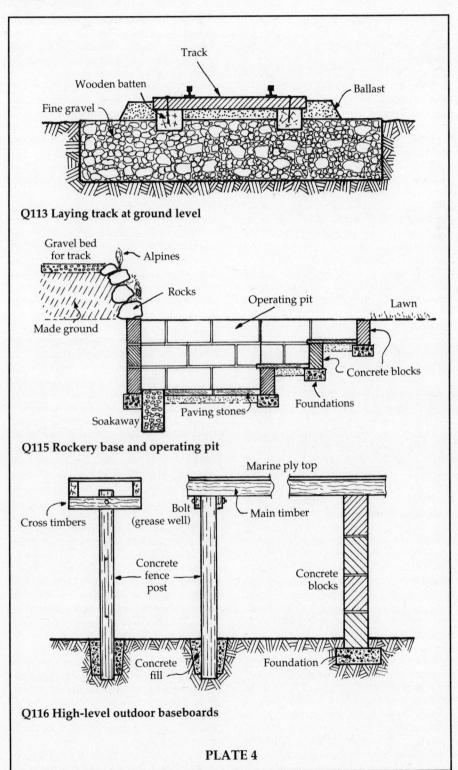

Q113 Laying track at ground level

Q115 Rockery base and operating pit

Q116 High-level outdoor baseboards

PLATE 4

can happen anywhere, even in a quiet, orderly residential suburb. Therefore it is not a good idea to have the railway visible from a public place. This is not a new phenomenon – vandalism of garden railways occurred in the 1930s.

Section 1:7
Research

122 I have heard it said that 'Research Must Come First'. Is this true?

As many of the finest model railways in the country have been built without the owner doing any formal research at all, it is self-evidently not true. However, here we define research as original investigation, generally based on primary sources. Reading a book or magazine is not research, it is merely study, and a certain amount of preliminary study is needed if you intend to scratchbuild a model, and some further cross-checking of photographs and other sources of information often comes in handy when building a kit, but if you're using ready- to-run models all you really need to know is that they are appropriate to the type of railway you have in mind. This is probably why you chose them in the first place!

It should never be forgotten that research interferes with modelling, and the best excuse for inaction is 'my researches are incomplete'!

123 Do I need to study the prototype in detail?

Some knowledge of full-sized railway practice and in particular the shape and form of the locomotives, rolling-stock and structures around the railway is helpful. However, if you intend to use finished models or kits, you only need know what models and kits are most suitable for your purpose. You can find out most of this from a well-illustrated book about your chosen railway. Start at your local public library, where you can borrow books for a period in order to find out if you need them. Many books include bibliographies, these provide clues to follow up.

124 Where can one get the more specialised railway books?

Advertisements in the model and railway press feature specialised bookshops. Some of these attend model railway exhibitions, which are good places to build up your library. Bookstalls at major stations also generally have a small but select range on view, but rarely stock anything from the more specialised publishers.

125 What information do I need to make a good model?

A reliable scale drawing and a few clear photographs are the main requirements. There are a few suppliers who can supply individual dye-line prints, but in the main you will find drawings in magazines and published collections of drawings. There is a growing tendency for the more specialised histories to include drawings, although not always to a recognised modelling scale. There are numerous railway picture books on hand to provide further information.

126 What information is needed to make an accurate model of a station?

An accurate track plan (not necessarily to scale) and good photographs of the principal buildings are needed at the outset. As most railways worked to standardised designs and used standard parts, details can usually be taken from either existing structures of similar appearance, or published drawings of such buildings.

It is best to select a station which still exists or is described in a readily available publication rather than choosing one at random. At this date there is no guarantee that sufficient information remains on many closed stations, for you can no longer visit the site with notebook, camera and tape-measure as we once could.

127 I have seen appeals for information in the model press. Isn't this a good idea?

By all means make such a request, but don't place any great reliance on getting results. If you should be lucky, remember not only to return all loaned material promptly, but to meet out-of-pocket expenses and thank the individual concerned. Regrettably, the failure of many people to do so has stopped a number of researchers from offering assistance.

128 Is there any other source of information? Is there any other way of getting this elusive information about closed stations?

Archives do exist, but in many cases records are not accessible. Regrettably, many have been destroyed, some by accident, others by deliberate policy, since such archives take up valuable space and not every railway official has a feeling for history. Even where efforts have been made to store drawings and photographs, lack of funds has often prevented proper cataloguing. Delving through old drawings and collections of photographs without a catalogue is both tedious and time-consuming. A very simple method of finding out what a demolished station was really like is to build the best model you can from published information and write it up for publication. Then wait to hear from those who know better. If nothing else, it does get the model finished!

129 Aren't there a lot of drawings stored at the National Railway Museum and other similar archives?

Yes, but in the main the collections are not readily available for study. Whilst fresh discoveries take place from time to time, there is no known way of turning up information on specific prototype features that have not been published or catalogued, nor is there any way of ensuring that specific information still exists.

130 Where do I find information on steam locomotives and rolling-stock?

The Railway Correspondence & Travel Society publishes a number of very detailed locomotive histories, and the range is growing steadily. Ian Allan has published a good range of illustrated accounts of the work of leading locomotive engineers, mostly written by Brian Haresnape; as aids to kitbuilding and general information on the major classes, they are extremely useful guides. Many photo albums have appeared and, in addition to drawings which have

appeared in the model press and elsewhere, several collections of locomotive drawings have been published. Whilst the coverage of coaches and wagons is not so exhaustive as that of locomotives, some excellent textbooks are now available, most of which include scale drawings to recognised modelling scales.

Although the British Library holds a copy of every book published in Britain since the dawn of railways, getting a Reader's Ticket is not easy. If, however, you proceed eastward from the new Library in Euston Road, London NW1, and take Pentonville Road, you will reach Calshot Street where you will find Keen House, the Model Railway Club's HQ. This houses a very comprehensive library which members of the club may consult on most Thursday evenings.

131 Is there any organisation or society devoted to railway research?

There are several, but for our purposes the Historical Model Railway Society, which was founded for just this reason, has been serving the hobby well for over 40 years. It publishes an authoritative journal as well as a number of very detailed studies of selected prototypes.

132 How do I obtain information on overseas railways?

Most developed countries have specialist publishers who issue books and magazines on their railways. USA material is simple enough, as it is published in English. However, if your interests are Continental, it helps to have some knowledge of the language in question. Specialist bookshops can provide the majority of recent publications. However, since the major European railway systems have support societies, the first step is to join the appropriate group.

Section 1:8
Photography

133 What is the best way of recording details of the prototype for subsequent use in modelmaking?

For all-round convenience and speed, there is nothing to touch a photograph. However, it is essential to note where and when you took the picture and to record any significant details of the shot. It also helps to take a few measurements of a building, if at all possible. Hence the vital tools for a field survey are camera, notebook, pocket tape and, above all, a good supply of pencils and/or ballpoint pens, plus a couple of erasers.

134 Is record photography difficult?

Only if you set out to make it so. George Eastman established the basic principles of trouble-free photography a century ago with the first Kodak camera; most cameras now follow his principles, and modern refinements have eliminated the limitations of the early instruments.

135 What sort of camera do you recommend for prototype photography?

Providing you do not want to take pictures of trains at speed, any of the modern compact 35 mm cameras will fit the bill very neatly and make little impact on the pocket – in more senses than one, since most of them are designed to slip into a roomy jacket pocket. The self-loading, auto-focus and auto-exposure type are to be preferred, and a two-stage or zoom lens is a help. This type of camera is advertised as foolproof; this is not so, but they do take care of the technicalities, so all one need do is load the film, compose the picture in the viewfinder, keep fingers and thumbs out of the way of the lens and gently press the button.

136 What is meant when a camera is described as focus free?

This means that the lens is set so that the picture is in reasonable focus from about 2 m to 40 m, readily attainable with a 35 mm focal length lens of limited aperture on 35 mm film. In short it is pre-set for the average snapshot picture. It is perfectly satisfactory for general record shots, but extreme close-up pictures could be a trifle fuzzy if enlarged. Prints up to 7 x 5 are quite satisfactory.

137 What is your opinion of cartridge and disc cameras for record photography?

They can do the job, but the results are likely to be indifferent. It is inadvisable to go beyond the standard processor's print and, as a check of their detailed services will show, most of the options for large prints are not available for these sizes since not only is the negative very small to begin with, but the method of loading the film is not precise enough. In addition, the lenses are only adequate, and the prints do not have the crispness one gets with better cameras.

138 I have noticed that expert photographers use expensive cameras. Is this the reason why their shots are better?

The key to successful photography is not the camera, but the photographer. The important point to remember is that no matter how advanced the camera may be, at rock bottom the results depend on the user pointing it in the right direction and, above all, getting the required picture in the viewfinder. If you can't take a decent picture with a simple compact camera, you'll fare no better with the latest costly, electronically-controlled gadget, whatever the advertising agency copywriter may imply in the carefully worded text.

139 What are the advantages of a single lens reflex camera (SLR)?

With a SLR you not only have greater control over the operation of the camera, but you can change lenses to suit the conditions. Against this, you do need to know the underlying principles of photography, for although an SLR can be used in snapshot mode, in this phase it is behaving in the same manner as a compact camera – at about three times the cost! There is also a more serious disadvantage – the camera is bulky and will not slip into a jacket pocket, whilst with the addition of spare lenses and other impedimenta, one ends up with a very large and heavy outfit which can get more than a little tiresome at the end of a day. However, there is one clear advantage – the SLR is an ideal camera for model photography.

140 What are the advantages of interchangeable lenses?

The focal length of the lens determines the area of scene covered by the camera.

In broad outline, wide-angle lenses (focal length 28-35 mm) are useful for overall shots of buildings or station layouts, since they cover a wider field. The camera must be held upright to prevent the verticals converging on the negative and so producing odd-looking prints. Telephoto or long-focus lenses, (focal length 70-200 mm) are invaluable for distance shots. The standard lens for 35 mm photography has a focal length of 50 mm and, in most cases today, has a very wide aperture suitable for work in poor light.

141   What exactly is a zoom lens?

This is a lens with a variable focal length. For 35 mm photography, two types are available: the short pattern, with ranges from 35-70 mm up to 28-85 mm; and the long-focus, generally 80-200 mm. Modern zoom lenses give good results over their entire range, hence the growing tendency for SLR cameras to be offered with a zoom lens as a standard package. For general-purpose work a 35-70 mm zoom is adequate, but the 28-85 mm is even better. There is a penalty, however – zoom lenses have a smaller aperture than a prime lens, which means that in poor light the camera may not be able to cope, but as the slowest zoom lens is as fast as the lenses used by press photographers 50 years ago, this is not really a limitation.

142   There are a lot of films on the market. Which make do you recommend?

If you subscribe to *Which?* you will from time to time see very detailed assessments of the various films on offer. The tables show variations between makes, and tell you which of the major companies produces own-brand films. What is not so obvious to the layman is that the variations are relatively small and are only detected because the test films are exposed under controlled conditions and then subjected to very detailed examination. This is not the case with normal photography and film purchased from a reputable outlet – and this includes supermarkets and kiosks on railway stations – will give good results. What is more important is the speed rating in ASA or DIN.

143   What on earth are ASA and DIN?

The initials stand for the names of bodies that have established speed ratings for films. They are both marked on the packet and also on the film cassette. The easiest to follow is the ASA, as the preferred steps are in hundreds, with ratings of ASA 100, 200, 400 and, in limited cases, 1000. The higher the number, the faster the film and, as one might expect, ASA 400 is four times as fast as ASA 100. This is a great improvement on earlier systems where the relationship between the film speed and the rating was not so obvious.

If your camera has a manually-set exposure control, you will see that it is marked in ASA or DIN. All you do is to set the dial to the rating of the film you are loading. To avoid confusion, stick to one speed of film. All modern compact cameras and many SLRs have DX facilities, and providing you use DX-rated film, you don't have to set the exposure. A DX film is easily recognised – the cassette has a large irregular area of bright metal along its side which makes contact with sensors inside the camera and tells the internal electronics what speed film is loaded.

144   I have a very simple camera with no exposure control. Which film should I use?

The safest choice is ASA 100, the type most commonly found on offer. With this you will still be able to take fair pictures in poor light, although ASA 200 would be a better choice for a winter's day.

145   What is the best all-round film for a camera with exposure control?

ASA 200 gives excellent results throughout the hours of daylight. Only under extreme conditions – generally photographs over water and snow in full sunlight – will it be over-exposed in a simple camera; with an SLR with high shutter speeds available, it is to be preferred.

146   What advantages and disadvantages are there in ASA 400 and ASA 1000 films?

Both films are intended for poor light

conditions. ASA 1000, which is fairly difficult to find, is primarily intended for work indoors and is only of value to the serious photographer. ASA 400 is much more useful and can be used out of doors with an SLR, or in winter with a good compact. It gives a grainier picture, but this is not very noticeable with normal-sized prints.

147 **I find questions of shutter speed and f numbers extremely confusing. Could you sort it out?**

If you are using a compact camera with automatic exposure control, or a simple camera without this feature or any means of adjusting the lens setting, you can simply forget the whole sorry business. Likewise, with an advanced programmed SLR you can leave the camera to sort out the optimum combination for a chosen type of photo.

In brief, the amount of light put on to the film through the lens is governed by the aperture of the lens, measured in stops, which for some arcane reason run f1.5, f2, f3.5, f4.5, f5.6, f8, f16 and f22, each number in the progression admitting half as much light as the stop before.

Shutter speeds also move in a similar fashion, each step slower and admitting double the amount of light. Thus if you set the shutter at 1/1000 second at f2 you will get the same exposure as if you used 1/60 second at f16 (these figures are for ASA 200 on a bright sunlit day). The larger the f number, the greater the depth of field; the higher the shutter speed, the better the camera will stop movement. Your camera handbook will provide a sound guide to the subject.

As a slight relief, modern colour emulsions have a good deal of exposure tolerance – you can over- or under-expose by a ratio of three and still get an acceptable print.

148 **What is an exposure meter and will I need one?**

An exposure metre is a device for measuring the amount of light present, and is provided with some means – generally a range of indications on a dial – of converting this into aperture and speed settings. With the growing tendency to have these facilities built into the camera, the principal users of these meters now appear to be cricket umpires who use them to determine whether an appeal for bad light should be granted.

149 **What is TTL metering?**

The initials stand for 'through the lens'. The light is measured through the camera lens on an SLR and the result displayed in the viewfinder. It is then necessary to twiddle either the aperture ring or the shutter speed dial to get the two lights to coincide, a fairly simple process. It is a halfway house to automatic exposure control, the only snag being that one has to remember to read the indication before pressing the shutter.

150 **What processing house would you recommend?**

The one you find most convenient. Generally, you will find that the postal firms offer keener prices, particularly for the larger-sized prints, but allow at least a week, longer in the busy season, for the return of your films. Handing film over the counter speeds matters, although 1 hour processing (at a premium), which may be attractive, is generally confined to 6 x 4 prints, whereas the slightly more expensive 7 x 5 print is to be preferred for record shots. Remember that it is cheaper to get an extra set of prints when having the film processed than it is to have additional prints made afterwards.

151 **Of what value are colour slides?**

These were the earliest form of colour material available for general photography, but since the advent of good colour negative material their popularity has diminished. They retain two invaluable features – first, the standard 50 mm square slide is extremely compact and easy to store and file for reference; second, it is quite easy to project the slide on to a large screen and study very small detail. For modelling, a good back-projector will give you a colour picture 300 mm wide, which is ideal for close study under normal working lighting.

152 **My collection of slides is getting out of hand. What do you advise?**

Now that all processors date the slide mounts, it is usually possible to identify the shot at a later date, providing you took notes at the time. It is essential to label all slides – the modern plastic mount can be written on, but many people find that a self-adhesive label is better. Currently, W. H. Smith stock a 12 x 38 mm white label which is clearly designed for this particular purpose. The boxes in which the slides are returned can be used for storage, provided that a larger label is used to identify the contents. Larger slide boxes provide excellent long-term storage; in addition, A4-sized plastic sheets with slip-in pockets, perforated to fit into ring-binders, are sold by photographic dealers to allow album-style presentation.

153 How do you avoid putting slides in upside down when projecting them?

By 'spotting' the slide. A small round self-adhesive dot is placed in the bottom left-hand corner of the mount, and this is then held between the thumb and forefinger of the right hand with the spot towards you when inserting the slide into the holder or magazine.

154 What is the best method of storing prints?

Whilst, for display purposes, the slip-in album provides a simple, flexible and convenient way of storing prints, a suitable filing cabinet or even a shoe box is cheap and in practice more effective for record purposes. In all cases the prints should be identified on the back while your memory is still fresh.

It is advisable to store negatives in a proper storage album and to identify them, but in any case you should note the date and location on the folder in which they are returned. Unless this is done, the value to later users is diminished, whereas a good collection of negatives, properly annotated, is of great value to future researchers. Even a commonplace picture becomes of interest when it is the only surviving record of a past event.

155 I have tried taking pictures late in the evening using flash, but they still come out too dark. What can I do?

If you must take night-time railway photographs, you need an SLR with a wide (f1.9) aperture prime lens, and even with this you need a good deal of know-how. Your flash will only be effective up to some 5 m from the camera – it is intended for use indoors. Record photography is best carried out in full daylight, ie from an hour after sunrise to an hour before sunset in temperate zones. Night photography is a very specialised subject and almost always requires the use of a tripod to allow long exposures. It is significant that most published night pictures of railway subjects are devoid of people.

156 I find that a lot of detail in my photographs gets lost in the shadows. What can I do?

There are three courses open to you. If the camera has control over the flash unit, set it to synchro-flash – this will put light into nearby shadows, but will not work outside the effective range of the flash and is therefore only effective for close-up pictures. The second is to get as much of the shadow as you can into the picture; even without automatic exposure control on the camera, the processors will compensate for the under-exposure. A more straightforward approach is, wherever possible, to make record photographs when the sun is hidden under a light overcast.

157 I understood that it was advisable to take photographs in bright sunlight, preferably with the sun at your back. Is this so?

In the early days of popular photography a century ago, when black and white film had an extremely slow speed, this was about the only way you could get an adequate exposure. Although by the 1930s photography had advanced sufficiently to enable one to work in dull daylight with a simple box camera, the advice persisted, which is why so many people in snapshots have their eyes screwed up. Modern cameras have fast lenses, the film emulsion is extremely fast and, much more to the point, with colour film you do not need high contrast to get an agreeable print. The only thing you should never do is to point the camera directly into the sun, and when photographing over water or snow in bright sunlight with a simple camera, it is advisable to use a slow (100 ASA) film.

158 Many of my photographs are fuzzy, even to the point of their being two faint images superimposed. Why is this?

This is the result of camera shake – in other words, moving the camera whilst the picture is being taken. This can be caused by setting too slow a shutter speed, but in the main is a result of two handling errors. When using an eye-level viewfinder, hold the camera with both hands and keep your elbows tucked into your sides. If you have to use speeds below 1/60 second, it is a good idea to loop the neck strap under one arm so that you can further steady the camera by pulling the strap tight. Above all, squeeze the shutter release gently – if you jab it hard you are almost certain to shake the camera.

159 What sort of camera is needed to take model photographs?

The basic requirement is a camera that can focus accurately at fairly short distances, that is capable of being stopped down to a small aperture, and that has a good range of shutter speeds as well as a socket for a tripod. All SLR cameras fit the bill admirably. As you will, initially at all events, be using colour film, the best light source is a flashgun, as this gives the correct colour temperature. The effective speed of an electronic flash, well under a thousandth of a second, ensures not only that there will be no camera movement, but that moving trains will be frozen.

The problems of colour balance with artificial lighting make black and white photography preferable for most serious layout pictures. Ilford XP1 film can be processed by all D&P firms, and is to be recommended. Its high speed, ASA 400, makes it particularly suited to our purpose. A tripod is advisable so that slow shutter speeds may be used.

160 My model photographs seem to lack the interest of those that appear in magazines. Have you any suggestions?

A good rule for model photography is to get in low and close; as SLR prime lenses will usually focus down to under 150 mm, this is quite easy. At this range the chart on your flashgun will inform you that you need something approaching f64, which, as the lens will only go down to f16, would be worrying but for the fact that when taking a flash picture with a normal flashgun at distances under 1 m, a good deal of the light is spread well outside the picture area. Indeed, it is possible to get partial under-exposure on the lower part of the picture because the flash has missed this bit completely.

161 Have you any general advice for a budding photographer?

The golden rule of photography, whether taking models or full-sized prototypes, is simple – what you see in the viewfinder is what you get on the picture. This not only refers to the subject, but also covers the light and shade thrown by the sun, the colours of the subject and, above all, the composition of the picture. This was true when one used a box camera and sighted the picture through something the size of a postage stamp, laughingly called a brilliant viewfinder, but it is equally true when you can buy a camera that focuses the lens and sorts out all the technicalities using an inboard computer. The end result still depends on the eye of the photographer.

PART 2
LAYING THE FOUNDATIONS

In this part of the book we deal with the foundations of the layout – baseboards, track, points and point control, and signals and their operation. This is an area where mistakes are easily made and can remain undetected until the layout is some way advanced. It is impossible to overstress the importance of well-laid track on soundly-built baseboards.

Signals are included here because, although often left as an afterthought, they should be regarded as the first scenic item to be added to the layout. You cannot work a full-sized railway without some form of signalling, and although you can happily run a layout for years without this important accessory, it is advisable to acknowledge their importance on the prototype.

Section 2:1
Baseboard construction

162 Why do I need a baseboard?
The baseboard is the foundation of a serious model railway. It allows you to assemble the various units of the layout into a congruent whole over a period of time. It marks the difference between a model railway and a toy train set, where the units are joined together each time the collection is used, and need to be put away afterwards.

163 What materials are required?
Timber, either in its natural state or in the form of man-made boards; normally ply, chipboard and insulation board are preferred. These materials are readily cut with hand tools and can be obtained from large DIY suppliers and timber merchants in any town. Frequently, suitable materials can be obtained as offcuts or even in the form of scrap timber, etc.

164 What tools do I need for baseboard construction?
The basic essentials are a tenon saw, a handbrace with a selection of small drills and a countersinking bit, a hammer, one or two screwdrivers, a steel tape, preferably 3 m in length, and, above all, a good square. A padsaw will be useful for certain applications; a heavy-duty trimming knife (Stanley pattern) and a bradawl

will assist construction; whilst a selection of screw clamps will help hold things together. These are the basic DIY tools – most are to be found in the average home.

165 What sort of workbench do you recommend?
It is possible to construct a baseboard on a firm flat-topped stool, especially if clamps are available. It is even practicable to work on an old wooden chair, but not one with a padded seat. The 'Workmate'-style portable workbench might well have been designed with model railway baseboard construction in mind, and since it is also invaluable for general house maintenance, it makes a very sound investment. It has many uses – it can even (with suitable padding) form a convenient seat whilst operating the layout!

166 Are there any other tools one might need?
A small selection of chisels, a mallet and a block plane will be needed if more advanced joinery is to be undertaken. Indeed, most woodworking tools can find their place in the modelmaker's tool kit, but they are far from essential.

167 Do you advise the use of power tools?

A power drill with a full range of attachments is a useful addition to the tool kit, but one should remember that a good many model railways were built before they became available. The jigsaw, or sabre saw, is extremely useful for cutting material in irregular shapes. Both tools save a good deal of time and effort and are extremely useful for household maintenance as well. In view of the number of screws that need to be inserted, a power screwdriver is another tool the railway modeller will find invaluable. A circular saw (preferably mounted in a sawbench) is very useful in advanced layout construction, as is a bandsaw, but neither is really justified except in a club context.

All power tools should be treated with respect – they can cause traumatic injury if carelessly handled. It is advisable to wear protective spectacles and, when using sanding attachments, a face-mask. Ensure that plugs and sockets are in good order and correctly wired, and that leads are kept out of the way of cutters, and clear of the working area, as a fall when holding a power tool can be extremely dangerous.

168 What is the best form of baseboard?

There are several methods of construction, each with advantages and disadvantages. Fortunately it is not necessary to stick rigidly to one method on a layout; a large layout may incorporate solid-top, open-top and L-girder construction. There will also be detail differences between permanent and portable layouts.

Baseboards consist of three elements: the framing, the top surface, and the support.

The framing is generally constructed of wood, either natural or plywood, and is normally the main strength member.

The top surface can be, in the simplest form, a sheet of man-made board – ply, chipboard or insulation board – but is frequently a composite of relatively narrow sub-bases carrying the track, and lighter landscaping to provide the scenic effect.

The supports need to be substantial and firm. They may be folding trestles, wooden legs of varying descriptions, or even old furniture, bookcases, chests of drawers, low cupboards, etc.

169 How do you construct the basic framework?

Framing consists of timber members screwed together to form a rectangle, with cross bracing at intervals. Several of these sections are joined together to form the main framework. The size of the timber is governed by the overall size of the frame; generally a baseboard section up to 1.5 m in length and 0.75 m in width can be built from 50 mm x 25 mm (nominal) softwood. The general form of the framing is shown in Plate 5. Screws are either No 8 or No 6, and the use of a PVA woodworking adhesive is advisable.

170 I am not a very good carpenter and I find difficulty in cutting squarely through the framing timbers, with the result that my joints are not true right-angles. Is there any simple way around this difficulty?

First of all it is advisable to mark both the top and sides of the timber before cutting, using a square. Unless this is done there is little hope of making a square cut solely by eye. However, a simple way of ensuring that cuts are made square and true is to use a mitre block (see Plate 5), which will guide the saw as you cut.

171 I have difficulty in screwing the timbers together – it takes a lot of effort to force the screws though two pieces of timber and occasionally the wood splits. There must be an easier way.

There is! You should drill a hole in the top timber to clear the screw and then countersink the hole with a suitable bit. A smaller hole drilled in the lower timber will ease the entry of the screw (see Plate 5). Special bits can be bought to drill and countersink all the holes at once.

172 I have considerable trouble holding two pieces of timber at right-angles and then wielding a screwdriver. What do you suggest?

One piece of wood can be held in the vice whilst the other is placed on top, but

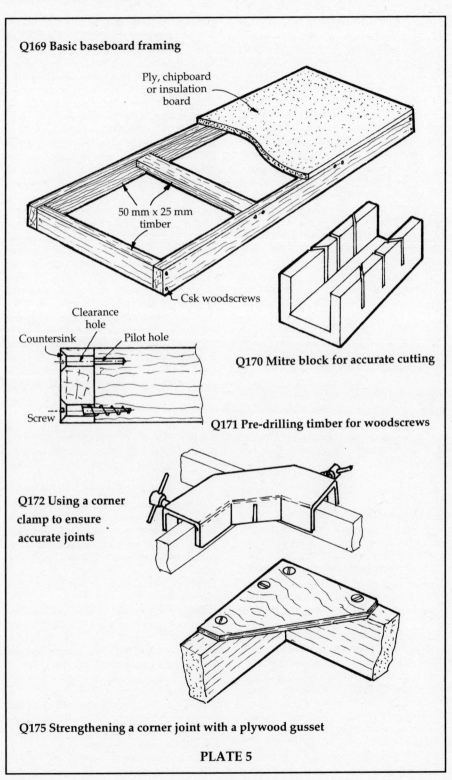

Q169 Basic baseboard framing

Ply, chipboard
or insulation
board

50 mm x 25 mm
timber

Csk woodscrews

Clearance
hole

Countersink   Pilot hole

Screw

Q170 Mitre block for accurate cutting

Q171 Pre-drilling timber for woodscrews

**Q172 Using a corner
clamp to ensure
accurate joints**

Q175 Strengthening a corner joint with a plywood gusset

PLATE 5

a more effective answer is to use a corner clamp, of the type sold for picture framing; this holds both pieces of timber at right-angles and provides a secure fixing (see Plate 5). Using workbench, vice and corner clamps makes life even easier.

173 What material do you recommend for baseboard surfaces?

Where the entire surface is to be covered, a single sheet of man-made board is best; you can use ply, chipboard or insulation board. Ply, in the thinner sections, tends to be noisy, but accepts fine pins and screws. Chipboard is strong, cheap and tends to be reasonably quiet, but will not take very fine pins and will not always hold screws. Insulation board accepts the finest pins, but will not hold screws and needs more support; however, it is an excellent sound deadener and is easily carved with a sharp knife for scenic effect. An ideal, if more expensive, solution is a base of 6 mm ply with a top covering of 9 mm semi-hard insulation board firmly pinned and glued it.

Hardboard is totally unsuitable since it tends to warp unpredictably and will not readily take fine pins.

174 Is it a good idea to build the layout in sections so that it can be easily dismantled and re-erected in the event of a move?

It is a very sound principle to use individual frames, allowing the track to be laid and wired and the basic scenery constructed in a separate workshop. Furthermore, the layout can then be dismantled and taken to an exhibition, and in the event of a move will be reasonably easy to dismantle. However, the chances of there being a place in the new home where the layout will fit without some modification are extremely remote. Therefore if there is any prospect of frequent moves, the layout should be designed to fit loosely in to the railway room, and any sections fitting into alcoves should be mainly scenic or, at the most, should only hold industrial sidings or other rail-linked features which can be repositioned or even omitted without affecting the main layout.

175 Although I took great care to make the corner joints square, I find

that my frames are tending to twist. What should I do?

This problem is caused by the fact that a simple right-angled butt joint has very little resistance to twisting. The problem mainly arises with open-top framing, and can be cured either by screwing ply gussets under the joints (see Plate 5) or by fitting proprietary metal corner brackets inside the framing. The latter can be found in any large DIY suppliers.

176 What is open-top construction?

With open-top construction, the tracks are carried on relatively narrow sub-bases supported on the main framing (see Plate 6). This form of construction is more or less mandatory for scenic areas, but it is of limited value around stations and yards.

177 How are sub-bases made?

Sub-bases are cut from a sheet of suitable man-made board, ideally with a power jigsaw. Composite construction is often used, with a wider ply or chipboard base and a narrower trackbed cut from insulation board or even cork sheet. In practice, many workers use a catch-as-catch-can approach and make the main sub-base from whatever happens to be to hand and fits the specific site (see Plate 6).

178 What is L-girder construction?

This is a system of open-top construction for permanent sites, where the main baseboard strength members are two long timber girders which have a number of joists fixed to their tops. Four stout legs provide the support and the joists are secured by screwing from underneath. The track bases are supported by risers and secured to them by cleats (see Plate 6).

179 What are the advantages of L-girder construction?

It is an extremely flexible system of baseboard assembly, as all adjustments may be carried out from underneath the layout. It is thus possible to move both joists and risers should this prove necessary. It is also possible to use a large amount of scrap offcuts, since the alignment of the sub-bases does not depend

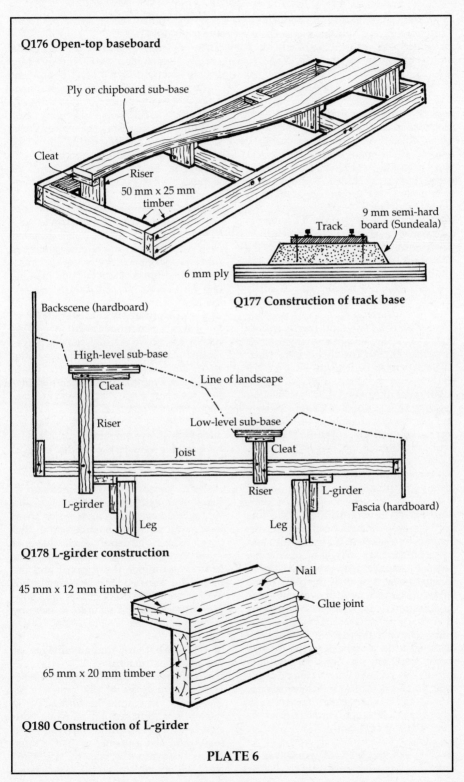

Q176 Open-top baseboard

Ply or chipboard sub-base

Cleat

Riser

50 mm x 25 mm timber

Track

9 mm semi-hard board (Sundeala)

6 mm ply

Q177 Construction of track base

Backscene (hardboard)

High-level sub-base

Cleat

Line of landscape

Riser

Low-level sub-base

Joist

Cleat

L-girder

Riser

L-girder

Leg

Leg

Fascia (hardboard)

Q178 L-girder construction

Nail

45 mm x 12 mm timber

Glue joint

65 mm x 20 mm timber

Q180 Construction of L-girder

PLATE 6

on all timbers being of compatible sizes. The screwed construction makes it easy to reduce the entire framework to its basic elements and rebuild the layout.

180 How is the L-girder made?

The original arrangement was to glue two sections of wood together, securing them temporarily with screws, but it was soon realised that skew nailing was quicker and cheaper than screwing. For spans of up to 3 m, the L-girder should be made from 65 mm x 20 mm timber with a 45 mm x 12 mm top (see Plate 6). For shorter spans, the depth of the vertical timber may be reduced. Where a sawbench is available, an L-girder can be cut from a single piece of timber. This method is slightly stronger, whilst the scrap cut out makes excellent joists.

181 Could I use metal angle for L-girder construction?

'Dexion' or 'Handy Angle' can be readily bolted together to form a strong and rigid framework. The main difficulty is cutting the material to size – a hacksaw is essential and, into the bargain, the cut edges must be smoothed. It is more convenient to use timber for the joists and to use round-headed screws and washers to give a proper fitting for the elongated holes in the girders.

182 Could I use aluminium sections for framing?

That would very much depend on your skills and the extent of your workshop, since the sections must be joined by bolting or riveting. There are few advantages, other than weight-saving on a portable layout, and many snags. If weight-saving is important, plywood is more convenient.

183 How do you make baseboard framing from plywood?

Ply frames need to be made from at least 6 mm thick material, generally with a depth of 75 mm (see Plate 7). If you don't have a sawbench, it is best to buy the ply from a timber merchant, rather than a DIY supplier, since the former is usually prepared to cut your sheet into whatever sizes you want for a small fee or, occasionally, no charge at all. This needs to be arranged prior to your visit.

184 How do you join the ply framing together?

There are two methods. The simplest is to use corner pieces cut from 20 mm square softwood, to which the ply frames are screwed. Alternatively, proprietary metal corner joints may be used.

185 What sort of legs should I use to support the baseboards?

Stout ones! They are ideally made from 50 mm square timber with 50 mm x 25 mm bracing, though in practice, providing all joints are firmly made with screws and glue, 50 mm x 25 mm legs with 50 mm x 12 mm bracing is adequate. Added security can be achieved by the use of metal shelf brackets to minimise swaying (see Plate 7).

186 How high should a baseboard be?

This is very much a personal decision. For comfort and convenience, something between waist height and chest height is advised. A lot has been said about the added realism of an 'eye-level' baseboard, but this has two severe disadvantages: the models to the rear of the layout are masked, and it is only possible to work on the layout when standing on a platform. In many sites fixed obstructions or other features may suggest an optimum height.

187 Should I bolt the baseboard to the walls for added strength?

When the layout is in a garage or other outhouse, there is some merit in this. It is not a good idea to fix the baseboard members directly to the walls, but rather to screw the supports to the fabric of the building. In a habitable room it is not such a good idea, since when you (or your heirs) need to dismantle the layout, the walls will need extensive replastering before the room can revert to its normal use.

188 How do I carry the baseboard across a door opening?

The classic solution is the lifting flap, a section of baseboard arranged on the principle of a bar flap. However, the hinges must be mounted at least 12mm above the surface, or the rails will hit against each other when the flap is lifted

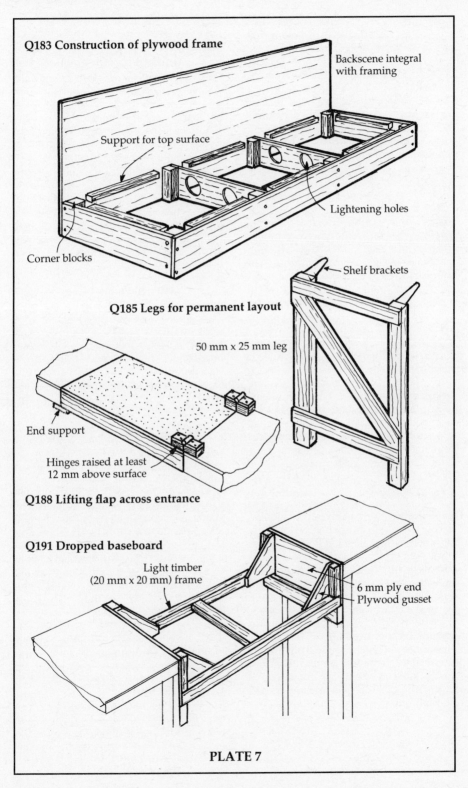

Q183 Construction of plywood frame

Backscene integral with framing

Support for top surface

Lightening holes

Corner blocks

Q185 Legs for permanent layout

Shelf brackets

50 mm x 25 mm leg

End support

Hinges raised at least 12 mm above surface

Q188 Lifting flap across entrance

Q191 Dropped baseboard

Light timber (20 mm x 20 mm) frame

6 mm ply end
Plywood gusset

PLATE 7

(see Plate 7). It is absolutely essential to provide a secure method of holding the flap in the vertical position.

189 Why should the lifting flap be secured?

Clearly, if the flap falls backwards on to the layout, it can damage whatever it hits. But this is as nothing to the trouble it can cause if it falls the other way, thus possibly preventing entry into the railway room.

190 Is there an alternative to a lifting flap?

A short section of baseboard can lift out, making it in effect a portable baseboard. When not in use, it can be stored under the main baseboard on runners. The main point to note is that the construction needs to be fairly lightweight and it is usually more convenient to make this a scenic section, often on a dropped baseboard.

191 What is a dropped baseboard?

A dropped baseboard is a section where the main framing is carried below the general level, so that a valley can be modelled and crossed by a long bridge or a short viaduct. Since the lower section is purely for scenic use, open frame construction is normally used (see Plate 7).

192 I have seen references to a 'duck under' on plans. What is this feature?

It is often more convenient to gain access to an operating well by ducking under the baseboard. This implies a reasonably high baseboard, generally offering at least 800 mm clearance, but providing the area is carpeted and possibly provided with handrails a clearance of 600 mm is adequate. The framing needs to be substantial and firmly fixed to the floor to prevent the layout being damaged should someone come up too soon. A little padding with foam plastic is also advised!

Section 2:2
Portable layouts

193 What is a portable layout?

A layout that can *easily* be taken apart and stored out of the way of the home and readily taken to another site or exhibition. Larger sectional layouts are transportable rather than portable. Whilst it is convenient if the entire layout can be carried to another site in the family car, this is not an absolute essential. What is vital is that the layout must be capable of being erected and dismantled in an evening, leaving time for a worthwhile running session, since if this is not possible the whole point of a portable scheme is lost.

194 Which gauge is most suited for portable layouts?

OO, HO, N and Z gauges, together with most narrow gauges, are equally suitable. The larger scales need bigger baseboards and are mostly confined to transportable schemes, but some limited O gauge schemes have been made on small baseboards. Gauges 1 and G are not really suited for this type of layout.

195 How large can I make a portable layout?

In practice, the upper limit is eight to ten baseboard sections. It is largely a matter of time – the more sections involved, the longer it takes to erect and dismantle the model, but the storage of the boards when not in use is also an important factor. You need to be able to erect the layout, enjoy a good operating session and put everything away in an evening. If it takes above 40 minutes to erect and a similar time to dismantle, the whole thing becomes a nuisance.

196 What do I do about locomotives, rolling-stock and other loose fittings when I dismantle the layout?

They could be kept in their original boxes, but most owners find it more convenient to provide special storage boxes with padded divisions into which the models are placed (see Plate 8). This not only speeds up the chore, but takes up less space in storage. There is the added

advantage that with 'a place for everything', there is less chance of overlooking
something at the end of the day.
Organisation is essential with portable
schemes.

197 How large can the baseboard sections be?

For home use the limits are set by the
difficulty of getting the baseboard unit
through a doorway measuring 2 m x
0.75 m. A baseboard measuring 1.25 m x
1.25 m is the optimum size, but 1 m x
0.5 m modules are growing in favour,
since they fit into most family cars.
However, the most significant factor is
the size of your storage area. Another
point to remember is that most portable
layouts have to be moved, erected and
dismantled by one person, so the all-up
weight of each unit needs to be kept low
enough for this to be done with ease.
Anything in excess of 12 kg is going to
become extremely irksome by the time the
final baseboard is back in its storage area.

198 I have seen layouts with folding baseboards. What are the reasons for this?

The folding baseboard protects the
models when closed and is slightly faster
to close up for storage (see Plate 8). It
calls for more careful construction, and
sets a maximum length of 1 m for each
folding section, although some very large
folding schemes have been built. These
are not strictly portable since the size and
all-up weight make it essential to have
two or more people to move the sections.

199 Is there any reason why I cannot build a portable layout on a single large baseboard?

The bigger the baseboard, the heavier it
becomes and the less portable it is. A
single baseboard for an OO/HO scheme
needs to be at least as big as a double
bed; for N one needs something about
the size of a door. Whilst these units can
be moved, they're hardly portable within
our terms of reference.

200 Where should one store a layout?

This depends on the design of the home.
A large cupboard is ideal, but at a pinch
the garage or the loft can be used. The

snag here is that it takes longer to bring
the sections into the living room.

201 I live in a small flat with limited storage space, all of which is needed. Where can I store the layout?

One popular solution is to build the
main station on two larger sections and
to store the rest of the baseboards underneath, sliding each section in on runners
(see Plate 8). The main baseboards need
to be provided with a solid cover so that
when they are not in use the models are
protected.

202 Would you recommend storing baseboard sections under the bed?

This is the worst place of all, since the
biggest enemy of model railways is fluff,
and most fluff in the home is found
under the beds. In any case, there is no
space under modern divan beds.

203 When my layout is erected it blocks the view of the TV and annoys the family. What can I do about this?

Move the layout into the bedroom!
Alternatively, lower the height of the
layout so that it is possible to see over it.

204 How should I connect baseboard sections together?

Where speed of assembly is of importance, there is nothing to beat the split
hinge (see Plate 9). A normal hinge has
its pivot removed and replaced by a
close-fitting pin – a round nail of suitable
size is ideal. The hinge is simply screwed
across the side of the joint, and to dismantle the sections the pins are removed.

205 This seems a trifle crude – wouldn't something more precise be needed to ensure accurate alignment of tracks?

A hinge is a very precise device – it
would not work satisfactorily if it were
not. Other precision devices, pattern-
maker's dowels for example, are more
difficult to locate precisely. In fact, pat-
tern-makers fit the dowels before completing the pattern.

206 How should I carry tracks across the joints?

The most favoured method is to assem-

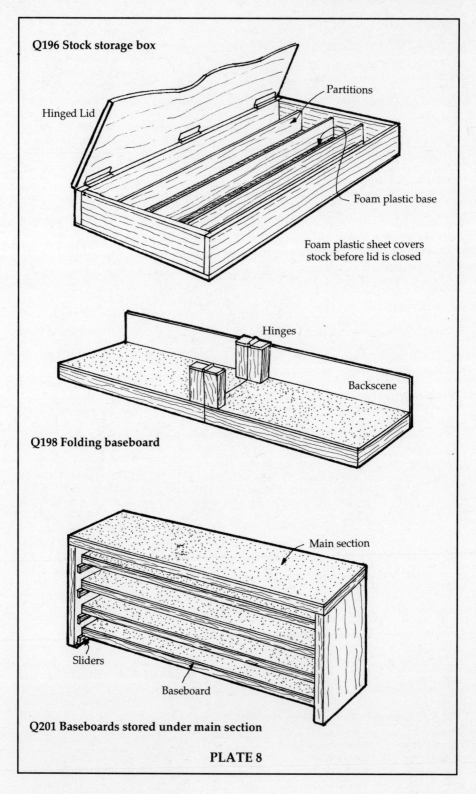

Q196 Stock storage box

Hinged Lid

Partitions

Foam plastic base

Foam plastic sheet covers
stock before lid is closed

Q198 Folding baseboard

Hinges

Backscene

Q201 Baseboards stored under main section

Main section

Sliders

Baseboard

PLATE 8

Q204 Split hinge for baseboard joint

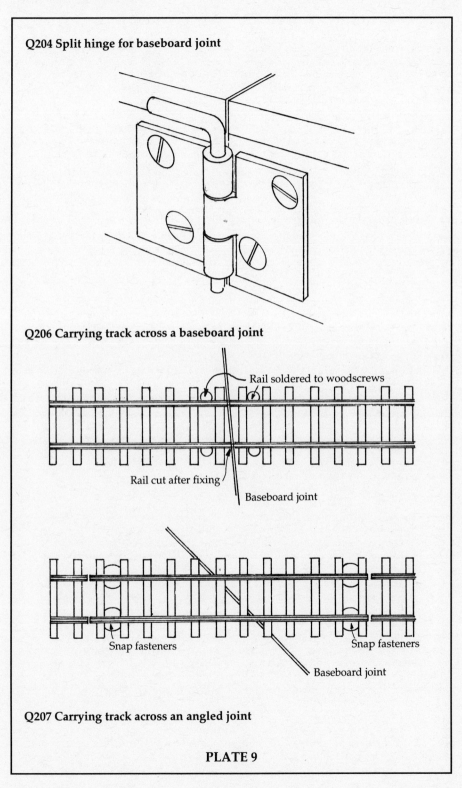

Q206 Carrying track across a baseboard joint

Rail soldered to woodscrews

Rail cut after fixing

Baseboard joint

Snap fasteners

Snap fasteners

Baseboard joint

Q207 Carrying track across an angled joint

PLATE 9

ble the baseboards first, lay the tracks across the joint, secure the rails on either side then cut through with a fine saw or a small abrasive disc. It is advisable to have the tracks crossing the joint at as near to a right-angle as possible (see Plate 9).

207 At corners, I find it is necessary to carry curves across at an oblique angle and derailments are frequent. What should I do?
Where an oblique crossing is unavoidable, there are two possibilities. One is to have a zigzag end to the baseboard, but this is troublesome to make and can cause problems in transit. The other is to have a short section of track, about 100 mm long, to bridge the joint (see Plate 9). A popular method of fixing this section of track is to use dressmaker's snap fasteners, with the base screwed to the baseboard and the top soldered to the rails. These devices are very precise and cheap.

208 How do you carry electrical circuits across baseboard joints?
There are three accepted methods. One is to fit mating spring contacts along the baseboard edges. Another is to provide jumper cables terminating in multi-pin plugs. The third is to control the layout from a separate panel and to link each baseboard to the panel with a long lead and multi-pin plug – the 'umbilical cord' approach. All three can be used on one layout. However, baseboard edge contacts, while cheap, are vulnerable, jumper cables can often be cumbersome, and the 'umbilical cord' system tends to get unwieldy on larger systems.

209 Should I mount the control panel on the baseboards or have a separate control box?
This is a matter of taste. The built-in panel is very convenient and affords the opportunity of applying one's ingenuity in disguising its presence. The central control box is particularly useful for exhibition work, since it is common practice to operate from the 'wrong' side to give visitors the better view of the model.

210 What sort of support should be provided for portable layouts?
There are three main types: the folding

trestle, the plug-in or screw-in leg, and the folding leg. There is no absolute best approach. It should be remembered, however, that only the initial section needs supports at each end – all subsequent sections have one end supported by the adjoining section.

211 What are trestles?
A pair of frames, hinged at the top and provided with a tie to hold the legs at a specific distance apart (see Plate 10). They are fairly cumbersome in use and only suitable for larger transportable systems.

212 How are hinged legs arranged?
A light frame is hinged at one end to the baseboard itself. It is necessary to provide some means of holding the legs flat against the base whilst in transit and to provide a modicum of bracing so that they remain upright (see Plate 10). Proprietary hinged stays can be found in any large DIY store.

213 What are plug-in legs?
They are what the name suggests, a simple frame which plugs into close-fitting slots fitted under the baseboard (see Plate 10). They require a certain amount of care in their construction, but have the undoubted virtues of simplicity and low cost.

214 How do I arrange screw-in legs?
These are neat tapered wooden legs which screw into metal plates; you can buy them at DIY stores (see Plate 10). However, the longer pattern need to be ordered – timber merchants with DIY counters are the best source here. However, the usual shorter pattern are useful for living-room layouts – the model does not then break the line of sight to the TV! A side advantage is that the legs take up little space in storage.

215 What is the ideal height for a portable layout?
This is again a personal choice, but in practice anything over 1 m is apt to be a shade unstable. Lower levels, around 6-700 mm, which are operated whilst sitting down, are very convenient in the living-room and are more stable.

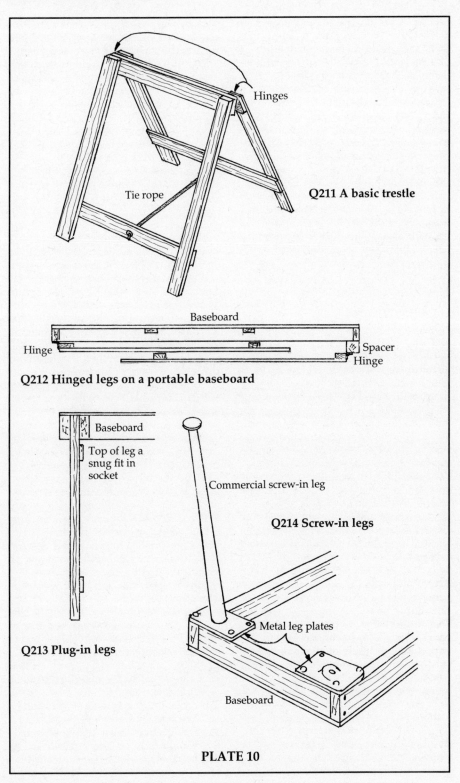

Q211 A basic trestle

Hinges

Tie rope

Baseboard

Hinge

Spacer
Hinge

Q212 Hinged legs on a portable baseboard

Baseboard

Top of leg a
snug fit in
socket

Commercial screw-in leg

Q214 Screw-in legs

Metal leg plates

Q213 Plug-in legs

Baseboard

PLATE 10

216 I am having some difficulty in getting my portable layout absolutely level. What would you recommend?
The main problems arise from uneven floors. There are three solutions. One is to fit some form of screw adjuster to each leg; this is best applied in the context of a club layout since such adjusters need to be specially made. A simpler arrangement is to provide a quantity of thin packing material and place this under the appropriate legs, a crude but extremely reliable system. The most sophisticated arrangement is to have each leg tailor made for the purpose, and the position of the first section marked by small tacks driven into the carpet.

Section 2:3
Tracklaying with ready-assembled track

217 I have a quantity of OO gauge toy train set track on hand. Is it possible to use this in a proper model railway?
Way back in the bad old days there was a very distinct difference between the track provided with train sets and that used by serious enthusiasts for model railways, so the first step one took when moving away from the toy was to lay scale track. However, modern sectional track, as supplied with the better-class train sets, is identical in appearance to the mainstream ready-assembled track for the serious market. In fact, there is no longer any real difference between the toy and the model – it is now a question of usage. The only significant practical difference is that sectional tracks have fairly sharp curves.

218 I have been trying for some time to produce an accurate track plan for a sectional track layout, but I am having considerable difficulty setting out the various sections. What advice can you give me?
If you *must* produce a track plan in this way, first and foremost you have to work to as large a scale as possible. The very small track templates provided by certain manufacturers are only very rough guides and even when used by experienced draughtsmen only produce approximate results. This is adequate for the main purpose of a track plan, to ensure that the proposed arrangement is practical, and in the case of sectional track to determine the number and types of track sections required. This can also be done, in the case of certain tracks, by using the small-scale plastic track planning kits which provide a plethora of track parts which one can assemble on a flat surface to try out one's ideas.

It is as well to realise that although sectional track appears to conform to a rigid geometry, there is a small but significant degree of flexibility in the joins and, except when one is dealing with a very small continuous circuit, it is possible to 'tweak' the formation into shape. To give an idea of what is possible, a square track formation, with 15 or more straight sections in each side between each quarter curve, could have a single straight section inserted in one side and still seem to line up accurately.

219 Is it possible to combine different makes of sectional track on the one layout?
Virtually all HO/OO sectional track uses Code 100 flat bottom rail, so the various sections can be connected together with no difficulty. However, the majority of sectional track manufacturers use different geometries, so the various individual sections are not directly interchangeable. In some cases the differences are negligible; for example, the main difference between Peco Setrack and Hornby track is the diamond crossing. Whilst this might seem a serious problem, these small variations can be of considerable value if you wish to get away from the strict geometric nature of the basic track formation.

220 Some sectional tracks are now being offered with integral ballast. What are the advantages of this?
The main advantage hits the eye – they look more realistic – though at present there is an unprototypical groove down the centre of double tracks. A less obvious, but equally important difference, is that they have greater strength, though this is only of importance when used in the basic toy mode, where it is customary to toss all track haphazardly into a

large box at the end of the day.

It is of interest that this provision of ballast is in effect a reversion to an older mode, since from the earliest days of 16.5 mm gauge, starting with the Bing table-top system, all sectional track made until the 1960s had some form of integral ballast – though in most cases this was lithographed tinplate.

221 Could I extend an existing layout with the new integral ballasted track, or must I relay everything?

The manufacturers have taken considerable pains to see that you can simply extend your layout for, much as they would like you to replace the entire track, they are realists and know that the continued support of satisfied customers is the most important factor in their continued prosperity. It can be taken for granted that unless there is a note to the contrary in the catalogue, all products from one manufacturer for a given gauge are completely compatible.

222 How does one arrange matters so that the ends of sectional tracks line up with the joins in a series of baseboard units?

Whilst in theory it might be possible to make baseboard joins coincide with the ends of sectional tracks, the practical difficulties are considerable. At the outset the units of track that cross the joins in the baseboard should not be pinned down to the baseboard; they can thus be removed when the layout is dismantled. This, however, can be bothersome and there is always the risk of losing or mislaying one of the sections. A slightly better solution is to carry on pinning the track down across the join and then, having added extra fastenings on either side of the gap, cut through the rails over the join (see Q206).

223 I have been attempting to construct a fairly complicated layout from sectional track, but I am unable to get all parts of my desired track formation to link up correctly. What am I doing wrong?

You aren't doing anything more dramatic than pushing what is of necessity both a rigid and limited system beyond its bounds. What you need are custom-made filler sections, which you can produce readily by cutting a section of track to fit. If you have several fillers to provide, you may prefer to buy a single length of flexible track and a packet of rail joiners for this purpose.

224 Is it possible to use both sectional and flexible track on the same layout?

If, as is usually the case, the rail section and sleeper thicknesses match, there will be no difficulty. Most sectional track manufacturers offer the option of plain flexible track.

225 What is the best way of cutting track?

There are two possible methods. The usual one is to use a fine metal-cutting saw, preferably whilst holding the section of track to be cut in a simple cutting jig or a vice (see Plate 11). Whilst many advocate a razor saw, I prefer a small hacksaw with pen-ended blades. However, a much better system is to cut through the rail with a thin abrasive disc mounted on an arbour held in a small low-voltage drill. It is advisable to wear goggles whilst doing this; should the brittle disc fracture, small bits of very hard material will fly off at high speed and some will head for your face. It is not a good idea to try to cut track with side cutters – they distort the end of the rail and often damage the fastenings.

It will be necessary to cut away the rail fastenings on the end sleepers to allow the rail joiners to be slid onto the rails (see Plate 11). If this isn't done there will be an unsightly gap in the sleepering. Whilst one can always insert a spare sleeper into the space, this will end up as one of those tedious little jobs one puts off in favour of more interesting projects.

226 Several track manufacturers are now offering OO/HO track with finer section rail. How does this differ from the standard track?

These tracks are laid with a finer section rail and, in most cases, also have more detailed rail fastenings, and are therefore a better choice for a high-quality layout. It is difficulty to account for all types of fine section track; there is, for example the Shinohara system, the earliest finer scale ready-assembled track, which is precisely to NMRA specifications and would not necessarily take all current ready-to-run HO or OO equipment. The finer Peco track is compatible with recent ready-to-run models, but early Triang stock may not run too smoothly unless the wheels are changed.

227 **Is it possible to extend a layout using standard section track together with this improved product?**
It is possible to use different rail sections on one layout, providing each section is kept to a specific area and the junction takes place in plain track so that there are not too many places where the necessary adjustments need to be made. A very simple method of making the adjustment in height is to join the two tracks together with normal rail joiners, solder these in place for added security, then file the head of the deeper rail for about 50-75 mm to form a reasonably gentle adjustment (see Plate 11). The relatively small difference in height, a matter of 0.75 mm at the most, makes this treatment fairly straightforward.

A better arrangement would be to make up short intermediate adaptor sections of track, where the two rail sections are joined together by filing and soldering. Whilst this involves more work at the outset, it will probably save effort in the long run.

This answer is only concerned with the mechanics of the process, not the wisdom of mixing both sections.

228 **Why do you imply that haphazard mixing of the older Code 100 track with the new finer section rails could be unwise? Will it affect the operation of the layout?**
The reason for the introduction of a more accurate rail section has no relation to the operation of the model – it is purely a cosmetic treatment and has come about in response to the steady improvement in the appearance of both the better ready-to-run models and, above all, the latest sophisticated kits now available. It is a finescale track of vastly improved appearance. One immediate effect of introducing more realistic-looking track on the layout will be to emphasise the overscale nature of Code 100 track. This is why it is advisable to keep the two types of track separate. However, it must be appreciated that once you introduce the finer section rail on to the layout, you will almost certainly find you want to replace the rest.

Provided that this is carried out systematically, as part of a carefully planned programme of improvement, using the short adaptor sections already described as links between the two types of track, the changeover will go ahead smoothly and the end result will be well worth the effort. However, don't expect a change of rail section to have any effect on the rest of the model – it will not improve an unrealistic layout with sharp curves and unprototypical track formations, and will only show up crude scenery; above all, it will not improve the running of stock still fitted with overscale wheels.

229 **I have a well established layout but I feel that the existing track, a somewhat hotch-potch mixture of various makes, some of it a little battered after sundry relaying sessions, is letting the rest of the model down. I would like to change to a finer section track, but am a little put off by the work involved. What do you suggest I do?**
Bearing in mind the golden rule of maintenance engineering, 'If it works, don't muck it about', you should think carefully before making any changes to your layout. To help you come to a decision, build a small separate trial section using the finescale track you favour, large enough to allow limited operation to help find out not only if the improvement will be worthwhile but also whether any of your stock will need rewheeling. Whilst you are doing this, draw up a written programme for conversion, make a careful costing of both the money and time involved, then double these estimates. Put them aside for a time and settle down to a serious operating session, possible involving an improved operating schedule. Whilst you are doing this, consider whether it might not be better to build an entirely new layout and then sell the old one as a going concern.

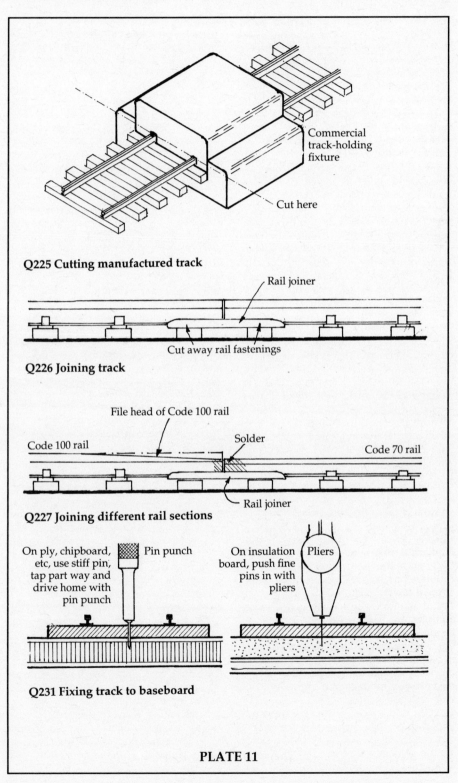

Commercial
track-holding
fixture

Cut here

Q225 Cutting manufactured track

Rail joiner

Cut away rail fastenings

Q226 Joining track

File head of Code 100 rail

Code 100 rail

Solder

Code 70 rail

Rail joiner

Q227 Joining different rail sections

On ply, chipboard, etc, use stiff pin, tap part way and drive home with pin punch

Pin punch

On insulation board, push fine pins in with pliers

Pliers

Q231 Fixing track to baseboard

PLATE 11

230 I am a little concerned as to the best way of fixing tracks to the baseboard. Various types of pin are offered for this purpose and I have seen references to the use of small screws. What is the correct method?

There is no one standard approach – you must select the one best suited to your needs. Older sectional tracks were intended to be screwed to the baseboard and suitable holes were provided. Screws, however, are costly, they take a considerable time to insert and unless you have a sectional track layout which changes formation with the phases of the moon there is little to recommend their use. The favoured method is pinning. The very fine blackened pins provided by Peco are intended for insertion into Sundeala board (blackened pins avoid any need to paint the track after laying). Other pins are stiff enough to be driven into chipboard or ply.

231 I am having some trouble driving pins into my chipboard base. Sometimes they bend, and I often hit the rail with the hammer. I feel that I'm making a mess of things – how do the experts cope?

First of all, use a light hammer, preferably of the cross pein pattern. Drive the pin down to a fraction of a millimetre above rail level, then proceed to the next pin along the track. Check the alignment carefully and, when you are satisfied, drive the pins firmly home with the help of a pin punch. The main reason Sundeala insulation board is recommended is that it is easy to push fine pins into it with a pair of flat-nosed pliers (see Plate 11).

232 I have covered my baseboard frames with a particularly hard variety of chipboard. After attempting to pin down some track, I have become converted to the virtues of Sundeala insulation board. Unfortunately I stuck the chipboard down – what can I do to salvage my baseboards?

You can lay Sundeala on top of the chipboard – this is probably the best all-round form of baseboard surface, combining the virtues of both materials. Except around stations and yards it is not necessary to cover the entire surface

with insulation board; sub-bases can be cut from the board to the required form and stuck in place with ample PVA adhesive.

233 How does one cope with flexible track which does not have pre-formed holes in the sleepers?

The sleepers on most tracks are moulded from a resilient plastic and it is possible to push fine pins through the material with only a moderate amount of pressure. It is also possible to drive stiff pins through the plastic, but this does tend to distort the sleeper locally and, whilst not affecting the gauge, does mar the appearance. Small holes can be made using a fine twist bit in a low-voltage drill.

234 What is 'floating track'?

This is track that is only lightly held down and which rests on a resilient underlay. It is claimed to provide better running, but this is a debatable point. The most common type of floating track today uses foam plastic ballast inlay. The track is first glued to the inlay and then the inlay is glued to the baseboard.

235 Is it possible to stick the track directly to the baseboard?

This is a perfectly acceptable method. Double-sided adhesive tape is best for this purpose, and it is essential to position the track dry and mark the location of the vital parts on the baseboard before the sticking down process begins. It will be more convenient to apply the tape to the baseboard first and to stick the track to this. You can usually separate track from baseboard by sliding the blade of an old table knife or a steel spatula between the sleepers and the baseboard.

236 If I pin the track firmly to the baseboard, how can I lift it for re-use?

By tackling the job with reasonable care. The track needs to be prised up gently – a screwdriver can be used to lift the sleepers sufficiently to ease the track pins out of the baseboard. Once the heads of the track pins are proud of the sleepers, a small pair of side cutters can be used to pull them cleanly out of the baseboard surface.

237 I have a quantity of old track with a few odd kinks in it. Is it OK to use this in tunnels and other hidden sections?

One reason why trains so frequently derail in tunnels and other inaccessible places is that it has been assumed that so long as you can't see any faults, they don't matter. With trackwork, 'out of sight, out of mind' is a sound principle, and the only way you can afford to ignore track is to ensure that it is absolutely free from blemish. Main lines should be laid with new track or track in 'as new' condition.

Where track is in poor condition, the only sensible thing to do is to follow prototype practice and use it for sidings. The kinks cannot be readily rectified – it is best to cut the defective section of rail clean away. In most cases the best way to salvage slightly defective plastic-sleepered track is to cut away the sharper kinks in the rail, then withdraw the rail from the sleepers. Once free of fixings, the rails can be carefully straightened, matched for length and threaded back on to the undamaged parts of the old bases.

238 I am having some difficulty keeping my double-track main lines parallel. How is this done?

The most straightforward method is to lay one track to the required alignment, then position the second using a simple gauge (see Plate 12). Peco now provides plastic spacing gauges for this purpose for standard double-track centres, but it is not difficult to make suitable gauges to provide the required track spacing for special circumstances.

239 Why are the recommended track centres for OO and EM 50 mm and 45 mm respectively, although both are to the same scale?

The standard 50 mm centres for OO are somewhat overscale to allow clearance on tighter-than-scale curves; a similar allowance needs to be made where EM tracks are laid to the sort of radii one finds in OO as a matter of course. Incidentally, the centres used for small-radius sectional track are even greater, 55 mm. Tables are produced for this widening; they are, however, only approximate since they assume a specific length of coach and locomotive overhang. It is perfectly feasible to lay OO gauge straight or large-radius double-track lines at 45 mm centres, but it will be necessary to modify any standard points used to make crossovers since these are set for 50 mm centres. For a quality model, this practice is to be recommended.

240 How does one curve flexible track to a pre-determined radius?

The most straightforward method is to use a proprietary track curve, a length of metal made to the chosen gauge and set to the required radius. Alternatively, a curved template may be cut from hardboard or ply to any desired radius (see Plate 12), around which the track is then gently curved. It is advisable on all but the most gentle of radii to slide the rail part way out of the sleepers and pre-curve it by hand before attempting to make the main curve. This reduces the natural tendency of the track to straighten itself out. It is important to remember that prototype track is not normally laid in a succession of geometric figures, but curves gently around the route in a succession of transition curves. Whilst it is possible to set out true transition curves mathematically, flexible track will, of its own volition, lie in an arc not far removed from a true transition curve if one end is curved to a selected radius and the other allowed to line up against a straight-edge positioned about 20 mm outside the tangent to the circle.

241 How does one make a curved template?

The first requirement is a suitable worktop which allows the template to be fixed down at the required distance from the centre of the curve – in other words, a length of wood at least 70 mm wide and some 150 mm longer than the radius to be struck. A nail is driven in near to one end and the template blank tacked the requisite distance from the centre pin. The radius is set out using a steel tape, then a length of string with a loop in one end is slipped over the nail and the other end is wound around a ballpoint pen or a pencil until the point of the pen or pencil is over the mark. The curve is then struck.

A slightly more formal arrangement is to take a metre- or yard-stick and drill a

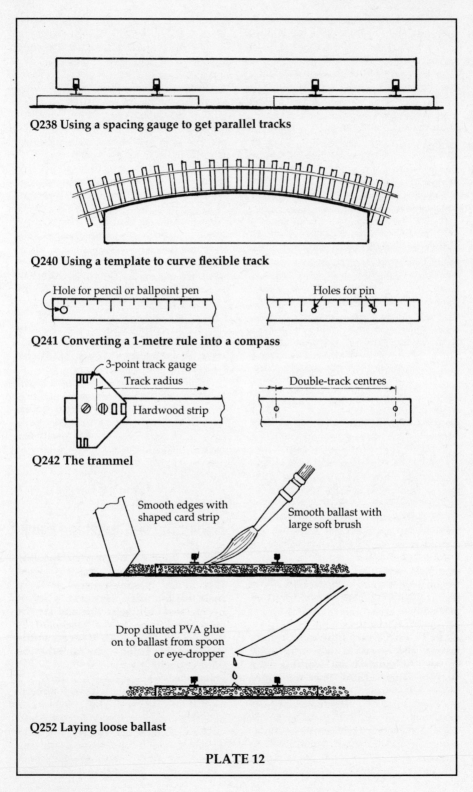

Q238 Using a spacing gauge to get parallel tracks

Q240 Using a template to curve flexible track

Hole for pencil or ballpoint pen

Holes for pin

Q241 Converting a 1-metre rule into a compass

3-point track gauge

Track radius

Double-track centres

Hardwood strip

Q242 The trammel

Smooth edges with
shaped card strip

Smooth ballast with
large soft brush

Drop diluted PVA glue
on to ballast from spoon
or eye-dropper

Q252 Laying loose ballast

PLATE 12

hole large enough to take a pencil or ballpoint pen snugly exactly on a mark at one end, then to drill a succession of smaller holes at the other end at 25 mm centres. These holes in no way detract from the normal use of the stick for measuring or as a straight-edge – they merely enhance its value as a tool (see Plate 12).

242 I have seen references to the use of a trammel for setting out curves. What is it, and how does one use it?

A trammel consists of a long bar, generally made of hardwood but for drawing office use frequently an extruded aluminium section. On it are two sliding units, one to hold a pivot point, the other to hold a pencil, stylus or bow pen. It is a specialised form of compass for drawing large radii (see Plate 12). A version can be produced by screwing a track gauge to one end of a wooden lath, with a series of holes at the other to allow the gauge to swing around in a series of arcs. This is then used to hold the rails in position as the track is laid to a true curve.

So far the idea is simplicity itself. There are, however, some practical snags. With the exception of a very simple solid baseboard layout, the centre of the curve is not only located off the baseboard but is usually in the very place the modeller needs to stand in order to work on the track with some degree of comfort. In other cases it may be situated beyond the walls of the room! Furthermore, it will only work if there is an unobstructed access to the curved track, which makes it useless for a multi-level system. In point of fact, trammels were used for the assembly of the obsolete pattern of battened track in the workshop, where these disadvantages do not arise.

243 I have very little room for my layout and need to use very tight curves. Although I am working to a slightly larger radius than the No 2 radius of sectional track, a number of my locomotives are decidedly unhappy with my curves, yet they will run around the very small No 1 curves without any difficulty. Why should there be this discrepancy?

It is almost certain that instead of a true arc, your track has been laid to an approximate parabola and the tightest curve is much less than you think. When very tight curves are required – under 600 mm in OO gauge – it is best to use sectional track. These are made with rail that has been pre-formed in special tools and a rigid plastic base which has been made in high-precision moulds. As a result the track is accurately curved to limits unobtainable in the home workshop.

244 Despite my upmost care I have a number of unrealistic, unprototypical kinks in my track. What should I do to eliminate them?

First of all, kinks are to be found in full-sized track. The reason we are unaware of this is that it is extremely difficult to see them unless you happen to be riding in the cab. However, it is as well not to ape this particular feature of the prototype.

To eliminate the kink you need to know exactly where it is, and the simplest method is to bring one eye down to track level. This is much more easily carried out on the prototype, so it is likely you will have to resort to using a small pocket mirror. Once you spot where the trouble is, the track alignment can be adjusted. Whilst a few small kinks can be tolerated, you must eliminate the sharper, more serious dog-leg, unless of course, you like derailments.

Part 2:4
Ballasting and finishing track

245 I am a little puzzled. Reading the catalogue, it appears that it is a good idea to lay plastic-sleepered track in foam ballast inlay. However, a lot of people seem to ignore this and lay the track directly on to the baseboard. Is this wrong? The catalogue seems a little vague on this point – why can't they be more explicit?

Foam plastic ballast inlay is a quick and neat method of improving the appearance of the track. It also has some sound-deadening qualities and is claimed to improve the running, though this point is impossible to determine with any degree of certainty. Naturally, the manufacturer would like you to buy as many of his products as you can afford, so implies that you should use their prepared ballast but, being a responsible concern, does not make any claims or issue instructions which are open to argument.

246 One manufacturer suggests that you should stick the ballast inlay to the baseboard and then stick the track into the ballast. Is this wholly satisfactory? Surely it would be better to pin the track through the ballast.

If you pin the track through the ballast, it is more than likely that you will compress it locally and the net result will be a gently undulating track; far from improving the running qualities, you will make matters worse. This can be overcome by pinning the track down at close intervals – say not greater than 60-70 mm centres. This will compress the foam sufficiently to eliminate ripples, though it will at the same time eliminate any sound-deadening from the ballast. Unfortunately the compression of the underlay puts the pins in tension and as a result they will tend to pull out. If the track is pinned to insulation board, as the manufacturer in question advises, there is a very distinct probability that some, but not all, of the pins will lift enough to create an undulating surface.

Gluing is simple and effective, it has been shown to be reliable and calls for no special skills on the part of the modeller. Obviously it is still necessary to take care when laying the track – in particular, the ballast inlay must be stuck to the track before it is stuck to the baseboard, otherwise it is highly unlikely that the sleepers will fit into the slots.

247 What glue do you recommend for sticking down track?

White PVA adhesive, as sold in bulk by DIY stores, is far and away the best and most economical adhesive you can get. Applied directly from the nozzle, a single, long and generous strip is perfectly adequate – there is no need to flood the ballast or baseboard.

248 What is the best way of fixing foam ballast inlay to the base – glue or double-sided adhesive tape?

Double-sided adhesive tape takes longer to use and doesn't allow you to slide the track sideways once it is in place. On the other hand, it is a lot easier to persuade the track to part company with the baseboard when double-sided tape is used.

249 If track and ballast are glued down, how can you lift them without damaging anything?

The simple answer is that you can't just lift it without tearing the foam inlay. It is usually possible to persuade the ballast to come away fairly cleanly from the baseboard by sliding the blade of a flat knife or a flat steel spatula underneath, but there may well be a little damage. Providing that it doesn't extend to the top surface, this is of no account. However, be prepared to spend a little time cutting away damaged ballast and replacing it with fresh material.

250 Try as I may, I do not seem to be able to get the degree of realism with my track that I would like. How do the experts produce such realistic-looking ballast?

For maximum realism it is essential not only to use loose ballast, but also to apply it realistically. Luckily, the fact that loose ballasting is inherently uneven aids this natural effect, but it is essential to study full-sized track carefully to see just how it looks on the prototype.

251 I have seen various materials suggested for loose ballast, ranging from actual stone chippings through cork chips to bird seed. Which is best?

Clearly, stone chippings or even fine sand are basically more realistic – you can't do better than use the real thing! However, cork granules, if fine enough, can often be extremely effective since, unlike natural stone, they are easy to colour. Dried coffee grounds also make good ballast and have the added attraction of costing nothing more than the trouble of saving the used filters and subsequently sorting the material.

Bird seed is bad – it can produce some very fine results but it encourages vermin. If this happens, the best you can hope for is that when they've eaten all the ballast, the little bugs will go away, but it is possible that they will then turn their attention to other parts of the model – they're quite partial to a tasty bit of cardboard.

With this one exception, it is not so much a case of a best product, but of careful selection of a material that produces the results you want. Always remember that you do not need to be absolutely consistent – indeed, if you look at a set of neglected sidings alongside the main line you will see that the difference in appearance is so marked that unless different materials are used on the model – say fine granite chips for the main line and coffee grounds in the siding – you will not get the correct effect.

252 I have been mixing my ballast with PVA adhesive and then applying it to the track. This is slow, tedious and messy, and the stuff seems to stick everywhere but where it is wanted. Is there a better way?

It is much easier to apply the ballast dry. Start by heaping it along the track much as is done in full-size practice when the material is dumped out of hopper wagons. It is then spread along the track with a slip of stiff card, again much as the plough fitted to the ballast brake van spreads prototype ballast. A broad, soft brush clears odd bits of ballast from the sleepers, the edges are neatened with a short straight-edge, and any small humps and hollows are evened out (see Plate 12). It is essential to remove even the smallest pieces of ballast from around point tiebars.

Once the results are satisfactory, the ballast needs to be secured in place. To do this, dilute PVA adhesive with an equal part of tap water, add a single drop of washing-up liquid to reduce surface tension, and apply the liquid to the ballast, using either a small spoon or an eye-dropper (see Plate 12). Soak the ballast thoroughly with the diluted adhesive and leave to dry for 24 hours. The diluted adhesive does not give a rock-hard bond, so it will be necessary, from time to time, to do a little judicious patching, particularly on portable layouts. An advantage is that it will be much easier to remove and relay track.

253 I am in the throes of remodelling part of the layout. Although I was able to lift the track out

of the ballast, how does one clean it away?

The favoured tool for this purpose is an old wood chisel – for once, a slightly blunt tool seems to work best; some modellers prefer a large screwdriver. A little vigorous scraping will remove most of the ballast, but after that it is often a case of getting to work with a small block of wood wrapped in coarse sandpaper to remove the last traces.

254 Is it advisable to paint track and, if so, what colours should I use?

It isn't absolutely necessary to paint the whole of the track, but it is certainly advisable to paint the rail to remove the bright finish along the sides and simulate the rust on the prototype. Track colour is available in tinlets, and represents an indication of public demand rather than any real necessity, since the actual colour of rail and fastenings is an indeterminate rust-mud brown of uneven hue. The classic formula for creating this colour is to mix all residues of dark coloured paint together and add thinners to taste. It is only necessary to slop this colour along the rail sides and over the fastenings, using a cheap paintbrush, as there is no need to attempt an even finish and, much more to the point, this particular usage is very hard on the bristles. If an airbrush is available, it makes the job that much faster.

Before the paint dries, the top surface of the rails should be wiped clean with a soft pad of cloth, then the running surface burnished with a track cleaner.

255 How does one get the effect of an overgrown siding?

This is done by running some narrow trails of PVA adhesive over the ballast and sprinkling model grass over the track and sleepers, using your favoured scenic modelling material. Here is a case where the final effect depends not only on the care taken with the actual modelling, but the amount of observation put into the study of overgrown sidings by the modeller.

256 How does one model inset tracks, as found in industrial sites and quaysides?

Basically, by covering the base with a

suitable surface material. However, as the sleepers are hidden, it is common practice to lay rails directly on to a subbase, for not only does this effect a small economy, but it also provides a more even surface on which to lay the roadway. There are two opposing schools of thought. One approach is to model the road surface either from card or from embossed plastic. In this case it is necessary to cut the surface material with great care so that the fit to the rail is good, although in practice small gaps can be hidden with modelling clay.

The other method is simply to apply plaster over the tracks; this is quick, cheap and straightforward, and the necessary flangeway is created by running an old wagon up and down the plaster just before it sets. A more sophisticated approach is to fit card slips to the face of the rail before applying the plaster, or to make up a simple scraping tool, generally by filing a notch in the side of a cheap electrician's screwdriver. The extra trouble of the first – card – method is well worth while if you wish to represent stone setts, for whilst these can be scribed into plaster, it is a very long and tedious business indeed (see Plate 13).

In either case it is advisable to depart from strict prototype practice and have the rail head at least 0.3 mm proud, so that it is possible to burnish the top surface without touching the modelled roadway.

Section 2:5
Scratchbuilt track

257   What is bullhead track?
Bullhead track was the principal form of track used in Britain until the late 1950s. It comprised a bulbous-section rail held in cast iron chairs by means of keys. These were originally hardwood wedges but in the 1930s were supplanted by special coiled sheet steel springs (see Plate 13). Originally the rail was double-headed, the idea being that when one surface had worn, the rail could be inverted for further use. Unfortunately, in use the bottom of the rail became pitted and when turned over produced a very rough ride. As a result the head was

deepened at the expense of the base.

Bullhead track was mainly confined to Britain, but some Continental lines built by British engineers, notably in France, also used it. The fact that the wide base of the chair spread the load over a larger area of the sleeper was considered to be an important advantage over simple flat bottom track (see Q258), whilst the chair also held the rail at a slight angle to improve running.

Although replaced by flat bottom rail in the 1950s, a considerable amount of bullhead track has remained in use on British railways. It is still standard on London Transport lines, where the ease of replacing worn rails is considered an advantage.

258   Could you give me some information concerning prototype flat bottom track?
Originally, flat bottom rail was intended to be spiked directly to the sleepers, and this is indeed still the practice for light and temporary railways, and on lines in developing countries. However, as locomotives became heavier, the tendency for the rail to bite into the relatively soft wooden sleeper became a serious problem. This was overcome by the insertion of a baseplate. Initially this was a piece of sheet iron with two holes punched for the spikes, but it was soon realised that a tapered sole plate could permit the rails to be angled inward to match the coning of the wheels and so improve running (see Plate 13). From here on the development of specialised fastenings to hold the rail more securely increased the complexity of construction. Modern flat bottom track for main-line use is a far cry from the original system, which naturally continues in use where economy is the watchword.

259   What is a Vignoles rail?
Up until the 1940s this term was commonly used in Britain to describe flat bottom rail. It acknowledges the fact that the section was introduced by the British civil engineer C. B. Vignoles in 1837, although its first recorded use was in 1830, by the US engineer, R. L. Stevens.

260   I have seen references to 'baulk road' in connection with the

GWR. Could you give me some information on this?

The GWR 'broad' (7-foot) gauge lines were, in the main, laid with bridge rail running on longitudinal timbers (baulks) which were spaced to gauge with transoms and tiebars (see Plate 13). Although mainly used on broad gauge lines, when the gauge was narrowed the original track remained in use for some years. Although all baulk road had gone from running lines by the early years of this century, a fair amount remained in sidings and on industrial sites. As a result, enough remained for the Great Western Society to be able to relay some broad gauge baulk road at their Didcot site. Although model bridge rail is not available from commercial sources, the Broad Gauge Society can often supply small quantities to members.

261 I have seen photographs of railway track laid with three running rails. What is this, and why is it done?

This is mixed gauge track, and was installed to allow trains of two different gauges to operate along the same track (see Plate 13). Needless to say, pointwork could be quite complicated and, in the largest installation of mixed gauge on the GWR in the latter part of the last century, it was not uncommon to separate broad and standard gauge pointwork. Today, mixed gauge is usually employed to allow stock of two gauges to use a common part of a yard, but a few cases of mixed gauge track exist on main running lines. In model form, mixed gauge track must be scratchbuilt.

262 I have carefully costed the components needed to construct a metre of track and find to my horror that they cost more than an equivalent length of assembled flexible track. Surely this cannot be right?

Flexible track consists of just two components, the plastic moulded sleepers, which are produced in long lengths, and the rails. These are drawn together in a specialised tool in a matter of seconds and, when assembled, can be packed in bulk, generally in batches of 25, in a stout card carton which only needs one simple label to complete the package. The resulting product is easy to store

directly on shelving and even easier to despatch to a customer individually or in bulk.

Hand-built track requires rail, sleepers and chairs or baseplates. Only the rails are easy to count and pack, but need reinforcing if sent through the post in small quantities. The sleepers and chairs are individually produced and then have to be counted accurately and placed in individual packages, which then need labelling and, ideally, an instruction sheet. These packages have to be stored in bins and are more difficult to pack for despatch. Hence it costs more to produce and this is reflected in the price to the user.

263 If there is no price advantage, why then does anyone bother to make their own track?

There are four reasons. The first is that it may be desired to have a very realistic track system which, it is believed, requires the extra detail of individual components. However, some extremely good assembled replicas of prototype track are now available and this trend is certain to continue. The second, and most common, reason is that the builder is using a non-standard track gauge and simply has to make his own. The third reason is that the builder produces his own sleepers and solders the rail either to flat-headed pins or to PCB sleepers and so saves some cost. The final, and probably the best, reason of all is that the builder likes making track. There is a much better case to be made for handmade turnouts where the saving is appreciable, although this is only true if the points are well made, since if derailments are frequent they are overpriced no matter how little they cost.

264 What is the meaning of the word 'code' in connection with rail? Wouldn't it be simpler to quote the gauge?

This is the standard method of distinguishing between various sections of rail (see Plate 13). The code number is the height of the rail in thousandths of an inch, and the term is of US origin. Thus Code 100 rail is 0.1 inches high. Although at one time it was common practice to refer to 'OO gauge bullhead

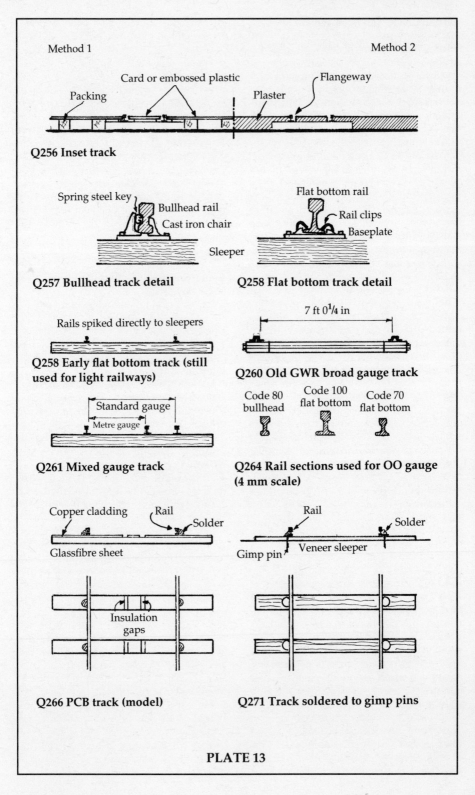

Method 1   Method 2

Q256 Inset track

Q257 Bullhead track detail   Q258 Flat bottom track detail

Q258 Early flat bottom track (still used for light railways)

Q260 Old GWR broad gauge track

Q261 Mixed gauge track

Q264 Rail sections used for OO gauge (4 mm scale)

Q266 PCB track (model)   Q271 Track soldered to gimp pins

PLATE 13

rail', the fact is that various sections of rail are used on the prototype and with a number of different sections now on the market, it is possible for a modeller to choose the section closest to his exact requirements. For example, a light railway or mineral line would use much lighter (and cheaper) rail than is used on the main lines, whilst a narrow gauge railway would use even lighter sections.

265 Is it possible to purchase plastic sleeper bases and rail separately for home assembly?

A few smaller manufacturers provide this option, generally for the more specialised gauges where the demand does not warrant the provision of a fully assembled track.

266 Could you explain exactly what is meant by PCB track?

This type of track consists of rail soldered directly to sleepers made from printed circuit board (PCB); this consists of a thin copper sheet bonded firmly to an insulating base and is supplied for the manufacture of circuit boards for electronic devices. For our purposes, the material is sawn into scale-sized sleepers, which have the centre part of the copper sheathing removed (see Plate 13). Long strips are also provided for point construction. Such sleepers can be produced in a small workshop equipped with a suitable circular saw bench; it is not easy to cut by hand, so most users rely on commercial products. Given a supply of sleepers and a suitable jig, PCB construction is fairly simple, if somewhat time-consuming.

267 What sort of jig is needed for PCB track assembly, and is it possible to make one in the home workshop?

Soldered track assembly jigs are not too difficult to manufacture at home. The most important requirement is a gauge lath, a length of ply or straight-grained hardwood some 3 mm thick, a little over 0.5 m long and accurately cut to the required gauge. It must also be straight. A length of softwood about 60-70 mm wide for 4 mm scale, and about 600 mm long is covered on one side with thin card. This is then carefully marked out to the required sleeper spacing, and slots

for the sleepers are cut though. The gauge lath is then secured in the exact centre by a number of small metal screws and nuts. In use, the slots are filled with sleepers and the gauge lath bolted down (see Plate 14). A length of rail is then placed on one side and soldered to the sleepers. The jig is then turned around so that the second rail can be soldered in place. The lath is then removed and the track extracted. It should then be washed to remove any traces of flux before being painted.

268 How does one make curved PCB track?

There are two methods. The simplest is to use the straight jig, but only to solder one rail in place. The resulting piece of half track can then be curved around a template and the second rail soldered in place. However, if a number of identical radius curves are needed, it is possible to make a curved assembly jig. Clearly this is nowhere near as easy to make as the standard straight jig and the idea is really only of interest to those individuals with a good craft background who enjoy making jigs.

269 There seem to be a number of different types of track gauges in use. Could you give me some information on these?

Track gauges fall into two main groups: those used for checking, and those for track assembly. In strict workshop parlance these are fixtures rather than gauges. The true gauge is something of a rarity – the 'Rogergauge', which could check OO or EM gauge track and which came out circa 1950 is no longer available. Nowadays a calliper gauge is preferred – this will tell you exactly how far the track is over or under gauge. An inexpensive pressed steel type, whilst by no means a precision instrument, is accurate to 0.1 mm, sufficient for our purposes.

Most commercial gauges today are based on a design initiated by Peco, and are of the turned roller pattern. Some recent types include spring loading and so ensure that the rail is held precisely to the specified gauge. The old three-point gauge, which produced a small gauge widening on curves, has virtually disappeared.

270 **Is it possible to make track gauges in the home workshop?**
The simplest form of track gauge is a block of wood, and this is always made in the home workshop. Although lacking slightly in absolute precision, it has one undeniable virtue when constructing soldered track in that it doesn't hold heat. Metal track gauges of various sorts can also be made in the home workshop but, except for the flat check gauge, they really require access to simple machine tools. In all cases we are moving into the realms of precision engineering and a prime essential is an accurate measuring tool such as a vernier gauge or micrometer.

271 **I have seen references to home-made track where the rail is soldered to pins. Can you give me any information on this system?**
This is a very old but relatively inexpensive method of track construction. Basically, the track is built up on a sub-base, usually cut from 3 mm ply. Sleepers, cut from thin wood veneer, are glued to the sub base and flat-headed pins driven into position about 1 mm outside of gauge (see Plate 13). Before the glue dries, ballast is spread over the base and pressed firmly home. When dry, surplus ballast is shaken off for reuse, then the rails are soldered to the pins. A more detailed description of this type of track is given in my book *Model Railways on a Budget* (see Bibliography). If you cut your sleepers from veneer, the overall cost is very low, little more than that of the rails, pins and plywood. The track units are similar to sectional track, hence it is relatively simple to lift and relay this type of track.

272 **Is it possible to spike flat bottomed track to wooden sleepers?**
This was a very popular method of tracklaying in the US, and enjoyed some vogue in the UK in the early days of flat bottomed track. It is essential to lay the track on a Sundeala base, as the spikes have to be pushed in with a pair of flat-nosed pliers.

273 **Could I stick flat bottomed rails directly to sleepers with superglue?**
If you can be certain of getting the rails

in the right place first time, yes. In fact, this particular idea has surfaced at regular intervals, and various adhesives have been used. The protagonists claim to have complete success, while others encounter problems. The fact that there appears to be a high failure rate doesn't deter experimenters. However, I would only advise the use of adhesives in conjunction with moulded chairs or baseplates, *and then only when the manufacturer recommends this course.*

274 **How many different makes of track components are there on the market?**
This is anybody's guess, for not only is this a popular field for the cottage industry manufacturer, who has a distressing tendency to cease trading after a few years, but it is also an area where specialist societies devoted to finescale modelling tend to provide excellent support. Most systems are alleged to be simple to use, though of late a few which have as their main aim extremely accurate replicas of prototype track, wisely omit to mention this but instead stress their main feature, considerable fidelity to prototype. Most manufacturers and all specialist societies provide instruction leaflets.

275 **Is it a good idea to construct hand-built track on a sub-base? If so, what do your recommend for this purpose?**
Whilst many systems of track construction do not require a sub-base, whenever one is building very accurate track and pointwork, the provision of a sub-base is well worth considering. The track is not only thoroughly supported during construction and at all times up to the moment when it is laid on the superior support of the baseboard proper, but it is also possible to lift and relay it without fear of undue damage. In addition, the track can be properly ballasted on the workbench, a much easier process than ballasting on the baseboard. The most suitable material for a sub-base is thin plywood, for hardboard, whilst cheaper in first cost, is prone to warp and is nowhere near so easy to cut. Although some people maintain that a bandsaw is an essential for this type of work, the

cheaper and less vicious power jigsaw is perfectly adequate, whilst a fretsaw or coping saw will enable you to do the job with the expenditure of a little effort and a small amount of time.

276 How are model railway rails made and why is nickel silver, a fairly expensive material, used for this purpose?

Model railway rails are produced by wire-drawing, where a billet of metal is pulled through a succession of dies until it reaches the required shape. As most of the cost is due to this process, the actual material is not quite as significant as might be thought. Nickel silver is favoured because it doesn't rust, is reasonably resistant to tarnish and looks right. Brass is no longer favoured – it tends to tarnish quickly and is the wrong colour. Steel can be used, but is prone to rust and has, therefore, to be pre-coated with a protective material. Steel is also more difficult to solder.

277 What exactly is battened track?

This is an obsolete system of track assembly where wooden sleepers were pinned to longitudinal wooden battens before chaired rails were fixed in place to gauge. This enabled one to construct scale track in sections in the workshop and to fit these in place on the layout, and was principally used by the early model railway manufacturers to offer a more realistic alternative assembled track. Most amateurs realised it was simpler and more economical to pin the sleepers directly to the baseboard. It was only used for O gauge and larger track systems and has been completely supplanted by flexible plastic-based track.

Section 2:6
Points and crossings

278 Why is turnout often used in place of the correct term, point?

In fact, turnout is the more correct form – point is the popular usage within the hobby, but it should be made clear that the word point has a very large number of meanings. Furthermore, it is worth pointing out that if you are discussing the hobby with an American enthusiast, it is pointless to talk about points, for even should you point to a point, you will be told very pointedly that it is a switch. You will then point to the control panel and point out to your friend that those are switches, and at that point he will probably agree that things can get confusing at times and possibly suggest that you both go off to watch a point-to-point meeting. However, if you attempt to write a similar piece of nonsense using turnout, it will turn out to be a rather pointless exercise.

Turnout – which has been used on the prototype from the outset of the railway age – is not only an unambiguous self-explanatory term but has the same meaning on both sides of the Atlantic.

279 What are stock rails, point blades, wing rails, checkrails, tiebars and, above all, what is a frog?

These are all parts of a turnout (see Plate 14). The stock rails are the outermost rails of the point. The point blades are the tapering tongues, which are connected by the tiebar at the toe of the point and which are moved from side to side to divert the vehicles to the side road or main track; they fit into joggles in the stock rails. The frog is the place where the rails cross at the rear of the point. The wing rails are the guard rails alongside the vee of the frog, and are connected to the closure rails which in turn connect the frog to the point blades. The checkrails are the guard rails mounted adjacent to the stock rails opposite to the frog.

It should be mentioned that in prototype parlance the point is a turnout, the point blades are known as the points – normally referred to as a pair of points – and the frog is the crossing. Purists have attempted to get these terms used and will doubtless keep on trying, but the terms in the initial paragraph are those in common usage within the hobby and are used by those railway engineers who make their work their hobby. Furthermore, the prototype tiebar bears no resemblance to the usual model pattern.

280 What is the difference between a crossing and a crossover?

A crossover is an arrangement of points to allow a train to cross over from one track to another. It is in most cases a pair of points placed back to back.

A crossing is where two tracks cross over each other without connection. As there can be some confusion with the crossover and, for that matter, with places where paths or roads cross railway tracks, the formation should be referred to as a diamond crossing, or diamond for short (see Plate 14).

281 Could you explain the difference between a facing and trailing crossover or point?

A facing point is one which is approached by the train when running in the normal direction – it is necessary to reverse when taking a trailing point. Facing and trailing crossovers are only found in double-track lines, where the trailing crossover is the more common, allowing a train to reverse on to the other track (see Plate 14). Until recently, facing crossovers were associated with entries to yards on busy lines and, more commonly, in conjunction with train reversals. Normally they allowed a train access to a bay or terminal platform; occasionally they allowed a terminating train to cross over on to the other line. This was usually done where the main station buildings and road access were on that side; normally stopping trains reverse over trailing crossovers.

282 Could you explain what a scissors crossover is, and what its function might be?

A scissors crossover consists of a pair of superimposed facing and trailing points which intersect with a central diamond crossing. It is a fairly complicated item of trackwork and is only found, in the UK, where space is tight. Its main function is to provide universal access to terminal platforms from either track (see Plate 14).

283 What is meant by a ladder junction?

Until recently, Ministry of Transport regulations insisted that any junction on a double-track line should take the form of a full double junction (see Plate 14), even

when the branch was single track. A similar condition occurred when crossover roads were provided between pairs of main and relief (fast and slow) tracks on a quadruple-track line. Today it is permissible to make such junctions with a succession of crossovers, and such junctions are known as ladder junctions (see Plate 14).

284 Is it a fact that facing points are barred by Ministry of Transport regulations?

The regulations, originally laid down in the early days of railways by the Board of Trade, state that before a train carrying fare-paying passengers may pass over a facing point, the blades must be securely locked to prevent their opening whilst the train is passing. Even before this, many railway engineers were extremely cautious about installing facing points in the main line. However, once a satisfactory facing point locking mechanism was devised, their use was accepted but the cost and complications of providing locking bars and their associated interlocking meant that they were only used when absolutely necessary. Whilst such considerations need not weigh so heavily on a model railway, there is the practical consideration that whereas it is simple to drop wagons into a trailing siding, to do the same with a facing siding either requires a run-round loop or the help of a shunting locomotive.

285 Why are points sometimes described by numbers rather than by quoting the radius?

In a sectional track system, points are defined by quoting the radius of the curved section they replace. This, however, is not the actual radius of the point; in practice the curve is struck between two intersecting tangents and is somewhat smaller than the true radius of the section of track. Prototype points are described by their crossing number.

This is only a rough description – other factors are involved and for a full explanation you should refer to the specialised literature provided by the finescale-oriented groups and manufacturers of finescale track components. In general, a No 4 point is very sharp

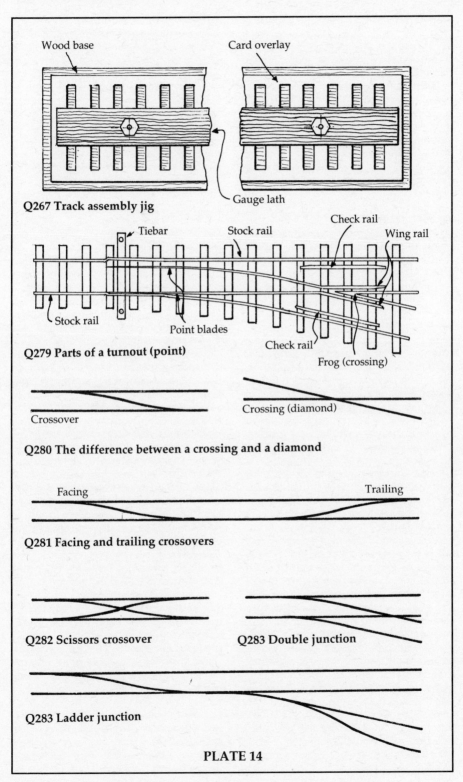

Wood base

Card overlay

Gauge lath

Q267 Track assembly jig

Tiebar

Stock rail

Check rail

Wing rail

Stock rail

Point blades

Check rail

Frog (crossing)

Q279 Parts of a turnout (point)

Crossover

Crossing (diamond)

Q280 The difference between a crossing and a diamond

Facing

Trailing

Q281 Facing and trailing crossovers

Q282 Scissors crossover

Q283 Double junction

Q283 Ladder junction

PLATE 14

indeed and would only be found in industrial yards. The smallest prototype turnout is usually a No 8; however, except for finescale use a No 6 is perfectly adequate.

Many track manufacturers – Peco for example – offer a range of points with a common crossing angle. This not only permits them all to be used with a standard diamond crossing, but allows large, medium and small radius points to be used together in a complex track formation without the need for small awkward filling units.

286 I am attracted to large-radius points by their superior appearance, but I only have a small room for the railway and must keep the radius well down. Am I compelled to use small-radius points?

Even when using sectional track with its fixed geometry, it is possible to use larger-radius points. There will have to be small adjustments here and there, that is all. If you are using flexible track, there is every reason to use large-radius points on a small layout. One useful tip is to make liberal use of large-radius curved points, particularly at the entry to loops where, in addition to a considerable improvement in appearance, the running will be smoother.

287 I have a small continuous layout on a single baseboard laid with sectional track. Wishing to get more sidings inside the oval, I purchased a curved point only to discover that the outer curve is laid to a much larger radius and as a result I cannot get the sidings in. I thought this was the reason curved points were made and feel a little cheated. What can I do?

The inner curve on your layout is very close to the absolute minimum and there is no way that you can take a curve inside this if you want to be able to run trains around the model. It is necessary to have a large differential between the two radii of a curved point. Were there only the difference of the standard track centres between the curves, the point would subtend a right-angle and the crossing angle would be so acute as to cause continuous derailments.

288 Why are the point blades and frogs on model three-way points staggered, when the prototype has them in the same line?

This is to simplify construction and two-rail electrification. It is worth mentioning that the prototype frequently adopted the same arrangement for the same reason. Strictly speaking, the formation is a pair of superimposed points, but it is felt – rightly I consider – that the majority of potential purchasers wouldn't understand what this meant, whereas the accepted name is self-explanatory.

289 What is a slip point and what is the difference between double and single slips?

The slip point is basically a diamond crossing with additional rails and point blades to enable trains to pass from one leg of the crossing to the other. With a single slip, this passage in only from one side of the crossing; the double slip provides either way movement (see Plate 15). It saves a good deal of length in complex track formations and on a model, where space is limited and cannot be readily increased, the relatively high cost of a slip point is more than justified. Slip points are extensively used on the Continent, where the approach to many large stations begins with a scissors crossover from which two diagonal routes link the running roads, loops and sidings through a succession of double slips.

290 I drew out my track plan with considerable care to 1/10th scale. However, now I have purchased the necessary points, I find to my horror that they do not quite fit. Are the manufacturer's published sizes wrong?

The most likely answer is that you relied on the scale drawing for your sizes. Correct drawing office practice is to *calculate* all dimensions and then produce the drawing from these. This is how model pointwork is designed for mass production. However, even skilled draughtsmen find it useful to work from a scale drawing, but in such cases the smallest scale used is full size. The working drawings for at least one leading make of track are anything up to five times full size. The simplest way for the

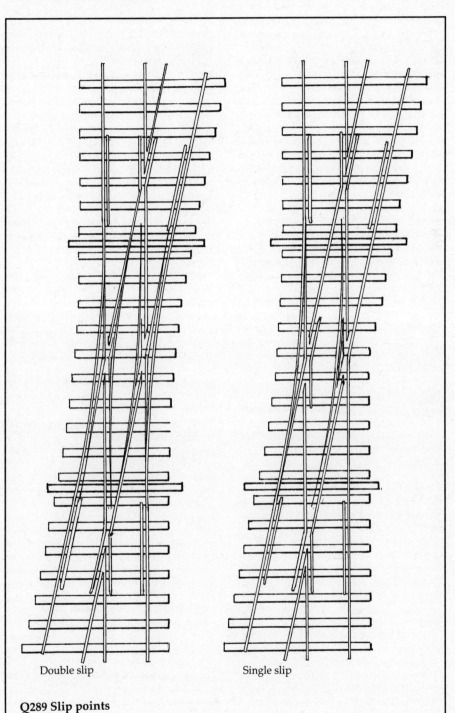

Double slip   Single slip

Q289 Slip points

PLATE 15

amateur to work out the size of a point formation is to use full-sized point plans.

291 Is it worth while making pointwork in the home workshop?

This is not an easy question to answer. There are two advantages – one, clearly, is cost. There is also the fact that it is usually possible to save quite an appreciable amount of space on all but the simplest of layouts. It is also possible to have any type of track formation you may care to build. This may not, however, be a real advantage – it is all too easy to create needless complications; moreover, if nothing can run through the pointwork without derailing, these advantages disappear instantaneously. Whilst this would only occur were the workmanship to be exceptionally botched, the more likely situation, where you could not be certain if a train would pass through the pointwork without something coming off, is hardly encouraging. Construction of simple points and crossings, singly or as a group, does call for a good deal of careful work and cannot be rushed.

292 Could you tell me how to build my own points?

This is something that needs more space than can be spared in this book, but the subject is covered in my book *Model Railways on a Budget* (see the Bibliography). In brief, there are two approaches. The most popular is to build up the points on a plan – this can be made from commercial point plans or drawn specially for the purpose, using accurate templates to fair in the curves. Where the track is to be mounted on a sub-base, the plans are first glued to it. In other cases – PCB track, for example – the plan can be mounted on a working board (a piece of Sundeala board is ideal) and covered with clear polythene sheet for protection.

It is also possible to assemble points in a jig. This calls for a certain amount of metalworking ability since the key parts are best made from aluminium sheet.

Section 2:7
Point control

293 Is it necessary to have points remotely controlled?

There is absolutely no reason why points should not be controlled by hand-levers alongside the tiebar, apart from the feeling that it is unprototypical to reach into the model. As this does not preclude the later addition of remote control, to dispense with such refinements can save a good deal of effort and some expenditure in the early stages, particularly as the more popular types of ready-made turnout have a simple self-locking mechanism and require no additions for direct manual operation.

There is, of course, a good reason for providing the more distant points with remote control, since they will be well outside the comfortable reach of the operator and it will probably be inconvenient to walk around the layout to change them over. However, if finances are stretched at the outset, the motorising of remote points can be put off for some time; the right moment to install the remote operating device is when you finally get fed up with walking around to change the setting.

294 Is there a simple way of operating points at a distance without going to the trouble of fitting full remote control?

The push-rod system of control is a very simple means of transferring the control of a point to the baseboard edge. In essence it consists of a length of stiff wire which is mounted under the baseboard and is provided with a knob at the outer end so it can be moved back and forth. The movement is taken to the tiebar by a length of springy wire passing through the baseboard (see Plate 16). This is best secured to the push-rod itself by a blob of epoxy resin, whilst a knob can be improvised from a sliver of ballpoint pen body secured with more epoxy resin. The main push-rod can be a cycle spoke, in which case the screwed nipple makes an excellent knob, but a cheaper source of supply is the ubiquitous wire coat-hanger provided by all good dry cleaning establishments. A wooden block on the push rod can be arranged to actuate a microswitch or switches to set polarity of the turnouts. Although the controls are still spread about along the layout, in practice they are much closer together than the levers in the full-sized lever frame needed to control the equivalent prototype station.

295 What is a microswitch and where does one obtain them?

A microswitch is a totally enclosed switch, generally having a set of changeover contacts, which is actuated by a very small movement of the operating device (see Plate 16). This is usually a small projecting button, but the switch may be fitted with a lever or rotary mechanism. They are available from good electrical suppliers, but the main source of supply for railway modellers is ex-equipment retailers. The principal advantage of the microswitch is that, being totally enclosed, there is virtually no chance that the contacts will fail to make circuit.

296 How can I control my points and signals from a central lever frame?

Broadly, there are two methods, electrical and mechanical, and each breaks down into a number of different approaches.

Electrical control can be by means of a commercial motor, and these in turn are divided into double solenoid types and motorised patterns. In addition, relays can be adapted to operate turnouts and signals.

Mechanical systems are divided into rod and crank, wire-in-tube, wire and spring, and cord and spring. There are numerous sub-divisions within the mechanical field largely brought about by the fact that the majority of these systems are produced in the home workshop.

297 What is the operating principle of a double solenoid point motor?

Two solenoids – coils of insulated wire wound around a core with a hollow centre – are placed side by side, or in opposition. One or more steel armatures are connected through a rocker mechanism to the tiebar, usually by an omega

loop. The application of ac current through a flash switch or other method of applying a momentary surge causes the armature to move to one side or the other, it is then held in place by a simple locking mechanism, generally a toggle spring (see Plate 16). In certain cases, the toggle spring is fitted to the point tiebar rather than to the motor itself.

The coils have a very low resistance, allowing a large amount of current to pass through. As a result, if the contacts on the switch should stick, the coils will overheat. Fortunately, they form a crude buzzer and the fault is generally noticed before too much heating occurs, but if left unattended for longer than 10 seconds, the risk of permanent damage is high. As a result, it is best to supply double solenoid motors through a capacitor discharge unit which not only gives more reliable operation, but also limits the current supply after the initial kick to safe levels. The device is a fine example of the 'crude but effective' school of engineering design.

298 What is an omega loop?

This is a length of wire with a loop formed into it, the resulting shape resembling the Greek letter omega (see Plate 16). The idea is to provide a degree of resilience in the wire so that a small difference between the throw of the point motor and the throw required by the point can be taken up. Furthermore, as the loop exerts a small amount of pressure on the system, the point blades are kept firmly in place against the stock rails.

299 What is a flash switch?

A flash switch, or passing contact switch, is a special type of switch which makes momentary contact when the operating lever is moved. For point control, the switch needs to make contact in one direction only, and the internal mechanism incorporates a biased toggle mechanism so that there is no reverse action.

300 Flash switches are fairly costly. Is there any cheaper method of operating double solenoid motors?

The cheapest system is the electric pencil control, used in conjunction with a track diagram. Two metal studs are placed

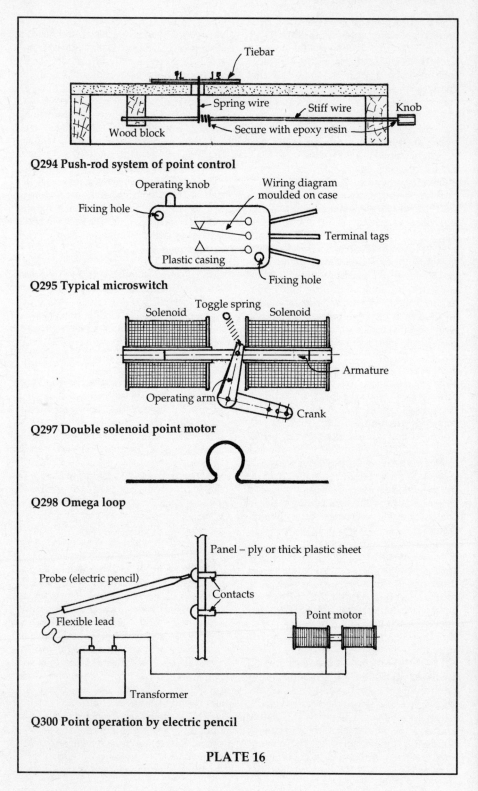

Q294 Push-rod system of point control

Q295 Typical microswitch

Q297 Double solenoid point motor

Q298 Omega loop

Q300 Point operation by electric pencil

PLATE 16

either on, or adjacent to, the track line, and these are connected to the coils of the point motor. The common return from the coils is then taken to the transformer or, better still, the capacitor discharge unit. The other terminal is connected to a small probe via a length of flexible wire. The operator then touches the appropriate stud with the probe (see Plate 16).

301 What exactly is a capacitor discharge unit and what benefits does it provide for point control?

A capacitor is a device of storing an electrical charge which can, if required, be dissipated in milliseconds. It is mainly used in electronic circuits for smoothing and delay, but is also employed to provide a massive pulse of electricity. There is a superb demonstration of this effect in the Science Museum, London, where an extremely large capacitor is charged with several million volts and then discharged to create artificial lightning. The same principle is employed in electronic flashguns, where a smaller capacitor empties its charge through a lighting tube in under a thousandth of a second, producing a brilliant flash of light. In a capacitor discharge unit, a large electrolytic capacitor is charged up to 20 volts and, when ready, this charge is sent through the point motor coil, resulting in a sudden kick that throws the turnout positively and safely, since once the charge has been dissipated, only a low bleed current is present and this cannot burn out the coil as might happen with a straight connection. In short, the unit boosts the normal 16 V ac supply, making for a more positive action at the point whilst at the same time protecting the coils against accidental overload. As a bonus, the fact that it delivers dc rather than ac makes it possible to control a fan of sidings through a diode matrix.

302 What is a diode matrix?

A diode matrix is an arrangement of diodes which allows a rank of push-buttons to energise selected solenoid coils in a number of point motors. It is difficult to describe in detail and even more difficult to design. For a full explanation I would refer you to *Practical Electronic Projects for Model Railroaders* (see the Bibliography) where the subject is explored in considerable detail. It is a simple form of logic control that does not rely on specialised integrated circuits and which can be worked out with the aid of a truth table.

303 What have logic circuits to do with point control; indeed, what is logical about such arrangements?

In this context the word logic is connected with Boolean algebra, a branch of pure mathematics employed in computer programming and very much dependant on binary arithmetic. The essence of this somewhat abstruse system is that all processes are reduced to an either/or (binary) state, and acted on by several functions, primarily 'and', 'or' and 'eor'. The relevance to model railways lies in the fact that a point is a perfect practical demonstration of an either/or system, in that the device is set either for the main line or the siding; there is no intermediate state. At least, there should not be, for where the blades are contacting neither stock rail we have an error condition – or in railway parlance, a derailment. As relays and switches are also either/or devices, their application is governed by Boolean logic. And I warrant that, like me, you thought it was just plain common sense!

304 What is a truth table?

This is an arrangement where one set of parameters (say the controlling devices) is set out in a vertical column and the other set of parameters (say the devices to be controlled) is set out horizontally. The various cells are then marked 'true' or 'false' according to the desired arrangements. Often 'true' is replaced by 'on' and 'false' by 'off' – the meaning remains the same. You will encounter such tables in treatises on track interlocking, here the terms are 'locked' and 'unlocked' or 'free'. It is a means of setting out one's ideas graphically and helps concentrate the mind no end. The probability is that you've used this arrangement often enough without realising.

305 What is a motor-driven point motor?

A motor-driven point-operating device

incorporates a small low-voltage motor which throws the operating crank very slowly and positively. There are two different mechanical arrangements: in one case the crank is driven directly through a small worm and wheel, while in the other it is moved by a small rod connected to a nut on a fine screw which is drive by the motor through reduction gears. Cut-out switches shut off the motor when the limit of throw is reached (see Plate 17). Usually physical stops are also provided as well as additional contacts for polarity change and point detection. It is identical in action to prototype devices and one version was, in fact, described in some detail in Henry Greenly's textbook *Model Electric Locomotives and Railways*, first published in 1922. Its practical application had to wait until inexpensive but reliable small motors became available.

Commercial units are more costly than the solenoid-operated pattern, but they are infinitely more reliable. In addition, this happens to be the pattern of point motor most suited for home construction, for not only are suitable motors sold very cheaply, but a fair number are to be found in broken toys. The small gears and screws are also not too difficult to find and, with the addition of a few microswitches, the total outlay will be less than the cost of the cheapest double solenoid device. They must be operated from a dc supply and are fairly bulky and noisy in operation. That is not regarded as a real disadvantage – it is nice to know that the device is actually working! The failure rate is so low that they are increasingly being used on exhibition layouts, where reliability over a long period of time is of prime importance.

306 How can you control points by means of a relay?

First and foremost the relay must not be mounted in a can and should not be a miniature type. The PO 3000 pattern relay is commonly employed for this purpose, mainly because it has been widely available ex-equipment. Other patterns of large relay have been used with considerable success. The relay is usually mounted under the baseboard and linked to the tiebar by means of a gain stroke arm (see Plate 17). A smooth dc supply, preferably independent of the main traction current, is needed to operate the relay and a standard on-off switch is employed to control it. In more advanced circuits, the relays can be controlled through other relays and, since the relay contacts can be used not only to set the polarity of the frog, but also for point detection and other functions, this form of control is particularly suited to automatic control. Unlike the double solenoid motor, the relay's current state can be detected directly from the control circuits. The system has disadvantages of which the need for a separate power supply is high on the list. Its popularity depends very much on the availability of suitable relays in the ex-equipment market.

307 What is a gain stroke arm?

This is a rod or lever connected to a mechanism to increase the throw or stroke. In the context of relay point control it is in most cases a length of stiff, springy wire soldered directly to the armature.

308 Can I use electric point motors out of doors?

Electric point motors have performed well in outdoor locations, providing they are protected against damp. Experience seems to indicate that total enclosure is not suitable, as this encourages condensation inside the casing. The favoured approach is to mount the motor above the baseboard on a block and to cover it with an inverted watertight casing. This can be a suitable strong plastic container (which could be fabricated from fibreglass) or a tinplate case with all joints completely sealed with soft solder (see Plate 17). Regular maintenance is imperative – a sparing but regular application of light oil on all working parts is essential. It helps to standardise on the motor and to make provision for easy replacement so that a sticky unit can be taken to the workshop for overhaul.

309 What is the wire-in-tube system of point control?

This consists of a length of piano wire threaded through small-bore copper tubing, which can then be gently curved

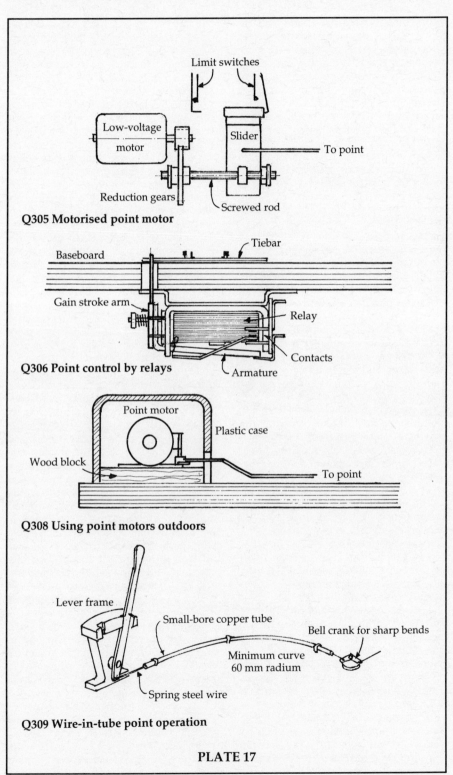

Q305 Motorised point motor

Limit switches
Low-voltage motor
Slider
To point
Reduction gears
Screwed rod

Q306 Point control by relays

Baseboard
Tiebar
Gain stroke arm
Relay
Contacts
Armature

Q308 Using point motors outdoors

Point motor
Plastic case
Wood block
To point

Q309 Wire-in-tube point operation

Lever frame
Small-bore copper tube
Bell crank for sharp bends
Minimum curve 60 mm radium
Spring steel wire

PLATE 17

to run between the lever frame and the tiebar. It is not possible to use curves below 60 mm radius and the maximum possible length is about 2 m, assuming no tight curves. Sharp turns can be arranged by means of bell-cranks (see Plate 17). The system is similar in principle to the Bowden cable used for cycle brakes and gear shifts.

310 I have seen references to choke control in old American publications. What exactly is this?

Manually controlled chokes on cars are operated by a pull-knob connected to a length of Bowden cable. A US enthusiast discovered that his local auto breaker had a large quantity of these available at bargain price and, with a flash of fine lateral thinking, realised that they were ideally suited for control of model railroad switches, bought the lot and sent an article to *Model Railroader*. The main snags are that it is necessary to make a special sub-baseboard mounting at the turnout to transfer the movement from the cable to the tiebar, and that unless you can get a supply at ridiculously low prices, the system is not really cost-effective.

311 I would like to operate the layout through a proper mechanical lever frame, preferably mounted in a model signal box. How should I set about this?

If you merely wish to operate the points and signals from a prototypical lever frame, there are a number of patterns on the market. The Gem frame consists of a series of cast frames which bolt together to form the frame proper – much as on the prototype – with pressed steel operating levers. It is small enough to fit into a 4 mm scale signal box shell, is reasonably priced and has been a firm favourite for longer than most people can remember. Model Signal Engineering produce etched and cast components for a large de luxe frame which is a close replica of the upper parts of a prototype frame, complete with locking latch – it appears costly until one looks at the amount of work involved in making the parts. Ratio, as part of their cord-operating system, provide a plastic lever that fits snugly into a 12 mm diameter hole in the baseboard together with a matching

rocker arm to bring the movement back up above the baseboard. The appearance is reasonable and, again, levers can be fitted into a model signal cabin (see Plate 18).

312 How can one modify a signal cabin kit to house a working lever frame?

With considerable difficulty, because the kit is not designed with this in mind. Where the cabin is to house a working frame – or, for that matter, a small switchboard – it is advisable to begin with a 3 mm ply shell to which the roof and the rear wall are hinged (see Plate 18). A strong shell is needed to take care of the inevitable knocks it will receive during the course of operation. It can be covered with plastic sheet, brick paper, etc, but the window frames are best produced from a sheet of etched frames – patterns for all major company's designs are available from specialist suppliers for 4 and 7 mm scale.

313 Can points be operated through prototypical rodding, with bell-cranks, etc?

This is possible providing that you do not expect, in 4 mm scale, to have scale-sized rodding. Indeed, in O gauge it helps to be fractionally overscale, but in Gauge 1 a scale-sized bell-crank is robust enough to do the job. However, it is a fiddly job calling for a good deal of skill and not a little patience and sheer determination, so most small-scale workers who opt for mechanical methods do so beneath the baseboard and provide cosmetic, non-working, point rodding above baseboard level. With below-baseboard rodding, the necessary cranks and rods can be well overscale and thus much easier to make from scrap. The ubiquitous wire coat-hanger is a good source for the rodding, while cranks and brackets can be fabricated from sheet aluminium. Movement should be well in excess of that needed for the actual throw – an unequal-arm rocking lever will reduce it to the amount needed.

314 Is it possible to operate points by means of cords?

The Ratio lever system is based on cord operation: a strong nylon thread links the lever and rocker arm and is taken around corners on small screw eyes. The rocker arms incorporate a return spring, and both lever and rocker arm fit snugly in 12 mm diameter holes The system is economical and effective up to distances of about 2 to 3 m, depending on the amount of twisting needed to take the throw from the lever to the point or signal. Full instructions are supplied with the kits. A similar system can be cobbled together in the home workshop, but two of the key items, the screw eyes and the nylon cord, are not that easy to track down in the High Street.

315 How can one carry a mechanical point-operating system over a baseboard joint?

Numerous arrangements involving some form of rocker arm on each side of the joint have been demonstrated as being completely reliable under exhibition conditions, the most testing of all circumstances. Unfortunately, the same arrangements have also been shown to be utterly unreliable in other hands. The simple fact is that any type of transfer mechanism relies for its success on extreme precision of workmanship. There is a lateral solution. It is usually possible to arrange matters so that the great majority of points at any one station are located on two adjacent baseboards, in which case two lever frames are located on either side of the common baseboard joint. The few points beyond the baseboard limits are then operated electrically. This incidentally was the approach adopted on the prototype where one or two points were beyond the practical limits of mechanical operation.

316 In Henry Greenly's *Model Railways* details are given of a pneumatic system of point operation. Has this ever been put into practice?

If the system described over 60 years ago was ever built, no record of it remains. However, a substantially similar hydraulic system, using neoprene tubing to connect the actuating rams, has been employed with considerable success on Gauge 1 garden railways, using car brake fluid as the medium. The system is ideal for outdoor use, as Henry Greenly said all those years ago, but its application depends on access to a well-equipped model engineering workshop since the small actuators need to be purpose-made.

Section 2:8
Signals and their control

317 I am having considerable difficulty trying to work out the correct signalling for my layout (track plan enclosed). Can you offer any advice?

The most common reason why a model layout is difficult to signal is that it is not designed in accordance with prototype practice, and your plan happens to be a case in point. The ideal solution is to redesign the layout – this should be the course if you have not begun construction because if the tracks are difficult to signal correctly, it is fairly certain that operation will not be easy if you wish to conform to normal full-sized practice. If you have built the model and are stuck with an unprototypical plan, you must arrange the signals as best you can, knowing that whilst they will impress your lay visitors, any knowledgeable friend will spot the errors anyway. However, an impressive array of signals can often fool even an expert into thinking that the model is more authentic than it actually is. It's certainly worth the effort.

318 Is there any reason to install signals? The layout will work equally well without them.

There is no actual need. Indeed, one senior signal engineer never got round to installing a complete set of signals he had specially made for his layout. However, one can also argue that boiler mountings have no function on an electrically-powered model of a steam locomotive, and so they can be left off the model if it is too much bother to make them!

Signals are a vital part of the railway scene and no layout should be considered complete without them. For this reason the correct procedure should be to provide signals at the earliest possible moment, having checked the accuracy of the station layout by working out where they should go before you even lay the first piece of track. Even if you do not consider that you have the time to erect working signals at the start, a selection of non-operative kit-built signals will turn a collection of tracks into a real railway.

319 **Can you tell me exactly what signals I should have on my railway?**
Unfortunately this is not a question one can answer fully in a few paragraphs. My book *Model Railway Signalling* (see the Bibliography) covers the major features of British practice in the current century, and this will meet the requirements of the overwhelming majority of modellers. Basically, you must choose between semaphore and colour light signals; the latter are simpler to understand and install, but the former have more character. A popular compromise is to install basic signalling using inexpensive plastic kits while you find out the type of signal most suited to your concept.

320 **Why did some semaphore signals move downwards and others upwards?**
Initially in Great Britain all semaphore arms moved downwards, in the lower quadrant, having developed from the three-aspect 'slotted post' signal. In the US the practice was to lift the arm and at the same time provide three aspects – stop, caution and clear. In the early years of the present century some US-pattern upper quadrants were installed in Britain, usually to provide three-aspect or 'speed' signalling. Whilst the three-aspect principle was abandoned for semaphore signals, it being considered that this was better carried out with colour light signalling, three of the grouped companies, the LMS, LNER and Southern, adopted upper quadrant signals for new installations (see Plate 18). The GWR continued to use lower quadrants, and on the other Groups lower quadrant systems remained in place until time-expired.

321 **What is a somersault signal?**
This is the popular name for the balanced arm signal adopted by the Great Northern Railway. The signal arm was pivoted in the centre, but was mounted

on a bracket extending from the signal post. It was a lower quadrant arm and, in the clear position, was almost vertical (see Plate 18). Whilst it did not perform a full somersault, the extreme degree of movement led to this term being applied. The GWR also used a balanced arm signal, but this was pivoted on the post and did not have the same degree of movement. Initially designed for cramped sites, mainly under platform canopies, its use spread, particularly after nationalisation.

322 **I have noticed that on many exhibition layouts the signals do not work. I feel this is rather unrealistic – could you comment on this?**
In an ideal world all signals would work, but having set about this task myself I am not prepared to criticise anyone who gives this aspect of the hobby a low priority. Having said that, there is no doubt that it is incongruous for trains to ignore signals, but I feel that until it is widely accepted that the essential difference between a serious model railway and a well-developed train set is that the former has working signals whereas the latter does not, we shall continue to see showpiece layouts with dummy signals. At least it is better than not having any signals at all. If, as one suspects, you feel strongly about this, you are free to make whatever comments you think appropriate the next time you see a train pass a signal set against it. It will not make you popular in the short term, but so long as your own signals work and you're prepared to share your expertise, you will be doing your bit towards improving the overall standards of the hobby.

323 **What is the best way of making a semaphore signal operate?**
Ratio supply a very simple cord operating system with full instructions. The subject is covered in some depth in my book *Model Railway Signalling* (see the Bibliography).

324 **Could you explain how to arrange a series of four-aspect colour light signals so that the correct indications are displayed on the signals?**
Although wiring diagrams which purport to show how this may be done have

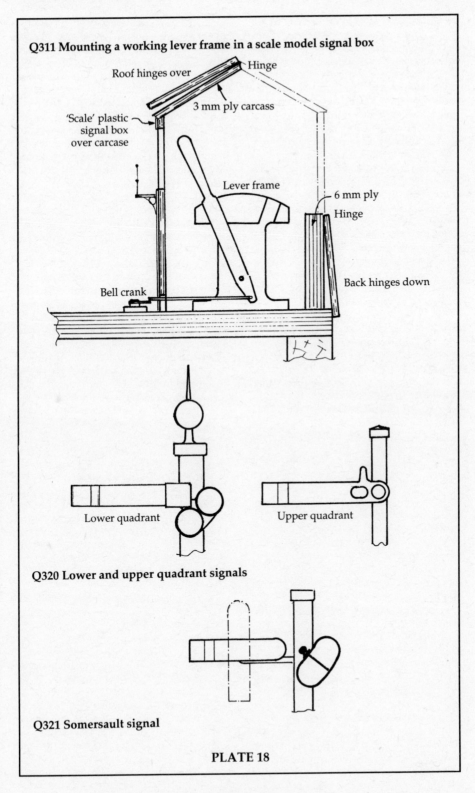

Q311 Mounting a working lever frame in a scale model signal box

Roof hinges over

Hinge

'Scale' plastic signal box over carcase

3 mm ply carcass

Lever frame

6 mm ply

Hinge

Back hinges down

Bell crank

Q320 Lower and upper quadrant signals

Lower quadrant

Upper quadrant

Q321 Somersault signal

PLATE 18

been published from time to time, I have considerable doubts whether any have been applied to a working model railway. The reason is simple – in order to have a full range of four-aspect signals, you need to have no fewer than four unencumbered block sections, each at least 10 per cent longer than your longest train. This is rather a lot of main line. The Model Railway Club's OO gauge New Annington layout has one of the longest lengths of plain main line on any exhibition layout, and yet it is insufficient to allow more than two blocks clear of the main station, and whilst four-aspect signals are installed and the indications cascade correctly, the wiring has had to be devised for this one specific site and it proved necessary to extensively modify the set-up after the early appearances at exhibitions.

325 Are there any rules for the location of signal boxes?

In the old pattern manual signal box, one of the signalman's duties was to observe the trains as they passed to see that the last vehicle carried a tail lamp, indicating that the train was complete. Therefore the box had to be placed close to the run-

ning lines and provided with large windows to give a good view of the railway. At the same time, the cost of rodding, together with the fact that the longer the length of the rodding, the harder it was to work the points, made it sensible to locate the frame as close as possible to the major collection of points. On single-track lines and at the junctions of single-track branches with the main line, it was also necessary to have the signal box and single-line tablet mechanisms close enough to the exchange point for the train tablets/staffs to ensure that this vital practice was efficiently carried out. It was not so much consideration for the signalman's feet, as that he must not be out of earshot of the block bells in the cabin.

Modern multiple-aspect systems are controlled from a remote box and this can be located wherever there is a suitable space. The fact that many have a sight of the main yard and are provided with large windows is more a case of tradition than fulfilling any operational need, for the signalmen rely entirely on illuminated panels for information on the location of trains.

PART 3
SETTING THE SCENE

Although by rights the next stage should be to connect the track to the power supply so we can start running trains, it is better to look at how the very gaunt structure we have considered up to now can be transformed into a miniature landscape.

Section 3:1
Landscape construction

326 I would like to include a viaduct in my layout but I do not have the room to allow the tracks to rise sufficiently to do this. How can I get round this problem?

By using the open-top system of base-board construction (see Q176), with the main framing sufficiently below the track datum level to give room for the viaduct. In many cases it is sufficient merely to lower one section of the framing, and this is usually referred to as a dropped base-board (see Plate 19 and Q191).

327 How is model landscape best supported?

There is no one generally accepted best system – a great deal depends on the specific circumstances. There are three common approaches, however: vertical profiles, wire support and hard shell. In practice modellers tend to employ an ad hoc approach, utilising whatever happens to be to hand and is felt to be suitable for the purpose.

328 What are profiles and how does one make them? Have they any connection with contours?

A profile is a vertical support, cut to the required profile of the landscape surface. They are often incorrectly described as contours, which as anyone who can remember their geography lessons will recall are horizontal lines joining points of equal height above datum level. The main requirement of a profile is that it should be reasonably stiff and cost as little as possible. Any handy material can be used – ply, chipboard, insulation board, expanded polystyrene, hard-board, even stiff cardboard – for as they will be covered by the landscape, their appearance is of no account. One advantage of ply framing is that it is possible to produce the main profiles at the same time as one makes the cross members (see Plate 19).

329 How does one support the landscape in between the profiles?

A very simple and inexpensive method is to weave a rough surface from long strips of thin card about 9-12 mm in width. Empty cereal cartons are ideal for this purpose, as are other types of packaging (see Plate 19). It is also possible to use old newspapers and worn bed-sheets for this purpose.

330 What is the best way of fixing the supports to the profiles?

The most effective method, providing that you have reasonably thick profiles, is to use a staple gun. As this is used in one hand, it leaves the other free to hold things in place. Apart from this, gluing or pinning is quite effective – it's really a case of what you find most convenient at the time.

331 I have heard of wire mesh supports. What is used for this purpose?

The favoured medium is chicken wire, a hexagonal-pattern wire mesh originally

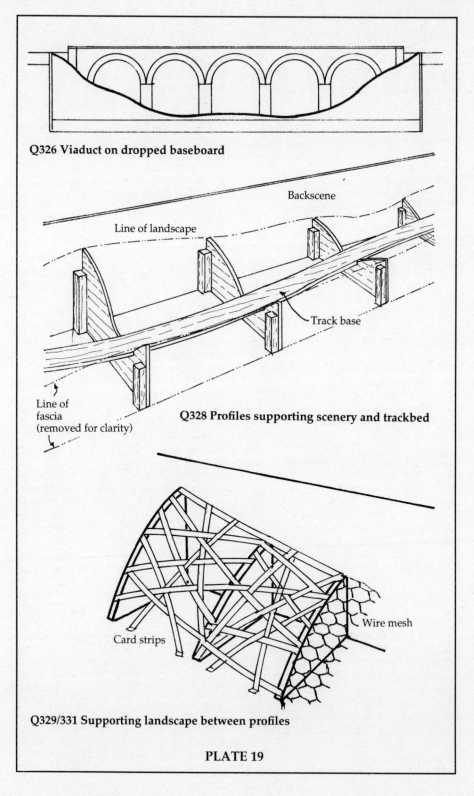

Q326 Viaduct on dropped baseboard

Backscene

Line of landscape

Track base

Line of
fascia
(removed for clarity)

Q328 Profiles supporting scenery and trackbed

Wire mesh

Card strips

Q329/331 Supporting landscape between profiles

PLATE 19

used to produce chicken coops. It can often be found in the larger garden centres and comes in rolls which can be cut to length. It is self-supporting up to about 600-700 mm gap, which means that on an open top framing little else is needed (see Plate 19). Adventitiously, the hexagonal mesh allows the material to be tweaked into any required shape by hand, and for modelling purposes it is usually secured with a staple gun. The wire can be cut into shape with tinsnips or side cutters, but as the end wires are very sharp it is advisable to wear stout gloves when cutting it. Then, once the edges have been trimmed and the end wires tucked neatly in and stapled in place, it is perfectly safe to mould to shape with the bare hands. The mesh is then covered with plaster to form the landscape base.

332 I have seen reference to screen wire in US publications. What is this and where does one get it?

In most parts of the USA it is the practice to have an internal screen door inside every external door to allow cool air to circulate through the house whilst keeping insects out – they are frequently seen in films and TV features. These doors are made from a light wooden frame covered with a fine wire mesh which is, not surprisingly, known as screen wire and is stocked by most hardware stores. There does not appear to be a readily obtainable European equivalent.

333 I have noticed references to different brands of plaster in various articles and books. What sort of plaster do you consider is best for landscape modelling?

Whatever plaster comes easiest to hand! The proprietary crack fillers, the best-known of which is Polyfilla, are reasonably fine, slow setting and, most important of all, easily available in small quantities. For this reason they are most widely used. Common plaster – sometimes known as Kean's Cement – is only obtainable in large sacks, which is fine if you have a large amount of landscape to cover. It is fairly quick setting, so you should only mix small quantities at a time. Larger builder's merchants can also supply sacks of hard-casting plaster

which is an excellent quick-setting material. Dental plaster is a very fine hard-casting plaster ideally suited for final finishing coats. The plaster sold for Linka building kits is also useful for finer landscape work.

334 How does one cover wire mesh with plaster without the stuff falling through the holes?

If the mesh is fairly small, a stiff plaster will stay in place, while chicken wire can be covered with old newspapers before applying plaster (see Plate 20).

335 I am having some difficulty in getting a consistent mix with my plaster. Have you any recommendations?

You need to use consistent measures. The Linka system provides a pair of mixing spoons for this purpose, but these are inconvenient for large quantities. Two identical measures are needed, one for water, the other for plaster, since the approved method of mixing is to add the plaster to the water. Clean empty cream cartons are a convenient size. Three parts water to one part plaster produces a stiff mixture, while four parts water will make a slightly creamier plaster. The thin plastic containers in which frozen foods and ice-cream are sold are the best mixing-bowls, since when the surplus plaster has dried out the unwanted mess can be removed by inverting the container over a sheet of newspaper and flexing the sides. Eventually the plastic breaks but you should have a fresh supply of containers long before this.

336 I am having considerable difficulty getting blobs of plaster off the tracks. Is there an easy way of doing this?

The easy way is to avoid getting plaster on the tracks in the first instance! This is done by covering them and the ballasted area with strips of polythene held in place with small pins. Map pins – short stiff pins with a round, brightly coloured plastic top, or their dressmaking equivalents – should be used, since they are much easier to remove when you've finished. The only way to get plaster off track is to chip it away with a small electrician's screwdriver. Ballast will have to

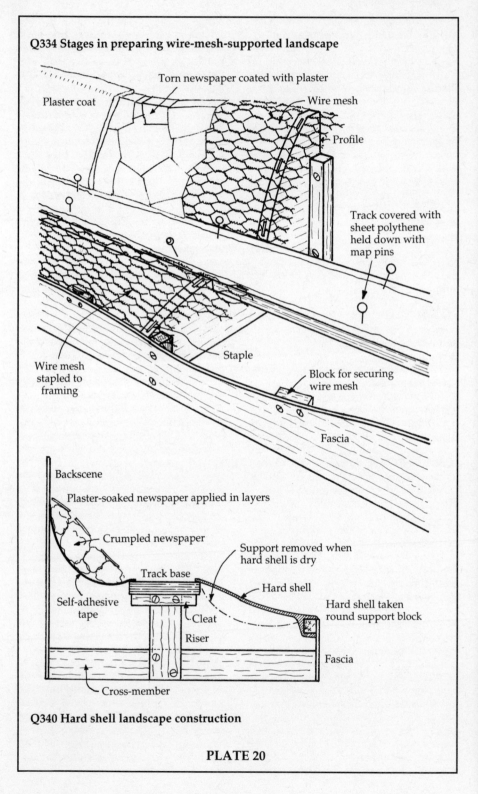

Q334 Stages in preparing wire-mesh-supported landscape

Torn newspaper coated with plaster

Plaster coat

Wire mesh

Profile

Track covered with sheet polythene held down with map pins

Wire mesh stapled to framing

Staple

Block for securing wire mesh

Fascia

Backscene

Plaster-soaked newspaper applied in layers

Crumpled newspaper

Support removed when hard shell is dry

Track base

Hard shell

Self-adhesive tape

Cleat

Hard shell taken round support block

Riser

Fascia

Cross-member

Q340 Hard shell landscape construction

PLATE 20

be repaired later. Small blobs can be disguised with a little track colour paint.

337 **I live in a small flat and am building a portable layout. I would like to add some plaster-based scenery, but am worried about the probable mess. What should I do?**
Go to your local DIY store and purchase a plastic cover sheet. Lay this down before erecting the baseboard section on which you intend to work, making sure that it extends well beyond the working area. Any plaster fallout will be on to the sheet. Be careful when lifting the sheet afterwards – it will almost certainly have to be shaken out of doors to remove the mess.

338 **What is the best tool for applying plaster to a scenic base? What is needed for subsequent forming of, say, a rock face?**
For the initial application in quantity, a miniature trowel as used for crack filling and obtainable in any DIY or other store catering for decorators' needs, is probably the most convienient. Final finishing can be carried out with small spatulas; suitable tools can often be located in specialist artists' suppliers where they are sold for clay modelling.

On the other hand, a quick raid on the cutlery drawer will reveal a lot of useful tools – spoons and knives are very versatile. Old EPNS cutlery which has lost its silver plating is particularly useful, as nickel silver base can be formed and filed into any shape one needs for a specific purpose.

339 **I have installed overhead electrification masts and catenary and am now having considerable difficulty in getting the landscape into position behind them. How do you recommend I set about it?**
You should follow prototype practice, where the landscape was there long before they put the wires in place! In other words, you will have to dismantle the overhead – there is no other choice.

340 **What is hard shell landscape made from?**
Hard shell is a system of landscape construction devised by Linn Westcott of *Model Railroader* and is widely used by advanced landscape builders. In essence, the main shape of the landscape is determined by filling the scenic spaces with crumpled newspaper lightly stuck on to and suspended by a masking-tape net. When the desired surface is complete, small scraps of torn paper towels soaked in a creamy mixture of quick-setting hard-casting plaster are applied to the supports and built up until a hard shell, at least 1 mm thick, is created over the entire surface (see Plate 20). When the shell has had at least 24 hours hardening, the underlying support is torn away and any defects corrected by applying extra strips. A final finishing surface is then applied before texturing and colouring is added. Hard shell is light and easily cut with a sharp trimming knife should it be desired to make alterations at some later date.

341 **I have seen references to the use of plaster bandage for a landscape base. What is it and how is it used?**
Basically it is the plaster-impregnated bandage used in hospitals for plaster casts. It is sold in small packs under various names for modelmaking, but can also usually be obtained to order in larger quantities from pharmacists. It produces a form of hard shell scenery but is slightly less messy in use. The usual instructions advise you to soak the bandage in water before applying it to the layout. This is of course the method used in hospitals, where it is also customary to spread polythene sheeting over the floor beforehand. A rather less messy system of using it on a layout is to put it in place whilst dry and then soak the surface with water applied with a wide soft brush. As with hard shell, it needs to be supported temporarily with crumpled newspaper whilst setting and subsequently covered with a finishing plaster coat.

342 **What is papier-mâché and can it be used for landscape modelling?**
True papier-mâché is produced by tearing paper into small fragments and soaking it in diluted size until it becomes a pulp. The pulp is then pounded to break up the fibres, the surplus liquid is drained off, and the pulp

is formed by pressure into the required shape. Whilst this could be used for scenic construction, a simpler method is to paste successive layers of newsprint over some simple former. Two to three layers can be applied in a session and then allowed to harden for 24 hours before applying a further layer. Whilst this is a fairly slow process, it is very cheap and the subsequent landscape foundation can be readily cut with a sharp trimming knife.

343 **I have tried making landscape by pasting newspapers, but I need a large quantity of paste. A bottle seems to go nowhere – what do you suggest?**
The best material is wallpaper paste. You should empty the packet into a large screw-top glass jar, label it accordingly and mix a small quantity in another jar. A large spoonful of paste powder to a cup of water is about the right proportion. Apply the paste with a cheap flat paintbrush, remembering to wash it thoroughly with water afterwards. A packet of paste will serve to provide scenery for a medium-sized layout.

344 **Long before I have got very far with scenic construction my hands are in a mess and I find it difficult to wipe them clean on a rag. What can I do to prevent this?**
You need a bucket two-thirds full of hot water and an old but serviceable towel. At regular intervals rinse your hands; the water should remain warm throughout a two-hour session.

345 **Can you use fibreglass for landscape construction?**
As long as money is no object and you are not allergic to the resins, plastic-impregnated fibreglass is an excellent way of creating a very strong, light and rigid shell and is often used by professional modellers where the model is going to be moved about a great deal. However, the material is not that easy to use and work *must be carried out in a very well-ventilated workshop*. It is not suitable for use inside the home.

346 **I have seen reference to the use of twin-part resins that produce an expanded foam plastic which can be**
used for landscape construction. Can you enlighten me?
These materials are those employed for certain types of wall insulation and were put on the market some time back. However, the chemicals involved are toxic and it has been discovered that, other than in expert hands, it can pose a distinct health hazard. To the best of my knowledge, the material has been withdrawn – certainly I would not recommend its use since, apart from any possible health hazards, it is extremely difficult to gauge exactly how far the stuff is going to expand, and the fine control needed for good landscape modelling is lacking. It is also fairly expensive.

347 **Is expanded polystyrene any use for landscape construction?**
Many modellers find it very easy to use this material – it is light and, if discarded packaging is used, very cheap (see Plate 21). There are some snags, however – it is very messy to cut other than with a hot wire, it is affected by many common solvents and, above all, it is flammable and, when alight, puts out toxic fumes. In addition, it has very little strength, so it is extremely easy to knock holes in a finished section of landscape.

348 **How do you cut expanded polystyrene without it breaking apart?**
Expanded polystyrene is most readily cut with a hot wire. From time to time this tool has been advertised, but it is fairly simple to make. A 'U'-shaped wooden frame is fixed to the cutting board and a length of thin resistance wire (fine nickel silver wire is ideal) is stretched tightly across the end of the frame. The wire is then connected to the 16 V ac output of your power unit, possibly through a wire-wound ballast resistor, and the power is switched on. The wire becomes hot and cuts through the expanded polystyrene (see Plate 21). Alternatively, a fretsaw can be modified by fitting a small insulating pad in place of the clamps so that a hot wire, connected to the transformer through a length of flex, can be strung between the end of the frame.

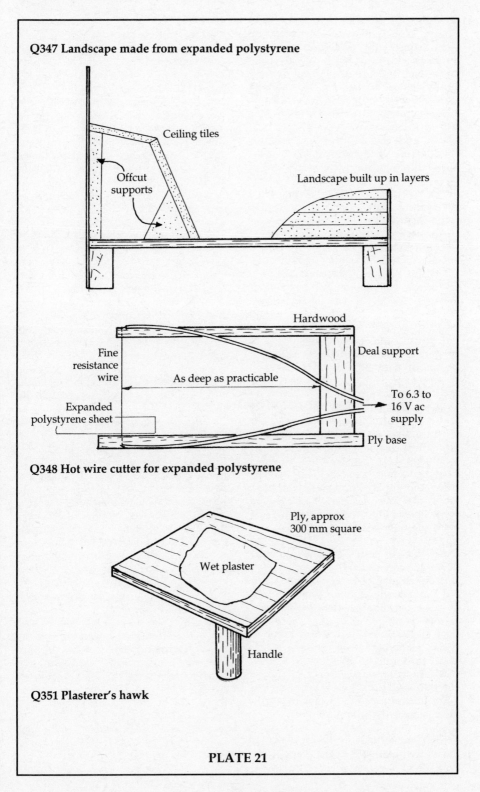

Q347 Landscape made from expanded polystyrene

Ceiling tiles

Offcut supports

Landscape built up in layers

Hardwood

Fine resistance wire

As deep as practicable

Deal support

Expanded polystyrene sheet

To 6.3 to 16 V ac supply

Ply base

Q348 Hot wire cutter for expanded polystyrene

Ply, approx 300 mm square

Wet plaster

Handle

Q351 Plasterer's hawk

PLATE 21

Section 3:2
Finishing the landscape

349 Having covered a wire netting foundation with plaster, I find the ground surface now has an all-over regular hexagonal pattern. How could I have avoided this?

Don't worry, it happens to everyone. What you have to do, now that the surface is hard, is to apply a finishing coat of plaster to smooth the surface. At the same time you can provide added detail to the landscape and correct any small errors in contour.

350 What is the best way of applying the final coat of plaster?

There are a variety of means – a small trowel, a palette knife, a set of clay modelling tools, or a flat brush. Much depends on the type of surface you want. It is probably easiest to apply the plaster with the trowel and use this to spread it over the surface before finishing it with a brush; wash the brush well before the plaster sets. Most of the tools mentioned can be purchased from an artist's supplier – they are used for sculpture, which when you consider things rationally, is what we are doing when creating a landscape.

351 I find it rather difficult to balance a container of wet plaster in one hand whilst I apply it to the scenery with the other. Can you suggest a better approach?

The plasterer's hawk has been used for this purpose since the days of the Pharaohs, and probably well before that. It is a square of wood measuring about 300 mm per side, with a handle screwed vertically in the exact centre which you hold in your left (or 'non-spreading') hand (see Plate 21). A generous dollop of plaster emptied into the centre will stay put whilst you manipulate it as you wish. You can scrape trowels or modelling tools clean on the side; it is even possible to mix small amounts of plaster on its surface.

352 Can I use ordinary plaster for the final coat, or must I get a special mix?

This is a matter of taste. There are several ready-mixed materials on the market and it is always worth carrying out a little experimentation with anything that happens to be handy after a home decorating session. The specialised modelling mixes which are sold by firms catering for scenic modelling equipment are also worth considering. These are not standard decorator's plasters sold in small quantities at inflated prices – they are specially formulated for specific tasks and, if used according to the maker's instructions, give excellent results.

353 How does one model a rock face?

There are several accepted methods of doing this, all of which work well in careful hands: you can use a ready-made rock section, you can carve or cast plaster, build up strata layer by layer out of a suitable material, or use natural rock. Each method has its advocates – the sensible course is to try a couple and decide which gives the best results in your hands.

354 I wasn't aware that one could buy ready-made rock faces. Where can you get them?

Like so many good things for the scenic modeller, these are made by German scenic specialists and may be a little difficult to track down in Britain. From time to time small British manufacturers have offered cast rock faces, but the twin problems of distribution and persuading the British to buy them seem to have defeated their best endeavours. The favoured ready-made rock face in Britain is cork bark (see Plate 22), sold by florists for flower arrangement. In small doses, carefully arranged, it can be very convincing – used in masses, the result is less happy.

355 Where can you get the moulds for casting rock faces?

You can't – you make them yourself, and there are two methods available. For the best results, look out for natural rocks with suitable striations and make a cold latex cast of the surface. This is done by mixing a two-part rubber-based compound in a throw-away container and pouring it over the surface. It will set fairly quickly, after which the resulting mould can be peeled off. In use, the latex mould is laid flat, supported and surrounded by plasticine, and a semi-liquid plaster mix is poured in. Several moulds are prepared and a variety of different rocks produced; these are then cut and fitted together on to the base plaster face, using fresh plaster as a cement. This is also used to cover the larger cracks, but a few narrow crevasses add to the effect.

It is also possible to make a very effective mould by folding aluminium kitchen foil, opening up the sheet and then applying it to a wet plaster surface. Crumpled foil is, however, a little erratic in its effects, but it is simple, cheap and remarkably effective on large or small surfaces (see Plate 22).

356 Is it very difficult to carve a rock face in plaster?

It is a lot easier than it looks. It is customary to do much of the preliminary work whilst the plaster is still workable; the finer detail is then cut into the surface with small craft knives (see Plate 22). This generates a good deal of fine powder which can only be effectively removed with a vacuum cleaner. Used judiciously on a rock face cast with crumpled foil, carving can create some excellent results.

357 Is there a simple way of creating the effect of regular strata, as one often finds in a limestone formation?

A quick and remarkably easy way of producing *short* stretches of rock strata is to break a sheet of insulation board into strips and lay these one on top of the other at the desired angle (see Plate 22). This method does not, however, work quite so well when larger stretches are required, for it is very unusual for strata to lay in even, regularly spaced layers over any appreciable distance.

358 Is it possible to make rocks and cliff faces out of expanded polystyrene?

If you aren't too bothered about fine details, you can make *anything* out of expanded polystyrene, so long as you don't want it to work or carry any weight! However, as any follower of *Star Trek* should be aware, even at full size polystyrene rocks lack ultimate realism, and in small scales the porous nature of the material is all too evident. There are a few very close-grained plastic sheets which could be used in this way, but there will still be a lot of carving to be done and a very large amount of small plastic debris to remove. Getting rid of this is, if anything, worse than carving the stuff!

359 I want to model an area of moorland with stony outcrops. What is the simplest way of modelling the rocks?

This is where real rock – in the form of suitable stones found in the garden – comes into its own. Begin by selecting a quantity of stones of about the required size and wash and dry them thoroughly before putting them into a box. They are then placed in position in the plaster when building up the landscape foundation (see Plate 22).

360 Plaster looks horrible in its natural state. How does one finish it off? What paint should be used or is it a good idea to colour the final coat?

It is difficult to get a realistic effect solely by colouring plaster, but there is some merit in the idea of giving it a base colour so that should it get chipped it will not show. Powder colours work well – brown, for a basic soil effect, is preferable to a green – and any paint that gives a flat finish is suitable; avoid anything with the slightest hint of gloss. Oil-based paints can be let down with white spirit to a much thinner consistency, and the absorbent nature of the plaster helps to soak them in. Acrylic paints are greatly favoured, but for large areas emulsion paint – which is the accepted material for painting plaster – is very popular. For smaller areas the small sample pots provided by many paint manufacturers to allow one to decide which of their latest shades best suits your home decor, are an ideal way of building up a fair range of hues at a reasonable price. However, if you should be modelling a Southern line, where there is a likelihood of encountering chalk cuttings, the plaster will only need a little weathering to look natural.

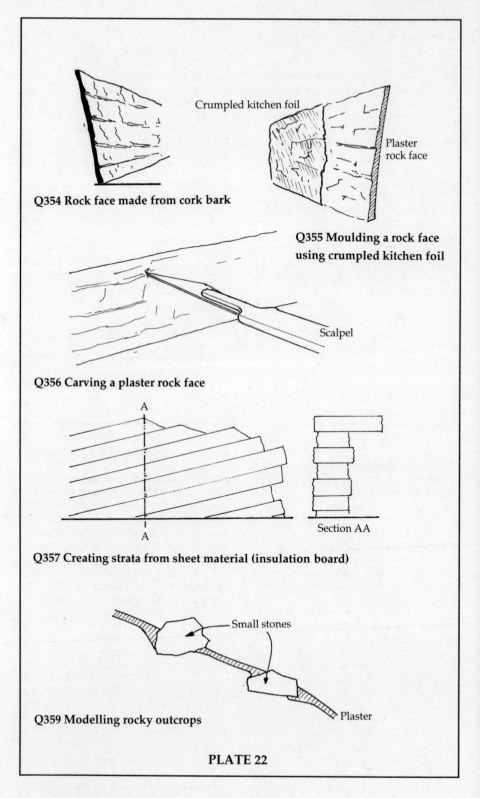

Crumpled kitchen foil

Plaster rock face

Q354 Rock face made from cork bark

Q355 Moulding a rock face using crumpled kitchen foil

Scalpel

Q356 Carving a plaster rock face

A

A

Section AA

Q357 Creating strata from sheet material (insulation board)

Small stones

Q359 Modelling rocky outcrops

Plaster

PLATE 22

361 I built some scenery with expanded polystyrene but when I painted it, it melted. What can I use for this purpose?

Most active solvents tend to attack this material, so the only safe paints are water-based. Emulsion paint is ideal, whilst acrylic paints are also suitable. A simpler solution is to apply a finishing coat of plaster which can then be painted with whatever paint you prefer.

Section 3:3
Grass, trees and foliage

362 What is your opinion of the scenic mats on offer? Are they mainly of value to the more casual worker, or do they have any value for the serious scenic modeller?

The scenic mat is clearly of considerable value to the individual who wants a quick fix for a plain area; it is also ideal for anyone who wants to change a sectional track system around. As a result, it is often regarded as only suitable for elementary work, but this is not so. As with all scenic materials, the end result depends more on what you do with the material than the material itself. It can, for example, be supported directly by a chicken wire foundation, cutting out any plastering, though it would be better to interpose a layer of pasted newspaper to help smooth the surface and make it easier to glue the mat in position. The even appearance of many 'grass' mats makes them the best material for modelling a tended lawn, whether this be a bowling green, a suburban garden or the tended verges along a housing estate.

363 My initial efforts with scenic mats have not been exactly successful as the material will form unrealistic folds no matter what I do. Can you offer any advice?

There is no way that a flat scenic mat will of its own accord lie smoothly over a contoured surface, any more than one can take a bolt of material and, without cutting or folding, produce a garment from it. As we do not want tucks or pleats, we must resort to judicious cutting, and this will inevitably produce

small joins which need disguising. As a scenic mat is normally made by gluing dyed flock on to a woven base, it is possible to scrape some from a spare offcut and then glue it over the join.

364 I find that most scenic mats produce a very unrealistic effect over large areas. Is there anything simple that can be done to rectify this?

Some careful work with a scraper will break up the even nature of the mat, and a little touching in with different colours will change the even hue. If an airbrush is available, a certain amount of shading can be carried out.

365 What is the best way of applying scatter material to my layout? I find the stuff will fall off and, since the layout is a portable one, areas of the landscape are beginning to get a trifle sparse.

Begin by applying PVA glue thickly to the landscape formation. Pour the scatter material liberally to the wet glue, then cover with a piece of newspaper and press home firmly over the entire area, repeating the process to make sure that every square centimetre of the ground has been covered at least once. Remove the newspaper and leave to dry. Don't worry if the glue squeezes out on top – it will not show when dry. After 24 hours check for bald patches and, if there are any, apply more PVA glue and scatter material. However, even with this technique scatter material will tend to fall off from time to time. Were you to see the actual setting up on an exhibition you would find layout operators busy applying fresh scatter material to their layouts.

366 Is it possible to make scatter materials at home?

Sawdust can be coloured with little difficulty. You can use dyes, or oil-based paints diluted generously with white spirit. A good method is to three-quarters fill a glass jar with sawdust and pour in a quantity of colorant to cover the sawdust. Allow to soak thoroughly, topping up if necessary, then pour away surplus liquid before spreading the sawdust to dry on a flat tray, covered with a sheet of polythene. Some modellers speed the drying by placing the tray in the oven, but this is not recommended if oil paint is used. If you wish to speed matters, place the tray over a source of heat in an outdoor location, such as the garage. The sawdust produced by a domestic circular saw is finer than that to be found in commercial woodworking shops.

367 I have seen some excellent rough grass on a number of layouts at exhibitions. It is quite long and has a wonderful overgrown effect. How is it produced?

Currently the favoured method is to coat the landscape base with PVA adhesive, then firmly press carpet felt on to it and allow it to dry hard. The felt is then torn off the base, leaving most of the hairs stuck down (see Plate 23). The grass so formed is then painted – to avoid too much flattening of the fibres it is best to use an airbrush. Other materials can be employed – medical lint gives a finer effect, and many cloths will also produce a similar result. A little experimenting could be quite rewarding.

368 I have tried producing grass by gluing carpet felt down and tearing it off again, but the results are very patchy and uneven. What should I do about this?

Persevere! If an area is bald, repeat the process until you are satisfied. Always be prepared to carry out a certain amount of trimming to create the effect you want.

369 What is zip texturing?

This is a very fast method of covering a plastered area with a realistic scenic texture developed in the USA. A mixture of powder colour and plaster is dropped on to the terrain by sifting it through a small sieve – a tea-strainer with a fine plastic mesh is ideal (see Plate 23). The surface can be dampened beforehand, but the favoured method is to spray with a fine mist, using a small spray sold for watering house plants.

370 My model grass is depressingly even. How do the experts get such delightful variegated colours. Do they paint the scatter material afterwards?

It is possible to paint the scatter materials, though for best results an airbrush should be used. It is a good deal easier to begin with a selection of different shades and, even more important, different textures of scatter materials and to mix them randomly over small areas of the landscape.

371 Are there any sources of scenic materials to be found around the home?

There are a large number of useful materials that can be culled or diverted from their original purpose. Dried used tea-leaves make very effective foliage – clearly the smaller Assam variety is to be preferred to the long-leaf Darjeeling. This is one scenic material that can be safety dried in the domestic oven. Scouring pads can be teased to form both foliage and hedges. Here cheaper varieties, as found on market stalls, seem to be superior to the branded pattern sold in supermarkets, largely because we want something that disintegrates readily! Foam plastic has limited uses, as it is very difficult to pull apart. Some effective hedging has been made from horsehair padding, as used in superior upholstery, but with the increased use of foam plastic this material is now difficult to find, although a small specialist upholsterer may be able to help.

372 I have some scatter material which appears to have been made from foam plastic, chopped up small. Is it possible to do this in the home?

Foam plastic can be chopped in a liquidiser, but it does impose a considerable load on the machine and is difficult to get out afterwards. This is likely to cause severe problems. As the price of a liquidiser which is intended solely for chopping plastic will outweigh any savings over the commercial product, this is not, in general, a cost-effective option. It is, however, worth bearing in mind if the question of replacing the food processor arises. Bargain-price liquidisers of unknown brands offered by cheap-jack concerns are not really suitable – they are usually cheap because they aren't that good to begin with.

373 Once a packet of scatter material has been opened, the contents tend to fall out no matter what I do to

seal the top. Have you any suggestions please?

Glass screw-top containers are ideal for this purpose. It is advisable to soak the original label off the body, so that the contents are clearly visible. This obviates the need to label most scenic materials. The larger jars, those containing instant coffee, for example, are particularly useful for holding dry plasters, since when the top is securely screwed home, the material is protected against damp for a very long time. Here labelling is advisable – the large self-adhesive address label is probably the best since the legend can then be clearly written in large block capitals with a felt-tip pen.

374 When I try to paint my grass and other foliage, I find I not only flatten the surface, but also frequently knock large quantities of material off the ground or branches. How can I get round this?

The obvious answer is to use an airbrush. For this purpose the inexpensive modeller's airbrush is adequate and could, for this application, be powered directly from a footpump since you are not seeking an even finish. Having said that, a number of modellers do paint scenery with ordinary brushes with excellent results – it is largely a matter of using a little care and, above all, filling a large soft brush with ample diluted paint so that it flows out rather than is placed in position.

375 I have seen some very realistic trees at exhibitions. How are they made?

To make an accurate model of a deciduous tree, you begin by constructing the trunk out of a bundle of multi-strand wire cable, using illustrations for a popular handbook on trees as a guide; the type that shows a tree in its winter and summer forms is clearly the best. Once the trunk and branches have been formed and painted, the branches are coated with adhesive and foliage is applied. This can be made at home – dried tea leaves are very good – or purchased in packets from your model shop. To get the best effect it is a good idea to glue individual pieces of foliage in position, using tube glue and tweezers.

376 I want a large number of trees to produce a model wood. Is there a simple and speedy way of achieving this aim?

A speedy method of producing large numbers of trees is to take a length of fine wire – copper is usually preferred – and fold it into loops a little longer than the intended height of the tree. One end of the bundle is twisted together to form the trunk, while the other ends are snipped and teased into a tree shape. This skeleton is painted bark colour, then, when dry, the branches are dipped in glue and then twirled in a heap of model foliage until a fair quantity is stuck in place. The finished trees are then laid aside to dry (see Plate 23).

When the trees are dry, they are sorted into three grades. A few will be found to be quite realistic – these will be reserved for prominent positions. A fair number will be quite reasonable, but many will look somewhat unconvincing. These last are used in the centre of the wood or copse and are surrounded by the better-quality trees.

377 How does one model a coniferous tree?

A very simple system is to form a long thin loop of stiffish wire. Bristles are then laid through the loop in slowly increasing lengths until the required girth of the tree is achieved. The open ends of the loop are then held in the chuck of a hand drill, the closed end is held in a vice, and the drill is turned until the wire is wound into a tight spiral and the bristles stick out in all directions. After any trimming has been carried out, the bristles are gently pulled downwards with the hand (see Plate 23).

Suitable bristles can be cut from a cheap nylon brush, or teased from sisal (not plastic) string. This type of construction, known as the 'bottle brush' tree, is that used to produce miniature conifers as Christmas cake decorations. It is best employed for masses of trees rather than individual specimens, but that's how most conifers are grown

It is possible to make a detailed model of a conifer from a tapered trunk into which indvidual branches are glued, but this is an extremely long process indeed.

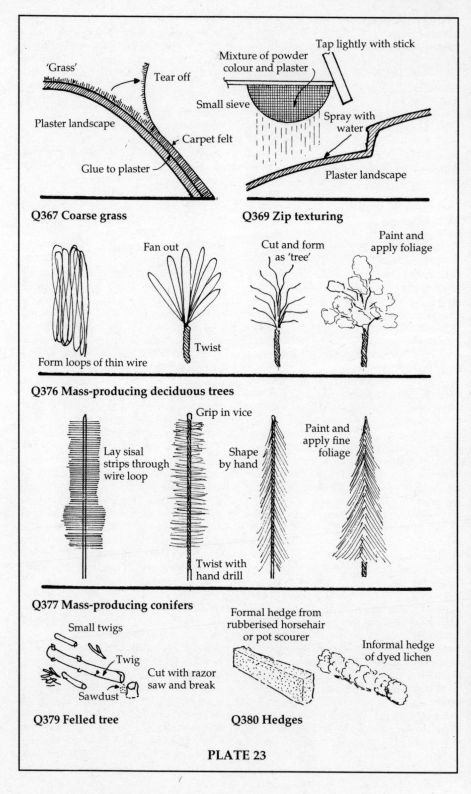

'Grass'

Tear off

Plaster landscape

Carpet felt

Glue to plaster

Q367 Coarse grass

Mixture of powder colour and plaster

Tap lightly with stick

Small sieve

Spray with water

Plaster landscape

Q369 Zip texturing

Fan out

Twist

Form loops of thin wire

Cut and form as 'tree'

Paint and apply foliage

Q376 Mass-producing deciduous trees

Lay sisal strips through wire loop

Grip in vice

Shape by hand

Paint and apply fine foliage

Twist with hand drill

Q377 Mass-producing conifers

Small twigs

Twig

Sawdust

Cut with razor saw and break

Q379 Felled tree

Formal hedge from rubberised horsehair or pot scourer

Informal hedge of dyed lichen

Q380 Hedges

PLATE 23

378 **Is it possible to use actual plants to reproduce trees. I've a feeling parsley might be suitable.**
Whilst some people have used plants – cow parsley is quite popular – it is difficult to prevent their wilting quite rapidly. However, it is possible to look out suitable twigs in the garden and use them as a basis for trees. As they lack finer branches, it is best to apply the foliage in the form of dyed lichen. This type of 'tree' is more effective in a mass than as individual specimens.

379 **I have seen models of felled trees on some layouts. How are these made?**
A model tree trunk can be produced from a suitable twig. Allow it to dry completely before use and saw the surplus away with a small razor saw. The stump and trunk would need to be cut almost through and then snapped to create the correct effect. Don't forget to get the felled trunk in correct alignment with the stump, and sprinkle a little fine sawdust around the spot (see Plate 23).

380 **How can one model hedges?**
There are two methods in vogue. One is to take a long strip of horsehair or pot scourer and tease it into the required shape. Another is to assemble the hedge from clumps of foliage base – dyed lichen is favoured for this. Trimmed hedges can be formed from foam plastic, the main difficulty here being to obtain a clean, straight cut. It is usually necessary to paint the hedge after assembly and a little additional foliage may be added if it is close to the baseboard edge (see Plate 23).

Small shrubs can be produced in much the same manner.

381 **How are garden plants produced?**
There are two opposing methods. One is to pull bits of foliage material, dyed lichen, etc, apart and then position them as realistically as possible. The flower heads can either be produced by gluing tiny scraps of appropriate coloured material in place, or by blobbing small dabs of oil paint in position. The object is to produce a broad effect rather than to make accurate models of specific plants –

viewers will make up their own minds on this matter.

The other is painstakingly to model an actual plant. This is time-consuming and is only reserved for the highest-quality models, such as those found in Pendon Museum.

382 **How does one model a vegetable garden?**
Peas and beans, which are very distinctive, are built around suitable frames made from wire or small stalks. Cabbages and lettuce must be made from modelling clay. In all cases it is vital to set the crops out in ordered rows. Few model vegetable gardens are very large for obvious reasons.

Section 3:4
Rivers and lakes

383 **How can one model water realistically?**
There are several approaches. For the still, murky waters found around industrial sites, a flat painted and varnished surface can be very effective (see Plate 24). Plaster surfaces, carefully painted and varnished, are also quite effective; indeed, this seems the only effective way of reproducing the effects of waves on a beach. In general, a moulded surface which has been properly painted and then varnished is an excellent all-round approach, given one simple proviso, that the builder has some artistic ability. It is all too easy to create a 'toytown' effect which sits badly with modern high-quality railway models. A different approach involves the use of transparent or translucent materials set in a modelled river or lake bed. These are probably the most straightforward ways of modelling rivers, streams and lakes.

384 **What are the basic principles for creating an effective waterway?**
Fundamentally, in a watercourse or lake the two elements, the bed and the banks, are joined by the level water surface. In the model one begins by deciding how translucent the water would be. In most cases it is only possible to see a short distance below the surface, so, even where

the bed is modelled, it is necessary to colour the modelled water to prevent the details being too crystal clear. This is where imagination and artistic insight, though not necessarily artistic skill, must be brought into play. In many cases it is not necessary to model the bed – a transparent surface over a flat painted base will suffice since one would not expect to be able to see more than perhaps 200 mm below the surface of the real thing, if that. This greatly simplifies construction since it is not necessary to match the banks to the bed. Indeed, it is really only necessary to go to the length of modelling the bed if you are modelling a placid lake fed by a crystal clear mountain stream or a swimming pool where the water, one would hope, is also clear.

385 How is the effect of running water simulated?

The effect of slow-moving water can be reproduced by painting the surface with flowing streaks of blue and green, simulating the flow marks (see Plate 24). This should be done below the reflective surface, that is to say before a varnish coat is applied, or underneath a transparent acetate sheet.

386 How can one represent rippled water?

Crumpled cellophane creates the illusion of rippled water very effectively, but it is more suitable for small streams and wide drainage ditches than wider rivers. However, these smaller waterways are probably more in tune with the usual cramped model site. The cellophane is laid over a flat painted bed and then the landscape is built over the edges (see Plate 24). Cellophane is extensively used for wrapping such diverse items as shirts, bouquets and even loaves of bread.

387 What is the best way of modelling a placid lake?

The usual method is to begin by modelling the bed using standard landscape techniques inside a hole cut into a sheet of ply fractionally larger than the finished shape of the lake. The bed is then painted in dark colours and any small details – stones, weeds, discarded junk, etc – added before the water. The

water is a sheet of transparent acetate sheet, generally painted on the underside with pale green and blue to reflect the sky (see Plate 24). Before securing this in place with cement, tape or staples, it is as well to look carefully to see that the modelled lake looks as you want it to, because it will be difficult to change your mind afterwards. If the ply support is not already part of the layout, it is then installed, taking care to see that it is absolutely level. The banks are then modelled to match the shape of the bed. The same technique is also used to model a limpid stream.

388 Should one model a swimming pool in the same way as one would model a lake?

It is better to build the walls of a swimming pool to their full depth and then cut and fit a sheet of acetate plastic before adding the bottom. The underwater portions of the pool should be given a blue tint and it is a good idea to reduce the slope of the bottom to simulate the effect of refraction. Any small gaps between the acetate sheet and the pool sides can be filled with a fine fillet of plastic cement (see Plate 24).

389 I have seen references to lakes being produced with setting resin. What is it and how is it used?

Setting resin is a slight misnomer – what is needed is clear encapsulating resin, a material initially offered to enable craftworkers to enclose an object in a clear plastic sheath. It is sold by the better artist's suppliers and consists of two liquids which are mixed together immediately before use in the proportions clearly stated in the accompanying instructions. Initially it is quite fluid and can be readily poured into a prepared bed, but it begins to harden by chemical reaction within minutes, so it is essential to mix only a fairly small quantity at a time. The most important thing to bear in mind is that unless the prepared bed is watertight, the resin will fall out of the bottom and make a mess on the floor. Check beforehand by filling the lake bed with water and, as a precaution, lay a sheet of polythene underneath in case of accidents.

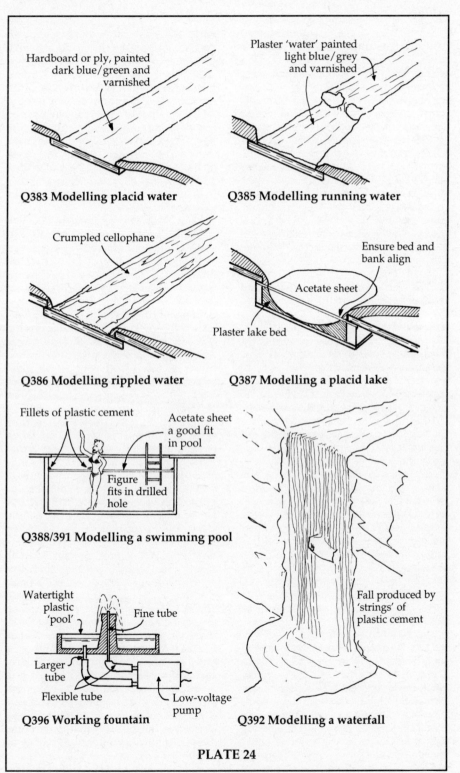

Hardboard or ply, painted dark blue/green and varnished

Q383 Modelling placid water

Plaster 'water' painted light blue/grey and varnished

Q385 Modelling running water

Crumpled cellophane

Q386 Modelling rippled water

Ensure bed and bank align

Acetate sheet

Plaster lake bed

Q387 Modelling a placid lake

Fillets of plastic cement

Acetate sheet a good fit in pool

Figure fits in drilled hole

Q388/391 Modelling a swimming pool

Watertight plastic 'pool'

Fine tube

Larger tube

Flexible tube

Low-voltage pump

Q396 Working fountain

Fall produced by 'strings' of plastic cement

Q392 Modelling a waterfall

PLATE 24

390 Is it possible to create the effect of deep water by pouring in a quantity of varnish and leaving it to dry?

Alas, this enticing scheme is doomed to failure. For a start, the varnish will only form a hard skin – the balance will remain fluid. Then over a period of time it will shrink, swell and crack. This also applies to the use of PVA adhesive which whilst, drying transparent, also shrinks and cracks. It is possible to apply several layers of varnish to build up a depth of about 1 mm, but this does take an inordinate time since it is advisable to allow each coat a week to dry and harden fully before the next coat is applied. The smell is none too pleasant either.

391 I have seen model lakes and swimming pools with bathers up to their waist in the water. How is this achieved?

The simplest method is to use clear encapsulating resin for the water. The bathers are cemented securely in place before the resin is poured into the lake. To arrange a swimmer, fill the pool to within 2-3 mm of the desired level, then put the figure in place just before the resin begins to harden. The final coat can then be applied to bring the water level up to the desired point. If the water is represented by a clear acrylic sheet, drill a small hole and file it to fit the figure; a little polystyrene cement seals the gap and produces the ripple effect one would expect (see Plate 24). Similar techniques can be used to insert piling for bridges and small piers.

392 How can one model a waterfall?

There are three basic approaches. The most difficult is to produce a realistic plaster torrent which is then painted to resemble running water and subsequently varnished. In expert hands this is extremely effective, but if the execution is less than perfect the result is unrealistic. The other methods model the falls themselves as if they were rock faces, but do not attempt to reproduce the water in plaster. In one case, the water is represented by fine slivers of cellophane hanging from the upper rim of the tor-

rent, ideally embedded in the clear encapsulating resin forming the upper part of the stream. If this is carefully done, the strips will move with air currents and create the illusion of movement. Another method takes advantage of the nature of polystyrene cement to produce long strips at the slightest provocation. Applying the tube at the top of the fall, strings of cement are drawn out and then allowed to drape down to the lower pool (see Plate 24). The effect of ripples on the latter created by concentric rings of cement.

393 Would it not be possible, by installing a small pump, to use real water to model a waterfall?

There is no technical difficulty – small pumps are available that work off the 16 V ac supply and give an effective head of some 100 mm if the pump and piping is carefully sited. Creating a wholly watertight bed is more of a problem; this is the one area where the cost of fibreglass is fully justified, particularly as a simple car-repair kit should provide sufficient material for the purpose. It would probably be necessary to make a plaster and stone original from which a further plaster mould is created for the fibreglass moulding if a good-quality model is required. However, there is one insuperable snag – the scale effect. Water in a model behaves exactly as it does in real situations, and there is considerable difference between a fall of some 7 m and one of only 100 mm, so the net result is somewhat unsatisfactory.

394 Can I model a cascade or set of rapids with running water?

This is a marginal case where it might be effective. Once again the stream bed is best made from fibreglass, but as most of the visible part will be made from small stones, it should be possible to mould it in situ. Although the stones need to show evidence of the smoothing associated with running water, if the torrent is rapid enough, one can account for freshly moved rocks with more jagged edges. One point that needs to be borne in mind at the outset is that open water does increase the humidity of the air in its immediate vicinity. In addition, many scenic materials will act as highly effective wicks, so it is vital that a small boundary between these and the water-course is maintained. Needless to say, real water creates a number of problems with portable layouts.

395 Is it possible to drive a model waterwheel realistically with running water?

The quick answer is no, the key word being realistically. Using a low-voltage pump it is possible to direct a stream of water over a model overshot wheel – indeed, a number of plastic kits incorporate this feature. Unfortunately, the stream is in practice only a trickle of water and the wheel simply does not run at a realistic speed. This can be overcome by driving the wheel by a separate motor. To overcome the visual problems that will arise if the wheel is running at a different speed from the water, you should model an undershot wheel which will tend to increase the speed of water leaving down the mill race. It is possible to make model waterwheels that work satisfactorily – there are examples in the Children's Gallery of the Science Museum – but to do this it is necessary to work to a much larger scale than we use.

396 Can I have a working fountain in my model townscape?

A number of kits are available for this attractive feature and it is not too difficult to make one's own fountain using a 16 V pump as the driving force, together with some plastic tubing. It will probably be best to use a short length of fine-bore copper tubing for the final jet. It is essential to create a watertight basin, and this could be modelled from sheet plastic; generous fillets of plastic cement along the joints will ensure it is water-tight (see Plate 24).

397 The small 16 V pumps have a very low flow rate. Is it possible to get something more powerful?

There is a large jump between the flow rate of the small model pumps and the more powerful low-voltage pumps sold for garden ponds; it is a case of either too little or too much. Whilst in theory it might be possible to have header and sump tanks and arrange both overflow pipes to divert excess water, and have

float-operated switches to regulate the flow, the probability of leakage is always present, and when several litres of water are involved, this is a significant point to keep in mind, particularly if the layout is situated in a loft or upper room, where even a cupful of water could stain a lower ceiling. For a large commercial exhibition layout the idea has possibilities, but it does seem to be one of those schemes that are much more attractive in theory than they would work out in practice.

398 Is it possible to incorporate running water into a garden layout?

It is not merely possible, but is highly desirable where the tracks run at or near ground level and can be incorporated into a specialised form of ornamental garden. The subject of water in the garden is fully covered in a number of excellent gardening manuals and touched upon in broad outline in many DIY manuals.

Section 3:5
Docks and inland waterways

399 I am thinking of including a canal into my layout. What is the best way to represent the water?

Canals are placid and, although relatively shallow, the waters are dark. A very simple method of reproducing canal water is to lay the bed from ply or hardboard, taking particular pains to see that the surface is level; water does not flow uphill. The base should be about 20 mm wider than the canal itself and must be perfectly smooth at the outset; any grain must be covered with filler and primer and rubbed smooth. It is then painted variegated blue-green with longitudinal brush strokes. Finally the surface is thickly coated with polyurethane varnish and left to harden. This is best done in an outdoor site as the pungent smell of the varnish takes days to dissipate. The same technique can be used for small harbours (see Plate 25).

400 How should one represent canal banks?

The prime essential to remember is that in

the prototype they are only 12 inches or so above the normal water level and reasonably even. The edging can be stone block or plain earth, and a towpath should be carried along one side of the channel, which should be wide enough for two narrow boats to pass (see Plate 25).

401 What features are found by the side of a lock?

The main essential is the lock-keeper's cottage; there may in addition be a canal-side inn. From around 1950, the probability is that the inn will have been improved and become a popular resort for nearby townsfolk, its original function, a staging post for the canal men and their families, only echoed in the name and decor. In a few cases the inn may even have been there before the canal – there is at least one example of a Tudor building by the Grand Union Canal.

402 How can one disguise the fact that the model canal doesn't go anywhere in particular?

Not only are canals crossed at frequent intervals by low road bridges, but also tunnels, whilst uncommon, were in sufficient numbers to allow one to use this type of exit without causing comment. Above all, it is quite legitimate to carry the railway over the canal by means of a bridge and loose the waterway on the far side.

403 I would like to include a lock on my model canal, but space is limited. Have you any ideas how I could arrange this?

There is no reason why either the railway or a road should not cross over the middle of the lock. In this way you only need model one pair of lock gates and half a narrow boat being locked through.

404 I wish to include a small harbour on my layout. Could you give me the approximate dimensions for such a feature in 4 mm scale?

A very small harbour, as one might find at the mouth of a river serving a fishing village, will, in 4 mm scale, measure at least 1 m x 0.5 m. This will only handle about eight small inshore trawlers or drifters and allow room for one coastal schooner or brig to tie up against the principal wharf, providing that all the fishing fleet isn't in port at the same time (see Plate 25).

405 What buildings are commonly found around small harbours?

The most important is the harbour office; this may be quite small but is likely to be something of an architectural feature. On southern and eastern coasts, a Customs House would also be in evidence, since a certain amount of traffic would be with Continental Europe. There would be at least one warehouse. In addition, all small ports had a boatyard; this was usually provided with a slip on which small craft could be hauled up out of the water for attention to the hulls. In recent years this yard would have turned over to maintaining pleasure craft. The slip and yard make a very attractive model feature.

406 Is it possible to have a modern marina alongside a steam age branch terminus, or are the two incompatible in time?

The time window is extremely narrow – 1960-65 – but as this means that one can have mixed steam and diesel traction on a track layout unaltered from the golden years of steam, it is possible to have the best of all worlds. Furthermore, as the boom years in yachting were yet to come at that time, the marina would not need to look like a marine version of the M25 on a summer Friday evening, and there would be room for the individual model yachts, dinghies and motor cruisers to be seen in isolation.

407 I have been hunting in vain for a suitable kit for a small coastal vessel. Have you any suggestions as to where I might find something?

The majority of plastic kits for ships are to relatively small scales and follow two themes: historic sailing ships and warships of the present century. However, several German kit manufacturers do offer kits for river craft suitable for HO or N gauge scenes. The differences between a coastal barge carrying cargo across the North Sea to small British ports and a Rhine barge plying its trade between Switzerland and Holland are too small to be noticed by anyone other than a ship modeller. Although the more specialised ship kits, intended for the serious marine modeller, offer a wider range of vessels, the bias remains towards historic vessels, warships and the more exotic types of commercial craft rather than the mundane, unglamorous general cargo carriers. A more serious consideration is that not only are such kits costly, but they are also aimed at the modeller who intends to spend an entire winter at the very least building the model. However, a visit to a model shop specialising in ship kits could prove worthwhile. Although 4 mm scale kits are very rare, the popular $1/8$ in scale (1:96) is compatible with both OO and HO gauge models.

408 **I have a fancy to include a paddle-steamer in my model harbour, but such kits as I have been able to track down seem to be too big for the space I have available. Have you any suggestions?**
The typical paddle-steamer that used to be found providing day trips for holidaymakers around our coasts and on the Thames and Clyde was a fair-sized vessel, ranging from some 60 m to well over 100 m from bow to stern. Furthermore, although the hulls were slender, the paddle-wheels in their sponsons added appreciably to the beam of the vessel. The result, even in $1/8$ in scale, which is to be recommended for use with a 4 mm scale model railway, is a large and, hopefully, impressive model. As a result, the best advice for anyone with a yen to include a model of one of these lovely vessels in a layout is to begin by allocating a berth for the ship to the rear of the baseboard and then to design the station complex around it.

409 **Why do you suggest that a ship model should be at the rear of the layout?**
There are two reasons for this. The first is that even a medium-sized model ship is a very large item and, if it is not to dominate the model, needs to be placed to the rear where it forms an excellent backdrop to the railway, whereas if placed in front of any tracks it will effectively hide the trains from view. The second and more practical consideration is that even

a steamship or motor vessel has masts and rigging; these are fairly delicate and so become a fragile obstacle to the operation of a model railway.

410 **What sort of model ships do you consider suitable for inclusion in what I appreciate is a cramped harbour?**
There are three suitable categories. First and foremost come the traditional coastal sailing vessels, and clearly these need to be carefully chosen, for it would never do to have a Norfolk wherry tied up in a West Highland port! Next we have small pleasure craft of all descriptions. In this connection it is worth mentioning that a large number of Second World War coastal patrol boats were converted into pleasure craft in the late 1940s. Finally there are the very small working craft, coastal barges and fishing vessels.

411 **I would like to add a small vessel to my model, but I do not feel inclined either to do a great deal of research or to spend a good deal of time and money on a craftsman kit. Have you any suggestions as to how I could produce something cheap, cheerful but reasonably authentic?**
The main factor in any model ship is the hull – get this right, add a neat superstructure using a couple of good clear photographs as a guide for detail, and you will have a reasonable model. This point has long been appreciated by toymakers, with the result that many cheap plastic boats, intended for the paddling pool and bath, are provided with a well-proportioned hull. All you need to do is to hunt diligently for a well-proportioned toy of the right size made from polystyrene or ABS. The next point to bear in mind is that masts and booms are quite slender in proportion to the hull, and that a mast either tapers towards the top, or else is made from several graded sections of tube, welded together. Moreover, it is braced to the hull with standing rigging. Over-thick masts and unrealistic rigging spoil many otherwise sound ship models.

412 **Is it possible to have real water in a model dock so that boats can move about realistically?**
This has been done on many occasions,

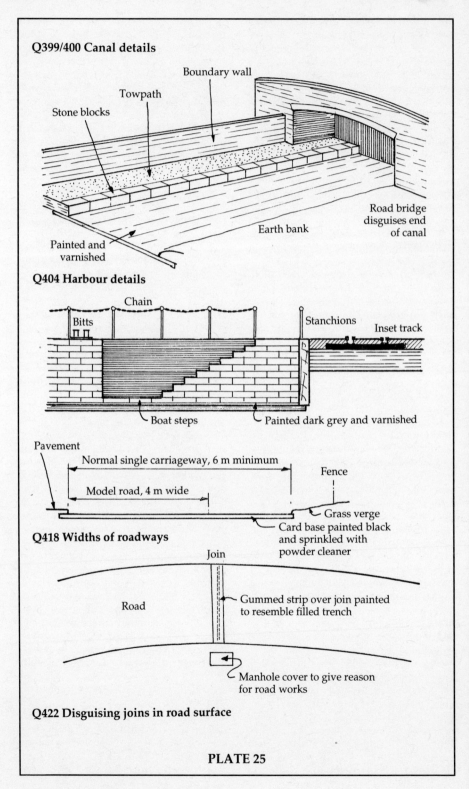

Q399/400 Canal details

Boundary wall

Towpath

Stone blocks

Road bridge
disguises end
of canal

Earth bank

Painted and
varnished

Q404 Harbour details

Chain

Bitts

Stanchions

Inset track

Boat steps

Painted dark grey and varnished

Pavement

Normal single carriageway, 6 m minimum

Fence

Model road, 4 m wide

Grass verge

Card base painted black
and sprinkled with
powder cleaner

Q418 Widths of roadways

Join

Road

Gummed strip over join painted
to resemble filled trench

Manhole cover to give reason
for road works

Q422 Disguising joins in road surface

PLATE 25

but does require a lot of space and not only must the tank be very strongly built, but also stout legs are needed to support it – water is heavy. Boats are moved by providing a magnetic link between the hull and a chain-driven mechanism below the tank. For constructional details you should refer to Dave Rowe's *Industrial and Mechanical Modelling*.

413 I would like to include a train ferry in my Southern Region model. How do you suggest I go about it?

Initially by modelling Dover, or else devising a convincing story for another ferry port – Richborough perhaps? A quick check in George Behrend's *Night Ferry*, a mine of information, reveals that the ferries held up to four Wagon Lits on each of four roads, so if you want a model of the ferry then you have space problems. These are not insuperable – a model Channel ferry in O gauge was exhibited at a pre-war model railway exhibition, and moreover it was a floating model in a tank, which is another story too long to relate here. Operationally the ferry will act as a specialised fiddle yard and so it might be possible to model no more than the stern and, of course, the special ramp connecting the dock tracks to the ship. The ferry could be moved some 300 mm away and a backdrop interposed to simulate sailing. Even if the unit were in water it would be advisable for the ferry to run on rails to ensure accurate alignment.

Smaller ferries have been built to move two or three boxcars on US-based layouts, since such freight-only ferries did exist. These have demonstrated that it is practicable to have a working ferry, but by any standards it is a major modelling project.

414 What type of cranes are provided at docks?

The normal dockside crane is a very large structure and really only appropriate in a major cargo-handling dock, where at least three would be provided. Indeed, until containerisation became the norm, the typical deep-water cargo ship was some 10,000 tons deadweight and had two holds ahead of the central superstructure and two holds aft, necessitating the attention of four cranes. Smaller ports generally relied on the ship's own equipment. A useful crane, commonly found around tiny harbours, is the Scotch derrick, which is relatively easy to model from square stripwood and very pleasant to look at.

415 How do ships discharge their own cargo?

Cargo vessels are always provided with booms which can be rigged to permit the unloading of cargo at any port where suitable cranes are not available. Twin booms and twin winches are provided so that one boom can be positioned over the dockside and the other over the hold. The lines from each boom are shackled together so that the cargo can be lifted from the hold by one winch, then hauled sideways and finally lowered on to the quay by the other. In practice both winchmen worked as a team and the goods sailed out of the hold in a graceful near parabolic curve.

416 What is the most common error to be found around a model harbour?

A failure to tie up the craft correctly. Unless a vessel is secured by bow and stern lines, it will veer away from the quayside erratically with changes of wind and current. Furthermore, to prevent damage to the paintwork, let alone the hull, fenders are interposed between the hull and the dockside. These are generally provided by the ship and although, in the past, these were made from rope, knotted in an elaborate pattern during the voyage, the more favoured device today is an old tyre. The mooring ropes are secured to twin bollards, or bitts, secured to the quayside and the deck of the ship. A mooring rope is generally provided with a loop at the landward end; on board it is hauled taut then wound in a figure of eight pattern around the twin bitts. It will, today, most often be a steel hawser rather than rope cordage.

417 I appreciate that I do not have room for a full-blown harbour on my layout, but I would like to create the impression of a port. Have you any suggestions?

The essence of a quay is that it is both

long and straight. This is also the characteristic of the baseboard edge, so it is not too difficult to turn what is an artificial boundary into a fair representation of a quayside. The quay would have inset tracks, lines which are all but buried in a roadway (see Q256). In older installations it was customary to surface the quay with stone setts, but for most of this century the tracks have been provided with inner rails to provide a flangeway and the space in between filled with tarmac.

Section 3:6
Roads, walls, fences and the railway right-of-way

418 How wide should a model road be?

This depends to a large extent on the purpose of the road – as you probably know, widths do vary. A typical modern single carriageway measures 10 m, more than the trackbed for a double track railway. As roads are only a secondary, scenic, feature on a model raiway, it is customary to reduce the width appreciably and to imply that they are secondary lanes or even cart-tracks leading to a farm (see Plate 25). Full-width main roads are best arranged at right-angles to the tracks, providing a good excuse for over- or under-bridges.

419 I am having considerable difficulty getting my roads to look at all realistic. In particular the changes in level look abrupt and toylike. What do you suggest?

A common error is to treat the baseboard top as the road surface and simply to put an overlay on top to create the gradient up to an overbridge. As very few roads are absolutely flat, the result is rather unrealistic. A road should be made from a continuous strip of card, thin ply or hardboard cut to the required plan and supported by packing. As, except on very small scenes, the roads need to be made from several units, this is only the foundation and a top cover should be applied.

420 What should be used for a top cover of a model road?

This depends very much on the type of road surface to be modelled. The simplest arrangement is to fill the joints with care so that they are not obvious and then paint the surface dark grey. This will suffice on larger layouts, where, if only for reasons of time, detailed attention to what is, after all, a secondary feature of the model would be too onerous.

421 I am finding it difficult to get an even finish to my road surfaces. Is there a simple way of achieving this?

Yes – don't bother! With the exception of newly finished road surfaces, the colour and texture of a road is uneven. However, it is important to suggest the pattern of normal road wear – this is most readily achieved by painting along the road rather than across it.

422 Try as I may I cannot hide the joint between two sections of road base. I have tried plaster, proprietary wood filler, even some car body filler with little success and, as the joint is rather prominent, what would you suggest?

An awkward joint can be disguised by covering it with a narrow strip of gummed paper which is then painted to look like one of those trenches public utilities will persist in digging across main roads, generally one week after the surface has been freshly renewed. The addition of a manhole along one edge will increase the realism and turn what is at present an embarrassment into an eye-catching piece of imaginative modelling (see Plate 25).

423 I have constructed a length of road alongside the open main line of my railway and, to increase realism, have added some of the excellent small-scale cars and lorries now available. However, their essentially static nature detracts from the realism of the model. What can I do?

To add movement to the scene you can install the excellent Faller road system, at the expense of some reconstruction and, of course, the cost of the models, but this restricts movement to coaches and lorries for the foreseeable future. As an alternative, consider the many ways road traffic is brought to a halt – road works, accidents, herds of cows, etc. One large club has a motorway feature on their OO layout and have installed a contraflow system on one carriageway and put contractors to work on the other, thus explaining why nothing is moving. In towns there are even more excuses for hold-ups. A side advantage of this is that instead of fuming impatiently the next time you're caught in a tailback, you can spend the time very profitably working out how to reproduce it on your model!

424 How does one get the effect of tarmac on a model road?

There are two popular methods. One is to cover the surface with fine wet-and-dry abrasive paper, which has the right texture and is quite good for colour. The other is to paint the surface black and then sprinkle white scouring powder over the top and leave to dry. This, however, produces a less even effect.

425 My layout is set around the turn of the century before road traffic became motorised. How should I finish my roads?

In towns there were three types of surface: stone setts, wood blocks and the macadamised surface which, in poorer areas, was very rutted. Side alleys and roads to industrial sites might be no more than a layer of coarse gravel over the natural ground. Outside the towns roads were intially macadamised, but after the middle of the 19th century and before the advent of the horseless carriage in any numbers, maintenance was patchy and potholes abounded.

426 How can one reproduce stone setts or wood blocks?

Apart from some sheets specially produced for road surfaces, there are a number of embossed plastic sheets which, whilst primariy intended for walls, can equally be applied horizontally as a ground surface. Brick, painted dark grey, makes a fair representation of wood blocks. For diorama-type models, where detailed examination is expected, some modellers cover the road with modelling clay and emboss the surface with a simple former.

427 What is a macadamised surface and how does one reproduce it on a model?

The basic principle of macadamisation was to lay graduated stones over the road foundations and then compact them with a heavy roller. This was capable of supporting horse-drawn vehicles providing that it was properly maintained and potholes were filled quickly. When motor traction arrived, the faster-moving wheels tore the loose surface away and threw up clouds of dust. The surface was then blinded with tar, and this led to the development of tar macadamising, or, as we now know it, tarmac. In model form, a macadamised road is the same as a tarmac road, but the colour is grey or brown and the surface is more likely to be rutted.

428 How does one produce a rutted lane?

First you need an old toy car or similar wheeled model with its wheels set the right distance apart. The lane is then coated with stiff plaster and before it is finally set the toy is pushed along the surface, producing realistic ruts in the mud; the plaster is then left to set. Wash most of the plaster off the toy before putting it away in the toolbox for the next lane. You can of course use a model vehicle, but it does get in a mess and is very difficult to clean up.

429 I am having considerable trouble painting the white lines along my roads. Try as I may, the final effect looks as if the contractors were drunk. How does one get a straight even line?

Several German firms offer pre-printed road surfaces with markings in place, though as these are for right-hand traffic their value for a British model is limited. There are two possibilities. Self-adhesive coloured tape, in various shades, is sold for commercial art and display work and is obtainable in white, yellow and red. Although this raises the line above the model road, the modern plastic lining is also slightly proud of the surface. Alternatively, the road should be masked with self-adhesive tape before the line is painted. Done with care, this produces a straighter, more even line.

Lettering is produced with white rub-down lettering.

430 My layout is set in the steam age, before the advent of modern road signs. Where do I get information about the older pattern signs so that I can model them accurately?

There may be an old copy of the Highway Code somewhere in the attic, failing which an early driving manual will give the information. However, Tiny Signs provide complete sets of early road signs, the purpose of which were self explanatory. In view of the tortuous nature of most model roads, even a small layout could use up all the warning signs for sharp bends and steep gradients.

431 How are pavements with stone slabs best modelled?

Plastic sheet embossed with paving stones is available; narrow strips cut along the length of the slabs makes excellent kerbstones. To reduce the round look of the slabs, the top surface can be rubbed down with abrasive paper. It is also possible to split such sheets into individual slabs by twisting along the grooves. These can then be stuck back on to a plastic base to create the irregular surface so often found in cities.

432 My pavements appear to be just resting on the roads. What should I do?

Follow prototype practice – put the pavements down first and then lay the road surface. Any small gaps can be hidden with a judicious smear of filler – plasticene is very good for this. Small irregularities go unnoticed because the gutter is usually covered with litter and presents a rough appearance.

433 Out in the country my road looks as if it has simply dropped on to the landscape. What should I do about this?

Unless there is a kerbstone along a road, the adjoining grass tends to lie on the edge of the road surface. Only when the road is freshly laid would the tarmac be appreciably above the land surface. The usual method of modelling is to lay the road first and then allow the edge of the final landscape finish to encroach irregularly along the side. It should be borne in mind that before 1960 few roads were provided with a kerbstone outside built-up areas, but drainage ditches were quite common and a distinct hazard for the unwary motorist.

434 How does one model manhole and drain covers effectively?

This is the sort of detail that is best reproduced by etching, and several concerns offer such detail for modellers.

435 Should the railway fence run at the top or bottom of an embankment?

The normal position for the fence is along the boundary of railway property, so it normally runs along the top of a cutting and at the foot of an embankment (see Plate 26). This does not rule out the addition of a safety fence on railway ground to keep people away from the running roads.

436 How can one get fences and walls to run realistically over undulating ground?

There are three types of commercial fencing that take account of this, the Peco post-and-rail and the Slater or Ratio post-and-wire.

The Peco fencing has an ingenious joint which permits a considerable degree of vertical flexibility and is quite simple to use. As the post-and-rail is the common type of railway boundary fence, this solves a good many problems in this direction.

The Slater and Ratio post-and-wire fencing is also a common railway pattern, but has to be assembled on site from plastic moulded posts and rod or monofilament. It is slightly more troublesome to erect, but the work is well worth the effort.

437 What is a drystone wall and how does one model it?

A drystone wall is made from individual stones skilfully locked together so that the resulting structure is firm and stable despite the fact that it has no mortar (see Plate 26). Such walls are common in areas where there is a good deal of stone in the ground; they were built by highly skilled farmworkers from material that was as often as not dug from the ground to improve the soil, and it is a tribute to their workmanship that they stand for well over a century. The courses of a drystone wall follow the lie of the ground, which makes then aesthetically pleasing, a feature enhanced by the fact that the material invariably blends with the locality.

There are two methods of modelling these features. One is to make small fragments of 'stone' and build the wall bit by bit, using a suitable tube cement to secure the stones in place. This system is the only really practical method for modelling the slate walls of North Wales, where the practice is to use real slate, which will split into narrow slivers with little trouble.

Limestone or granite walls are more readily made by scribing the stones into modelling clay blanks. If a large number of walls are required, it could be worth the trouble of making a simple embossing tool to enable lengths of walling to be embossed on a nearby working surface before being gently placed in situ on the model.

438 Is it possible to make post-and-rail fencing in the home workshop?

It is tedious rather than difficult to build up most types of fencing from styrene sheet. The posts are built from three layers of sheet cemented together, the middle layer having gaps to form the housing for the horizontal rails. It is best to make up a strip at least 100 mm long from which individual posts are sawn, rather than try to make each post individually. The rails can be cut from the sheet, or made from commercial plastic microstrip (see Plate 26). A methodical approach will pay dividends here.

439 Can one make paling fencing in the workshop?

Any type of fence can be built up by following the constructional methods of the prototype, using plastic or wood sheet and strip of scale dimensions (see Plate 26). However, a wide variety of fencing is available from various sources and in view of the sheer work involved in making individual fence parts, these will prove an attractive alternative.

440 I want to carry a commercial wood panel fence along some undulating ground. How can I overcome the fact that it is supplied in a level strip?

This type of fencing is stepped to deal with slopes. It is therefore necessary to cut the strip at a joint. For a quick but effective step, cut beside the post on the falling side with a very sharp knife and make the necessary adjustment (see Plate 26). A more accurate method is to cut through the post with a razor saw, smooth each adjacent panel with a fine file to remove all traces of the post, and then supply a new longer plastic post. This is really only necessary when the fencing is in a position where it comes under close scrutiny.

The same procedure will apply to concrete panel fencing.

441 How can I make a realistic brick wall?

The most common error when making model brick walls is to fail to include piers at regular intervals of approximately 3 m scale, since without these the wall would certainly collapse. It is also important to consider the thickness – a single brick wall in 4 mm scale will be 1 mm thick, while bonded walls are generally a scale 140 mm (2 mm in 4 mm scale) in thickness and, unless over 2 m in prototype height, are not provided with piers. Most important of all, a brick wall is almost always provided with some form of capping, the most common being edge bricks, but stone or concrete slabs are also to be found covering the wall proper and the piers.

442 The fencing along the edge of the baseboard is frequently broken as friends rest their weight here. What can I do?

A fairly realistic fencing can be made by driving long panel pins into the framing at regular intervals and then winding copper wire around each successive pin, using a simple spacing jig to ensure a uniform level of the wires (see Plate 26). If the tops of the pins are cut off with side cutters, they will remind everyone that they should not lean on the base-

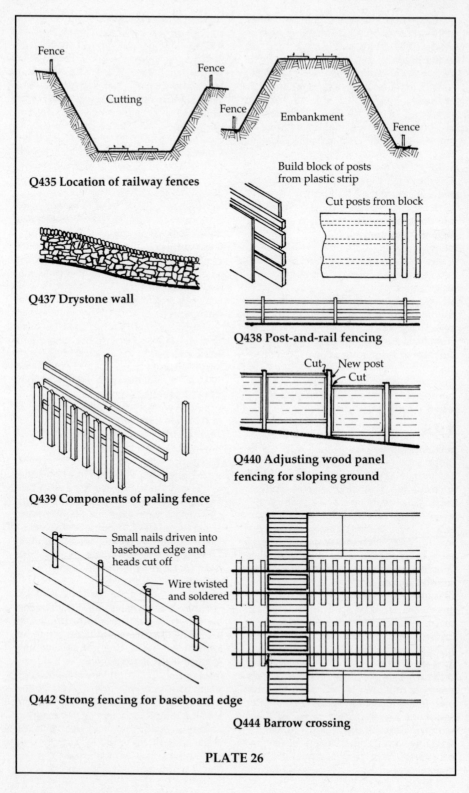

Fence

Fence

Cutting

Fence

Embankment

Fence

Q435 Location of railway fences

Q437 Drystone wall

Build block of posts
from plastic strip

Cut posts from block

Q438 Post-and-rail fencing

Q439 Components of paling fence

Cut New post
Cut

**Q440 Adjusting wood panel
fencing for sloping ground**

Small nails driven into
baseboard edge and
heads cut off

Wire twisted
and soldered

Q442 Strong fencing for baseboard edge

Q444 Barrow crossing

PLATE 26

board. In addition, this type of fence will usually prevent locomotives and rolling-stock from falling over the edge after a derailment, since some part almost invariably becomes snagged on the wire.

443 What is an occupation crossing?

An occupation crossing is provided to link farms and estates which have been severed by the railway. It is not provided with a crossing-keeper's box, nor is it protected other than by a notice warning users to watch out for trains. In most cases old sleepers form the path between the rails, while the approach might be tarmac but is more likely to be gravel or ballast. The width is around 3 m, sufficient for a single vehicle.

Such crossings do not normally form part of a public right-of-way and, should the separate halves of the estate fall into different ownership, the railway concerned looses no time in closing the crossing.

Some minor public roads and foot-paths also cross railways in this fashion, but the tendency today is to fit automatic half-barrier crossings and, in the case of heavily used footpaths, a footbridge.

444 What is a barrow crossing?

A barrow crossing is about 2.5 m in width and is situated at one end of a pair of platforms (see Plate 26). It is normally made from discarded sleepers and is provided to enable barrows to be wheeled across the track by the station staff. Most stations are provided with this crossing and, in many cases, the path to the signal cabin is linked to it. Where on minor lines no footbridge or subway is provided, this crossing is used by passengers; elsewhere a cast iron or enamelled iron notice bluntly informs passengers that they must not pass any further. Etched plates for this common fitting are available.

445 Why are some level crossings provided with a pair of gates on each side, and some only a single gate. There seems to be no connection with the width of the crossing.

The essential difference lies in the method of operation on the prototype. Where the gates are opened manually by a porter, single gates are provided, as this allows one man to open or close each gate in succession. Where they are mechanically operated by means of a handwheel in the signal cabin coupled to rods and gears, a pair of gates is provided so that all four gates may swing simultaneously.

Section 3:7
Buildings

446 Which type of building kit would you recommend for a beginner – plastic or card?

This must be a matter for personal preference. In general card kits are cheaper, but some are very crude and more correctly classed as child's toys than model kits. The Bilteezi range retains its popularity despite the fact that it produces extremely flat structures and, because the card used is very thin, needs judicious reinforcing if the structure is not to bow. The Superquick range is on thicker card and is partly punched out. Both ranges are extensively used and make good models; the fact they are still in production some 30 odd years after their first introduction is an indication of their value.

Another card kit series worth getting is the Prototype range of railway structures, each based on an actual example. Plastic kits of any quality are rather more costly than card but they provide much more relief detail and in many cases are more complex. They are marginally easier to build, but unless they are well painted, they betray their origins.

447 I have been building card kits for some time but I find the white edges rather annoying, particularly as the examples I've seen at exhibitions do not exhibit this fault. Can you tell me how these kits are assembled?

The trick is not in the assembly, but in the stage just beforehand. The white card edge is coloured using a matching felt-tip pen, taken from one of those sets of coloured pens available from most stationers.

448 Many otherwise excellent model railways seem to me to be spoiled because they all have the same buildings in the background. Is it possible to modify kits to make different types of building?

Modifying kit-based buildings is almost a hobby in its own right. However, it is as well to make up a couple of kits strictly according to the manufacturer's instructions before heading out into the wilds of 'kit-bashing' and 'cross-kitting'.

449 I have bought a plastic building kit of German origin. I am slightly mystified by the instruction sheet, not because of a language problem, but because it consists of a series of rather crude exploded diagrams with the parts numbered and no explanation. What should be the order of assembly?

The golden rule for kit assembly is to study the parts carefully in conjunction with the instructions and work out how you think they should go together. Even the best instructions have been known to be ambiguous, and most experienced kit-builders like to go their own way.

It is generally best to fix the glazing to the window frames and doors and then insert these in place before assembling the sides. Apart from the fact that it is a trifle difficult to get them in place later, it is much easier to apply plastic solvent to the rear edge of the frame and so get a good joint.

Generally, the walls will be assembled in numerical order; these are usually the lowest numbers on the kit. It is advisable to check not only that they are square with the base and each other, but that the corner join is unobtrusive. It may be advantageous to smooth this with a flat file beforehand; certainly all nibs left after removal from the sprue must be cleaned off.

When the walls are securely in place, leave the kit for at least half an hour for the cement to harden sufficiently for you to be able to get the roof on without disturbing the alignment. Pay particular care to the fit of the roof ridge – this is extremely prominent – and also see that the roof sits securely on the sides. Again, leave the building to harden, preferably overnight, before adding the smaller details. A pair of long tweezers or fine-nose pliers make this a much simpler task.

This is only a broad outline of the process and needs detail modification, particularly with the more complicated kits. It is advisable to begin with something simple to gain experience, but if you take things steadily and think carefully about every step, there is no reason why you should not start off by tackling one of the exciting and ambitious kits for a large station building or extensive factory. They are no more difficult – there are merely a lot more parts to fit together.

450 How do you check that the corners of a building kit are square? I've tried using an engineer's square but it is rather too big for comfort?

A standard 50 mm square plastic colour slide body can be cut to form two very small squares (see Plate 27). I have made myself a similar-sized square from a piece of flat 3 mm thick copper which is even more useful, particularly as one corner is filed away to clear the usual projections inside a building kit wall. Any metal will serve – I just happened to have the copper to hand.

451 The majority of kit-built plastic buildings have a slight sheen, but I have seen some where not only are the surfaces beautifully matt, but I only realised that the buildings were made from kits because I recognised the design. How is this achieved?

The kits have been painted with flat paints, either acrylic or oils, neither of which have an adverse affect on plastic. In the main, they are painted before assembly, often whilst the parts are still on the sprues. This is not a quick process; it can take twice as long to paint a plastic kit as it does to assemble it. When, as is often the case, painting is combined with a degree of modification or cross-kitting, the preparatory work can take even longer. It is no exaggeration to say that the final results depend far more on what is done before the model is assembled than anything else.

452 What is 'cross-kitting'?

Cross-kitting is a technique for producing an original model building by combining the parts of two or more kits. It is advisable to use products from a single manufacturer since the wall finish and other details will be congruent. Indeed, many building kits have major components, as well as details such as windows and doors, in common. It is a convenient halfway house between straightforward kit assembly and scratchbuilding. For obvious reasons, it is a good idea to make one's first essay into cross-kitting with a pair of kits bought cheaply at an exhibition.

453 How does one set about modifying a plastic building kit?

First and foremost, it is a good idea to start with a clear picture in your mind of the final result you wish to achieve. However, it is not always advisable to stick with this original scheme through thick and thin, as it is possible that, during the development, a new idea may spring up. Experienced kit-bashers occasionally begin with a pile of odd parts and create something out of what is to another just scrap, although this is usually more effective with SF and Fantasy models than with building kits. However, it could be a good route to a Gothic ruin or an 18th-century Folly. After that, it is largely a matter of personal inclination. You may prefer to make a detailed sketch of your proposals, or merely to rough out a pencil outline as a guide. With experience, you will probably make the main cuts in the walls and bases, then fit the other parts to these as you go along.

454 I can't find a kit that quite fits my requirements. Is it difficult to scratchbuild a model building?

A good deal depends on the building you are modelling. It is best to begin by modelling a simple hut to get an idea of what is involved. The construction of the basic carcase is fairly straightforward – the majority of the work involved is dealing with details.

455 What material is recommended for model building construction?

The traditional materials are thin wood, generally 2 or 3 mm ply, and card, but the advent of sheet plastics, particularly those with embossed or moulded surface detail, has widened the scope considerably. There is no doubt that for large structures, especially those with large openings, such as locomotive and goods sheds, plywood, cut to shape with a fretsaw, has considerable advantages, at least for the basic structure. Most card and all thin plastic needs a certain amount of internal stiffening, but if floors and internal walls are fitted, these generally suffice; indeed, there is considerable virtue in doing this, as it prevents the viewer from seeing right through a hollow shell. Most modellers experiment and then settle for a material with which they are happy and, in general, one that they can obtain without too much trouble.

456 Where can I find information on attractive buildings to model?

A number of architectural publications include elevations; whilst many are very expensive, there are popular surveys which are affordable. Guidebooks and nostalgic albums cover most parts of Britain, though many of the best are local publications produced by small independent publishers and only sold in the immediate locality.

However, the most pleasant way of finding attractive buildings is the field trip. This need not be an expedition – I live in a post-war new town, but within a comfortable 5-minute stroll of my home I can study innumerable examples of attractive buildings as well as a number of excellent modern designs; not all modern architecture is bad. Of course, Hemel Hempstead may be an exception, but even when, as a boy, I lived in the centre of one of the most stereotyped estates ever built, the LCC Becontree estate, I had little trouble in finding attractive buildings to look at and sketch. It is just a matter of opening your eyes, using your brain and, above all, ignoring the prejudices of the experts.

457 I have seen references to brickpaper. What is it and where does one get it?

Brickpaper is, as the name suggests, thin, good-quality matt paper printed with a brick or stone pattern. Early patterns – the Merco series, for example – were somewhat overscale, but more recent versions have much smaller bricks and frequently offer a variety of bonds in the brickwork. Colouring is good, but the finished building lacks texture, so it is not greatly favoured by finescale modellers. Nevertheless, the work of such masters as John H. Ahern and Peter Denny demonstrates clearly that in careful hands brickpaper produces excellent results. It is mainly employed on card or wooden carcases, but can also be applied to a plain plastic shell. It can be obtained from most good model shops.

458 How does one apply brickpaper to a model building?

Brickpaper is more easily applied one wall at a time – attempts to fit a continuous sheet around the various corners are rarely even marginally successful. Use a glue with slip – Cow Gum is ideal – but the maker's instructions should not be followed; coat the paper evenly using a plastic spatula and apply this to the building. To deal with window and door openings, cover them with the paper then cut two diagonal slits and fold back the paper triangles into the opening, thus covering the returns with brick (see Plate 27). Since you are applying the paper one wall at a time, pay particular attention not only to align the courses of brick at corners, but also take pains to ensure that the courses are level.

459 I have some difficulty making the corners of my buildings fit snugly. Is there any simple and straightforward way round this problem?

There are several solutions. The best is to persevere and master the technique of cutting the corners squarely and bevelling the sides to fit (see Plate 27). Where card buildings are to be covered with brickpaper, a good sharp corner can be made by taking a narrow strip of gummed paper and folding it down the centre. This produces a neat sharp angle and, when stuck to the walls, gives a good finish. Alternatively, the corner can be covered by a row of 'quoins', contrasting stones which, on the prototype, are both ornamental and practical edgings to a wall.

460 How are model bow windows made?

It is necessary to make these out of several layouts of card or plastic, cut out where necessary for the windows. One good method is to take the base sheet, which must be cut oversize, and secure it to a suitable curved surface, generally a glass jar, by means of self-adhesive tape. The upper layers are then secured in place by a generous layer of adhesive or solvent. Some strategically located elastic bands help hold things in place (see Plate 27). The sandwich is left to harden for at least 24 hours, after which it will be found to have taken the required curve. It is then backed by curved formers.

It is also possible to build a bow window around a set of curved formers; again, the multi-layer construction allows the skin to take a permanent curved arc.

461 How are the very fine glazing bars to be seen on many model buildings produced?

Frequently they are brass etchings – a number of small manufacturers offer packs of varying-sized windows at prices which seem remarkably reasonable to anyone who has ever cut a set out the hard way from plastic sheet. There is also the old, tried and tested alternative of scribing the bars in the acetate sheet and filling the grooves so formed with paint (see Plate 27). The glazing bars should be drawn out in pencil or ballpoint pen on a piece of paper – graph paper is ideal – and the acetate sheet taped in place for scribing. Surplus paint must be removed with a soft dry cloth before it hardens on the acetate. Whilst this method does not stand up to close inspection as well as the etched bars, at normal viewing distance it is, as it always has been, remarkably effective.

462 Where can I obtain thin transparent sheets for building construction?

Any model shop should carry a stock. However, thin acetate sheet is now extensively used in packaging, and whilst a lot of it is shaped into intricate forms which are only of interest to Fantasy modelmakers, a fair amount has sufficiently large flat surfaces to make a spot of recycling well worth while.

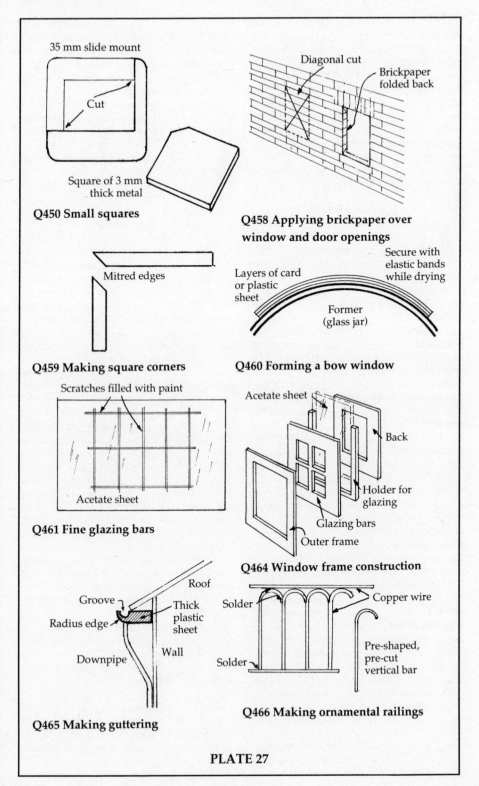

35 mm slide mount

Cut

Square of 3 mm thick metal

Q450 Small squares

Diagonal cut

Brickpaper folded back

Q458 Applying brickpaper over window and door openings

Mitred edges

Q459 Making square corners

Secure with elastic bands while drying

Layers of card or plastic sheet

Former (glass jar)

Q460 Forming a bow window

Scratches filled with paint

Acetate sheet

Q461 Fine glazing bars

Acetate sheet

Back

Holder for glazing

Glazing bars

Outer frame

Q464 Window frame construction

Roof

Groove

Radius edge

Thick plastic sheet

Downpipe

Wall

Q465 Making guttering

Solder

Copper wire

Solder

Pre-shaped, pre-cut vertical bar

Q466 Making ornamental railings

PLATE 27

463 **Is it possible to use real glass in a model building?**
There is nothing that looks more like glass than glass itself. In addition, very thin glass is obtainable, either as microscope slides or as cover glasses for photographic slides. The only problem is that this ultra-thin glass is even more difficult to cut than normal 24 oz window glass. A diamond cutter is essential, and they are not cheap. The possibility is, however, well worth considering if one is producing a very good building.

464 **I cemented my widow glazing in place firmly enough as I thought, but after a while it fell out. Whilst I can do little with the present models, what should I do in future to avoid this happening again?**
In the case of plastic window frames, the use of one of the more powerful solvents is advisable and, when the window frames and glazing are in place but before the walls have been assembled, a fillet of plastic cement around the outer edge of the glazing should do the trick. With a scratchbuilt model, where a mixture of materials is being used, it is often well worth while going to the trouble to produce a proper housing for the glazing, so that the material is slipped into a groove rather than being just stuck in place (see Plate 27). A similar procedure can be used with a kit with very large windows; these seem to be more prone to this particular trouble that those with relatively small areas of glazing. Whichever approach is favoured, take great care to secure glazing in place firmly; it is next to impossible, with a full body model building, to get it back after the building is finished.

465 **How does one arrange realistic gutters on a model building?**
Small specialist manufacturers can provide plastic and cast white metal guttering for prominent buildings constructed to a high standard, where the cost of such fittings may well be justified. Alternatively, the section ribs from a broken umbrella can be used to produce a fairly convincing gutter.

A good, though slightly tedious, method of making guttering is to take a strip of fairly thick plastic sheet and cut a groove along its edge with a small saw. This is then hollowed out with a small round file and the front edge rounded off. The strip is then cut approximately 2 mm from the front, and cemented under the eaves as shown in Plate 27. It is more convenient to produce several strips about 75-100 mm in length rather than attempt to produce a longer gutter in one go.

466 **What is the best material for downpipes?**
Copper wire, stripped from an electric cable, is a popular material; it is easy to shape, remains rigid and can be fixed in place with epoxy resin or cyanoacrylate glue. Thin plastic rod is available; this will retain bends to a remarkable extent and is very easily attached to plastic buildings. Square downpipes are probably best made from strips cut from plastic sheet of a suitable thickness, as square wire is difficult to find.

467 **How are those attractive wrought iron railings made?**
In the main they are bought in sheets as etchings. It is, however, possible to make them with copper wire and patience. The usual source of the wire is scrap electrical cable – the wire is straightened by gripping one end in a vice and pulling the other end hard using a pair of pliers. The wire is then patiently twisted into the required shape. A simple pin jig can be constructed over a full-sized drawing of the scrollwork to hold the wires in place whilst they are being soldered (see Plate 27). It is worth pointing out that copper wire can be hammered flat on a small anvil or on the rear of a vice. This not only produces flat strip but, if the wire has already been formed, it can also create intricately-shaped items. A little experimentation can prove extremely profitable.

Section 3:8
The townscape

468 **There isn't a great deal of room for my model railway and I would like to save all the space I can. Is it necessary to have a town alongside the station?**
Although it is often said that a town pro-

vides the reason for having a station in the first place, the only justification for including one in a model is that you enjoy constructing buildings. It is not difficult to find examples of large and important stations set in open countryside; whilst such situations were more common in the steam age, a Parkway station can appear in a green field site. However, it is often a good idea to site a townscape over a sharp curve – it hides the unrealistic corner without obstructing anything of importance, since it can be on a light sub-base designed to lift off to give clear access underneath.

469 I need to carry a road directly into the backscene. How can this be done realistically?

The painted road on the backscene has to be rendered in perspective, and will only look right from one angle. To ensure this, it is necessary to have buildings or other obstructions on either side of the road so that it is only possible to see that part of the backscene from a narrow angle. One very popular arrangement is to take the road through an archway (see Plate 28).

470 Is it possible to introduce perspective modelling into a model railway scene where one is supposed to be working to a uniform scale throughout?

Full perspective modelling, as can be seen in dioramas, is virtually impossible. However, it is often possible to arrange zonal perspective with buildings and figures towards the back modelled in a smaller scale. It is even possible to have N gauge tracks at the rear and OO gauge tracks in the foreground to create the illusion of a large town, though this is more a case of architectural modelling with railway features than true railway modelling. Some form of zonal perspective is needed where the railway is set in wild and rugged countryside. Vertical perspective can be arranged by mounting a small-scale aircraft or balloon in the sky.

471 What suggestions can you give for creating an attractive and interesting townscape?

Begin by looking for attractive scenes in your own locality. There are some well-tried schemes that are worth consider-

ing. One is the busy town centre; if this can face on to your main station buildings so much the better, but it is even more attractive if a large public building can balance the station. A row of detailed shop fronts never fails to attract the eye, especially if the shops are owned by friends and acquaintances, or firms with appropriate names (*Private Eye*'s favourite solicitors, Sue, Grabbit & Run, for example). Gentle curves, old buildings and fascinating alleyways that seem to be leading to even more interesting parts of the town all add to the atmosphere.

472 I want to include a church in the village I am modelling as part of my layout, but such plans as I have located are too large for my purpose. Could you suggest where I could find a suitable plan?

Churches are very large buildings indeed and, to add to the problems, they are almost invariably set in extensive grounds. A 4 mm scale model of a modest parish church would take up most of a 1 m x 0.5 m baseboard and, with the addition of the churchyard, church hall and vicarage, it would spread well beyond such restricted confines. Fortunately, not many people know this until it is pointed out to them, and they are perfectly happy to accept a 3 or even 2 mm scale model as being absolutely right providing a few small details are fudged. In the main this means taking care that the smaller doors and any paths and steps are not too far below the nominal scale, since a model figure will immediately reveal the subterfuge. The main architectural details – the West Door and the windows – are so large that a considerable reduction in scale is not noticeable; the important thing is to get the proportions right. The term 'God's Acre' is if anything an underestimate for a churchyard, so it is essential to avoid giving the impression that the site is cramped.

473 I really do not have room to fit a church into the tiny space I can allocate for my model village, yet I feel that without one the community is incomplete. What do you suggest?

The most prominent feature of a parish

church is the tower and, where present, the spire. A bas relief tower placed against the back scene behind a low-relief backdrop, modelled to a smaller scale to provide a perspective effect, will not only provide a church but also create the illusion of depth (see Plate 28). It is worth remembering that many Nonconformist chapels have an impressive facade facing the street and only a narrow passageway on either side. Occasionally one can find the parish church similarly hemmed in, with only the main doorway clearly visible. This forms an excellent subject for low-relief modelling.

474   What is a low-relief model?

A model consisting mainly of the facade, with perhaps as little as 9 mm total depth, placed along the rear of the layout to create the illusion of a townscape (see Plate 28). In general, side walls are devoid of detail, and frequently a range of buildings are run together to create a continuous block. With only a quarter of the wall surface to model, it is not difficult to add a good deal of additional detail to the structure. There is a strong affinity to the film set here since 'anything goes' behind the model! A popular method of creating low-relief models is to cut the side walls and bases of a plastic kit in half, thus producing two buildings for the price of one!

475   I am constructing a low-relief backdrop to run for some 3 metres behind the main station. A little over a third of the way along, I am somewhat dissatisfied – the results do not seem to be as effective as many I have seen. Have you any suggestions?

Excluding poor workmanship, which one assumes you would see for yourself, there are two points to watch for in this type of modelling. The first is the choice of prototype. A lot of streets are quite banal, with all buildings much of a muchness; this applies in particular force to roads bordering on railways. If you're copying this sort of scene the result must be equally banal in the model. Model interesting buildings and the model is well on the way to being interesting.

The second possible reason is lack of human interest. As the small details that

give life to the townscape are usually added towards the end, this could be part of the reason for your dissatisfaction. There is also the distinct possibility that, having spent some time with each model, you are only too aware how it falls short of your ideals, whereas with other people's work you are impressed by the good features.

476   Is it necessary to add internal detail to a model building?

This depends on three factors: the position of the model on the baseboard and its relative importance, the size of any windows or other openings, and, above all, the overall size of the layout, which determines the number of buildings that might need such treatment. If internal detail is included, then it is essential to provide lighting so that the work can be seen and appreciated. As fitting full internal detail to a model building can take more time and effort than the construction of the building itself, it is not a project upon which one should lightly embark, but in the final analysis it comes down to the fundamental question: do you get pleasure from adding such detail? The only case where some internal detail is essential is where, as in a shop window, or on a station concourse, the viewer is certain to notice the omission.

477   How does one arrange lighting for model buildings?

In general this needs to be planned during construction. Most plastic buildings need blanking out internally so that the light doesn't shine through the walls, for although this can produce the illusion of floodlighting, if this is required, then model floodlights should be provided. However, even when a building has been assembled without provision for lighting, it can often be arranged by pushing a light source inside from underneath.

478   If I put lamps in inaccessible places, what can I do when they burn out?

The best solution is not to burn them out in the first instance. Small lamps are rated to work off 16 V ac, but at this voltage not only is their life threatened, but the light output is that of a powerful

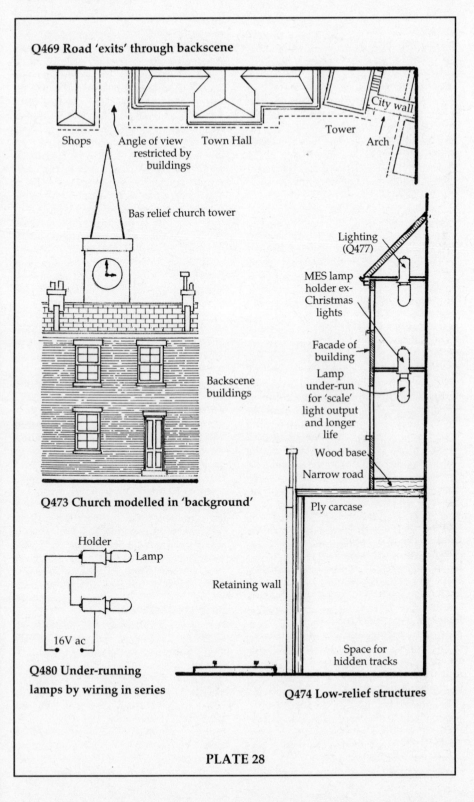

Q469 Road 'exits' through backscene

Shops

Angle of view restricted by buildings

Town Hall

Tower

Arch

City wall

Bas relief church tower

Backscene buildings

Q473 Church modelled in 'background'

Lighting (Q477)

MES lamp holder ex-Christmas lights

Facade of building

Lamp under-run for 'scale' light output and longer life

Wood base

Narrow road

Ply carcase

Holder

Lamp

16V ac

Q480 Under-running lamps by wiring in series

Retaining wall

Space for hidden tracks

Q474 Low-relief structures

PLATE 28

floodlamp. On a lower voltage, 9 V or
even 6.3 V, their light has a lovely
mellow glow and their life is almost
infinite. Although the output is down, it
is still enough to show in a darkened
room. It can help to have the lights fed
from two or three circuits so that the
town can be illuminated in stages.

479 How does one get a 6.3-volt transformer?

This is the standard voltage for radio
valve heaters and, as a result, 6.3-volt
transformers, with an output of up to 1.5
amps, are not only still advertised by
electronic suppliers but, more to the
point, can also be salvaged from broken
mains radios of which there are still
quite a few around. Electronic catalogues
list quite a range of transformers at varying output voltages, but make sure that
the output is high enough; many for
transistor use only give output in mil-
liamps. If the va rating is less than the
voltage, the transformer is no use to us.

480 Is there any other way of reducing the voltage applied to small lamps? Could I introduce a dropping resistance?

A dropping resistance will work, but
unless it is matched to a fixed load the
voltage drop will be variable. A better
solution is to wire pairs of the lamps in
series so that each lamp, of necessity
matched in demand, only gets half the
line voltage (see Plate 28).

481 The cost of small lamps is high – is there an alternative?

LEDs are considerably cheaper, especially when bought in bulk. However, a
very cheap source of small lamps and
screw-in sockets is a redundant string of
Christmas tree lights, which provide an
added incentive to replace a set as soon
as there is the slightest suspicion that the
wires may be getting loose or frayed. As
these small lamps are designed to short
out when they blow, they should only be
used on lowered voltage, and a wire
blow-out fuse must be fitted in the circuit to protect the transformer.

482 Is it possible to use fibre optics to light buildings?

Fibre optics do not transmit a lot of light
along a single strand and as a result are
best used where the tip is visible. One
common use is to illuminate street lights,
the lamp post being made around a
length of fine-bore tube. A lamp body
carved from perspex can be made to
glow very realistically by a single fibre
optic strand inserted into a hole drilled in
its base. Several strands should be taken
to a single light source mounted in an
accessible place. A large 16 V lamp in a
screw holder running on full voltage is
required for this purpose, but size is
clearly of no significance and the lamp
can be easily replaced should it fail. Fibre
optics can also be used to illuminate rings
of lights around a noticeboard, and with
the aid of colour filters and mechanised
shutters some very dramatic effects can
be achieved. It would even be possible to
reproduce the lights of Piccadilly Circus,
if one had sufficient patience.

483 I have acquired a large number of figures for my layout, but when set out they look rather uninter-esting even though each one, individu-ally, is fine. Have you any idea why this should be so?

The probability is that you have set then
out in rows. Although this will happen
just before a train is due at a crowded
station, people usually stand about in
groups, or walk along in twos and
threes. As your townsfolk must be static,
it is a good idea to arrange them in small
groups which appear to have some purpose. Whilst it might seem difficult to
arrange natural groupings, you should
start by asking yourself what a particular
figure might be doing, something we
find relatively easy since this is how we
view our fellow citizens. Once you've an
insight into your tiny figure, you're well
on the way to discovering how to make
best use of it. Obviously you do not have
to create a rounded character – merely
slot the figures into easily recognisable
stereotypes.

484 Most of the better figures come without stands. Why is this and what can I do about it?

Figures come without stands because
very few of us have our feet stuck in concrete blocks. Stands are needed for
miniature soldiers used for wargaming,

since they have to be repositioned during the battle, otherwise this is primarily a toy usage. Figures should be either cemented in place or secured with a small pin driven into the leg through a small-bore hole, which in 4 mm scale is easier to suggest than to perform. Stands need to be cut away with care, making sure that the model's feet do not get lost at the same time.

485 My layout is set at the turn of the century. What can I do to ensure that the figures are correctly dressed?

Period figures for 4 and 7 mm scales are produced in white metal by a number of specialist concerns and can usually be found at major exhibitions. In addition, women's skirts can be lengthened – the two-part modelling putties such as Milliput are ideal for this purpose; it will then be necessary to paint the figures. Preiser have produced an extensive range of turn-of-the-century figures and, as well as providing them in ready-painted sets, provide a complete unpainted pack at a very reasonable cost. Every figure is an individual character – there are elegant ladies of fashion, military gentlemen, a period seaside party, tall, short, fat and thin people, a truly wonderful collection. Although to 3.5 mm scale, they can be used, with discretion, in a 4 mm scale scene.

486 Is it possible to mix 3.5 and 4 mm scale figures on one layout?

As human beings come in a variety of sizes, the discrepancy is not too obvious, providing that you do not mix the two scales in the same group.

487 Where can I get authentic workmen for my OO gauge railway? I particularly need action figures.

Dapol are now marketing the range of railway workmen originally produced by Airfix. These were based on a series of pre-war LMS posters featuring railwaymen at work and are extremely authentic. The mouldings are unpainted. In 3.5 mm scale, Preiser have a wide selection of working figures and even offer a pack of unpainted workmen.

488 Is it possible to modify the stance of a miniature figure in the way

military modellers adapt their larger-scale figures?

It is always possible to modify the stance of a plastic figure. Even the rather wooden Slaters figures can be brought to life by a little manipulation. It is less easy to do this with cast figures, but even here simple alterations are possible. Except for the business of size, the techniques of the military modeller transfer faultlessly, and a lot of good ideas can be gleaned from one of their textbooks.

489 How does one paint small figures? It looks very difficult, but there must be a way of doing it without too much trouble.

Apart from the obvious necessities, a selection of paints and an array of fine brushes and the necessary thinners, two things are needed: a pair of self-closing tweezers to hold the figure whilst painting, and an illuminated magnifying glass on a swivelling stand. It helps to do as much painting as possible whilst the figures are on a sprue; certainly flesh colours and main clothing can be put in at this stage. It is easier to work in batches – this not only allows you to paint a lot of figures with one colour, but also gives time for the paint to dry off in between. Acrylic colours are greatly favoured for figure painting, but flat oil paints are equally good.

Section 3:9
Railway structures

490 How high should a model platform be above the baseboard?

The height should be measured above rail level, not from some other datum. The prototype dimension varies in practice, but is usually around 1 m (3 ft 3 in) above rail level (see Plate 29). Early stations had lower platforms and it was possible to find country stations with two distinct heights, but this is the standard for British usage and elsewhere where raised platforms are employed. However, in most of the rest of the world platforms are rarely more than 100 mm above rail level.

491 How does one set out the correct arc for a curved platform?

Begin by cutting a piece of thin card to fit roughly between the rails; if need be, stick several pieces together with self-adhesive tape. Take a wooden pencil and pare one side away almost to the inner lead and place this against that part of the locomotive or coach that is most likely to foul the platform. In general, the outside cylinders of express steam locomotives give most trouble on internal curves, and the centre of long coaches on external curves. By running the model up and down whilst pressing the pencil on to the card you establish the basic curve (see Plate 29). You then use the card as a template for the platform, but as a check offer it up on temporary supports and run trains alongside on both tracks, making any necessary adjustments. A similar check is advisable when the platform surface has been finally cut out – it's easier to make alterations before the supports are fixed in place.

492 What is the best material for a platform surface?

Ply, hardboard, thick card and plastic sheet have all been used with success; it is largely a matter of ready availability and the modelling techniques favoured.

493 What is the best way of supporting the platform surface?

Again, this is largely a matter of ready availability. In OO gauge, a 3 mm top surface placed on a 12 mm base gives a reasonable result when normal plastic-sleepered track is laid direct on to the same surface, so a combination of a hardboard top and a chipboard sub-base works very nicely. A slightly better method is to cut a strip of material to the required height and then build up side walls braced by cross-pieces. Where plastic is preferred, the sides should be cut from brick or stone embossed sheet. Wooden supports are very strong and if a saw bench is available it is a very simple matter to cut a large quantity of accurate strips from ply offcuts or odd lengths of stripwood.

494 What is the correct angle for the end ramps of platforms?

1 in 4 is a reasonable guide, but is by no means critical.

495 Is a footbridge absolutely essential on a double-track station?

Except on quiet branches, means were always provided to allow passengers access to either platform without crossing the tracks. This was usually arranged by a footbridge, but could be a subway, though this was rarely found outside major stations, or stations on an embankment. Many suburban stations have the offices set across the tracks against an overbridge, with direct stairway access. An exceptional arrangement in Docklands saw the buildings erected on girders above the running rails even though there was no overbridge; this was purely to save space.

496 Where the station building is situated on one side of the tracks, is it normally on the up or down platform?

There is no hard and fast rule. In most cases it was situated on the town side of the tracks when built, so that it was directly accessible for the majority of users; this could be modified as the town grew and in some cases auxiliary offices were added to the other side. On occasions the lie of the land determined the position.

497 Why do so many small stations have a large two-storey station building?

In most cases the structure not only housed the station offices, but also had the station house attached, a roomy dwelling for the station master who was expected to live on the job and be on call 24 hours a day. The station house could be separate, and in addition there was frequently a row of substantial terraced cottages for other railway staff – it was convenient to have them near at hand. A few small stations close to a large country house were provided with elaborate fittings and built to a high standard solely to placate an influential landowner.

498 Why have some goods sheds an internal road and others merely an outside platform and awning?

The internal road not only enabled the

wagons and vans to be dealt with under cover in all weathers, but it was easier to arrange an internal crane. In addition, until the main doors were allowed to deteriorate in the latter years of steam, the contents could be secured overnight. The simpler side-road shed was usually chosen for economy, but there are cases where very large side-sheds were combined with extensive awnings; this was particularly common where the majority of the traffic came in vans rather than open wagons. It was always more important to protect merchandise from rain damage than to keep the men dry.

499 Why do the tracks almost invariably extend beyond a goods shed?

This is to allow wagons that have been loaded or unloaded to be moved to one side to allow others to be brought in. Very few goods sheds are capable of holding all wagons to be handled in a shift at any one time (see Plate 29).

500 I understand that only the largest yards had permanent shunting engines allocated. How were wagons moved in the small stations?

The train engine of the local goods – usually called the pick-up – would collect any wagons it needed and then drop those it had brought to the station, leaving them as close as possible to the desired unloading position. After that it was usually a case of muscle power, one reason why railways continued to use horses well after the Second World War. At a pinch, three hefty men could get a four-wheeled wagon moving, and after that one man could keep it in motion on level track. This sort of arrangement is difficult to model – possibly the forefinger is the best substitute.

501 Why are tracks so widely separated in a goods yard?

So that carts and lorries can be brought up against the wagons for unloading purposes. The width is needed not only to allow two wagons to pass but, more importantly, to allow a horse-drawn cart to turn around since, unlike a motor lorry, it cannot be reversed. It is virtually impossible on a model to over-emphasise this feature.

502 Why do some goods yards have cranes and others not?

This is governed entirely by the usual traffic offered at the station. Where this was confined to mineral (eg coal), general merchandise and agricultural produce, a crane was not needed since, until comparatively recently, loads were largely kept down to one hundredweight, the practical limit for a strong man to lift continuously through a working day. However, many stations had a crane neatly hidden within the goods shed.

503 How did they manage at a craneless station when an exceptionally large load was offered?

With considerable difficulty. In extreme cases the railway would, for a fee, provide a mobile crane. Towards the end of the 19th century traction engines became available and these were frequently designed so that a simple crane could be rigged off the rear. However, the usual answer was to jury rig a derrick, using three long posts, a set of block-and-tackle and a good deal of rope. With this simple equipment and plenty of hefty men, considerable loads could be shifted. Remember that when you had got the load on to the lorry, you still had to get it off again at the other end.

504 Why are some sidings provided with a ramp up to the top of the buffer stop?

This is the end-loading dock. Until the end of the steam age road vehicles were carried around the country by rail and in order to load and unload them special vehicles were constructed which had end-loading facilities. These were complemented by the end-loading facilities at the stations, which were often combined with a raised section of loading platforms, such as the cattle dock. All model steam age goods yards should have one to permit this type of traffic to be handled.

505 Should coal bins be placed alongside the coal siding or on the other side of the coal yard?

Both arrangements have been used, for although it might seem more convenient to empty the wagons directly into the

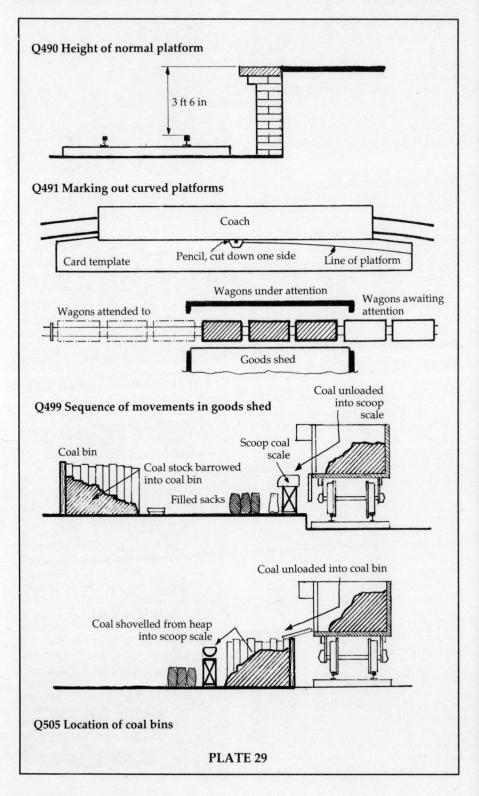

Q490 Height of normal platform

3 ft 6 in

Q491 Marking out curved platforms

Coach

Card template   Pencil, cut down one side   Line of platform

Wagons under attention

Wagons attended to   Wagons awaiting attention

Goods shed

Q499 Sequence of movements in goods shed

Coal unloaded into scoop scale

Coal bin

Scoop coal scale

Coal stock barrowed into coal bin

Filled sacks

Coal unloaded into coal bin

Coal shovelled from heap into scoop scale

Q505 Location of coal bins

PLATE 29

bins when they are alongside the track, the most common practice in the steam age was to keep the coal in the wagons – hence the use of privately-owned wagons – and to shovel the coal directly into a coal scale for immediate bagging. This eliminated the need to lift the coal up to put it into the scoop. The bins were only employed as a back-up to enable a wagon to be freed to collect more coal (see Plate 29).

506 What sort of scales were used in coal yards?

Two specialised coal scales were authorised for this particular use, a low check-weighing scale, normally placed on the rear of coal cars and lorries so that the customer could, on demand, see that the sacks were the correct weight, and the scoop-pattern scale intended for filling the sacks. Both were pre-set accelerating scales which tripped abruptly when the predetermined loads were reached. The scoop scale had a large iron scoop mounted on top of the mechanism that would hold and retain slightly more than the maximum load. It was carried on a pivot and could, when full, be tipped directly into a waiting sack. Both pattern scales are still in production. The steelyard type of scale, often included in model coal yard sets, would only be used as a check-weigher; it would not only be inconvenient to fill a sack on the scale, but the probability of dislodging the steelyard from its pivots would also be too great.

507 What is the purpose of the weighbridge to be found in many railway goods yards?

When goods are loaded in bulk on to a lorry or cart, the vehicle is weighed empty and then weighed when loaded, the difference being the weight of the load. For much of the steam age, the railway weighbridge was the only means of accurate mass weighing in the town and was a very important factor in its commercial life. Weighbridges had, and still have, be to an approved pattern and verified by Weights & Measures Inspectors.

508 What is the purpose of the length of rail set alongside a weighbridge?

The older pattern lever weighbridge is a relatively delicate mechanism and could only be entered from the ends, so a barrier was provided to prevent a carter or lorry-driver from going off the side and so dislodging the table from the knife-edges. Modern weighbridges are mounted on weigh cells and have only a very limited amount of movement, so are more stable.

Section 3:10
Civil engineering

509 What is the difference between a bridge and a viaduct?

A viaduct is a long bridge, generally spanning a valley. The main factor is normally the number of arches, three being taken as the break point. However, a number of large single- span railway bridges have been called viaducts without anyone raising objections.

510 I would like to incorporate a viaduct on my layout but I am worried about the gradients needed to raise the tracks sufficiently. Is there another answer to this?

As usual, the best solution to the problem is to go back to the prototype, for with the exception of the case where a line has to be carried over a waterway in flat territory, bridges and viaducts are there to span valleys. Therefore a section of the baseboard framing is lowered to allow the landscaping to be carried well below the datum line of the railway and to form a valley of the desired cross-section. The viaduct piers are built up from the lower level – the railway can be dead level if you so desire.

511 What is the difference between a bridge and a culvert?

A culvert is a small bridge which carries a stream or drainage ditch under an embankment. It can be a simple half circle but most modern culverts are made from sections of concrete tubes, and are usually terminated in a plain vertical face cast in situ or built from pre-cast blocks. Modelling this type of culvert is fairly simple, providing that you can find a suitable piece of tube. Many tube culverts end some distance above the main watercourse, and a tiny waterfall takes the drainage down to the stream. This can be easily represented by squeezing a quantity of plastic cement into the end of the tube and allowing it to fall down by gravity (see Plate 30).

512 **I intend to model a section of my layout on arches. Is there a standard dimension for these?**

Most continuous railway viaducts had a standard span of approximately 30 feet with 5-foot wide piers. However, as the model structure will be under scale length, it is permissible to reduce these figures slightly to get more spans in a given length. Clearly this cannot be taken too far, since the majority of arches are occupied and it is necessary to be able to put in a convincing facade.

513 **What sort of concerns might one find in occupied arches?**

It is slightly quicker to list what one is not likely to find in such a location, though it is ironic that the purpose first put forward, low-cost dwelling, is one of the exceptions. However, there is at least one public house and one well-known theatre to be found under a railway. In general, arches directly below a station are often used for small shops and for station offices; further along the line small industries make good use of them, and their value as storage units is undeniable.

514 **Most of the bridge kits in my local model shop are of Continental origin. Can I use these on a British layout?**

A bridge is a bridge is a bridge, and there is more variation between the work of different designers than there is between masonry bridges in different continents, let alone in Europe where, since the 19th century, civil engineering has been at the forefront of cultural unity. Girder bridges follow recognised engineering principles and although the major spans are distinctive, the shorter patterns featured in kits are basic designs which are found all over the world. There is a little more variation in masonry structures, but again most of the designs are of standard structures and the main differences lie not so much in the shape but in the colour of the local stone.

515 **What are the main problems encountered in scratchbuilding a model bridge?**

Principally, getting reliable information on the chosen prototype, although in recent years the number of drawings available from various sources has increased appreciably. However, given some good photographs and the span of the main arch or arches, it is not too difficult to deduce the elevation. Construction only involves basic scratchbuilding techniques. The main structure can be built from ply, wood, card, plastic sheet or any combination of these. Suitable stone or brick cladding for the abutments and arches is available; the major difficulty lies in the reproduction of the masonry arch. This must be correctly reproduced if the structure is to look right.

Some modellers have gone to the length of laying individual 'stones' in place to produce accurate models of masonry arches – fitting thin plastic rectangles on to a plastic base with a solvent adhesive is not too difficult, but the worst part is cutting out the stones in the first place. Other modellers cover a wooden body with Das modelling clay and scribe the stones on this. It's a matter of personal preference.

516 **Could I use a model lifting bridge to cross the doorway?**

Lifting bridges are provided to span navigable waterways at a low level and are raised to permit the passage of ships. Whilst this is stating the obvious, it follows that they have a fairly short span and as a result it is only possible to provide a wide enough gap by this means in 7 mm scale – and even that will be a very narrow opening.

Having said that, lifting bridges have been used in this fashion in OO gauge. The best-known example was on the late Edward Beal's West Midland – it was built for him by a civil engineer friend and, although a model of no known prototype, it was constructed according to engineering principles and looked right to anyone not familiar with prototype practice.

517 **I would like to carry a length of railway line over a model navigable river. What sort of moveable bridge should I provide?**
If you intend to use a kit, you have a rather restricted choice – a simple bascule bridge is the limit. If you are prepared to scratchbuild, then you can not only choose between swing bridges, lifting bridges and telescopic bridges, but within these categories that are sub-divisions (see Plate 30).

Swing bridges can have equal arms, in which case it is usual for the pivot to be on a large pier in the centre of the river and, most important of all, the operating cabin is usually placed over the top of the bridge. Some have unequal arms – these have their pivots on one shore and the control mechanism is in a cabin beside the bridge.

Lifting bridges can either be simple bascules, mounted on massive trunnions, or the rolling lift type where the span ran back on a large cogged track. In addition there are straight lifting bridges where the span is raised vertically in a girder frame; these, however, are confined to canals where the lower headroom is not a serious bar. Rowe, in his book *Industrial and Mechanised Modelling*, describes the construction of a working telescopic bridge, the ideal choice for the adventurous modelmaker since it performs some extremely complicated manoeuvres which cannot fail to impress a visitor.

518 **Can I join two lattice girder bridge kits together to produce a longer span?**
Inasmuch as the model bridge is unlikely to fall down, you can, but it will always look as if it were about to collapse. It is not merely that the resulting girder will be far too slender to support the load in reality – the model stays up partly though the scale effect, but mainly because the principal strength member is a strip of 3 of 4 mm ply – but the arrangement of the bracing girders will be completely wrong. Girder bridge panels, whether braced or plate, are designed according to complex principles which ensure that the load is correctly spread throughout the structure. Obviously in a short answer it is impossible to begin to compress a major part of a civil engineer's training – the basic principles occupy a solid chapter in an elementary engineering textbook and require a good groundwork in mathematics in order to follow them. For the amateur the answer is to study the prototype.

519 **I want to include a model of a local braced girder bridge in my layout, but I cannot locate a kit which looks anything like it. Would it be a difficult task to scratchbuild the structure?**
As you have the original close to hand for reference, and you can presumably take enough photographs to show not merely the overall arrangement, but also the details of girders, braces and gusset plates, then it is more a matter of getting organised and then settling down to a long, but ultimately rewarding, task. The first requirement is an accurate, but not necessarily detailed, full-sized elevation of the girder panel, pasted on to a piece of Sundeala board. This should be covered with polythene sheet to protect the paper and prevent anything sticking to it, and then used as the master for a pin jig. This is nothing more than a series of small pins pushed into the board on either side of the line of girders. The girders can then be built up from strips of styrene sheet plastic. A simple cutting jig to ensure that you can make numerous strips of the correct width will be a boon, as will lengths of stripwood around which angles, tees channel and I-section girders can be made. It is then a question of cutting the girders to size and fixing them to the gusset plates. It will only be necessary to use 0.020 in thick sheet for this purpose for, by following the design of the prototype bridge, you will produce a model girder which will be, if anything, stronger in proportion than the original.

It is a very elementary scratchbuilding project, for there is nothing particularly difficult about any step – it is just the sheer quantity of parts that makes this a major modelling project.

520 I am attracted to the elegant Brunel timber fan viaducts that were such a feature of the West Country in the steam age. Is there a kit available for one of these?

Many years ago a kit was produced for a $1/8$ in scale model of two fans of the most advanced design, Walkham viaduct, but it has been discontinued. However, modelling any timber structure is not difficult, providing that you can make full-sized elevations of the various bents – the individual timber frames. These are used to produce a pin jig (see Q519 on girder bridges above) and the frames are built up on these. Whilst balsa wood strips, as sold for aircraft construction, can be used, it is better to hunt down a source of basswood sections, usually of American origin. If a small sawbench is available you could produce your own timbers – here a good straight-grained hardwood is ideal. Joints are normally made with acetate cement, but it is possible to add small pins if the holes are pre-drilled; a 12 V electric drill will be found invaluable for this. A drawing of two spans of Walkham viaduct appears in my *Model Railways on a Budget* (see the Bibliography), and outline drawings for the Cornish viaducts appear in Dick Woodfin's *History of the Cornwall Railway*. Although the end product is a very complex model, the techniques are simple enough to put it in the elementary category, and are ideal for a determined beginner prepared to put a fair number of hours into the project.

521 Why are railway tunnels oval in section? Wouldn't a circular bore be stronger?

Most rail tunnels were built to take steam locomotives, and the greater height of the oval bore provided the necessary ventilation space required to prevent the locomotive crew being completely asphyxiated (see Plate 30). Even so, in long single-track bores there could be difficulties. Tunnels built for electric traction can be circular and mostly are, though often this is because they are built with tunnelling shields and, as in the case of the Channel Tunnel, boring machines. Furthermore, where motorways cross rail tracks it is now common practice to carry the lines

in pre-cast concrete or ribbed steel tubes. An example of this type of construction can be viewed in detail by taking a ride on the Beer Heights Light Railway at Pecorama in Devon.

522 Why were so many early tunnel facades constructed to look like medieval castles? Surely it cannot have been merely to impress?

Believe it or not, that was the main reason, but the towers usually served as buttresses and strengthened the structure. There is the recorded example on the GWR where Brunel designed such a facade but when, halfway though construction, a massive slip made it unnecessary to go further, left the half-completed structure as a Gothic ruin. The Faller kit of the Lorelei tunnels on the Rhine is an extremely popular model, providing a pair of extremely elaborate facades which do not look out of place on a British model.

523 Isn't there a risk of derailment inside model tunnels? What should be done to prevent this?

Clearly, all tunnelled track needs to be carefully laid, but trouble can occur from time to time so it is essential to provide access to the tracks (see Plate 30). Often this can be done by arranging for some portion of the landscape above to lift away; where tracks are carried under stations, it is best to build the upper portion on lightweight sub-bases which can be easily detached to gain access to the lower level. Where open-top construction has been used it is usually easy to get at derailed trains from underneath. To prevent a train falling to the floor, it is customary to provide side protection in the form of strips of hardboard, projecting approximately 25 mm upwards on each side of the track base. It is not a good idea to site turnouts in inaccessible positions.

524 What is the correct slope for cuttings and embankments?

The exact angle of a cutting side depends on the type of soil, but is rarely steeper than 40 degrees except in rock formations – chalk is classified as a rock in this context (see Plate 30). Embankments, being formed by tipping, are invariably

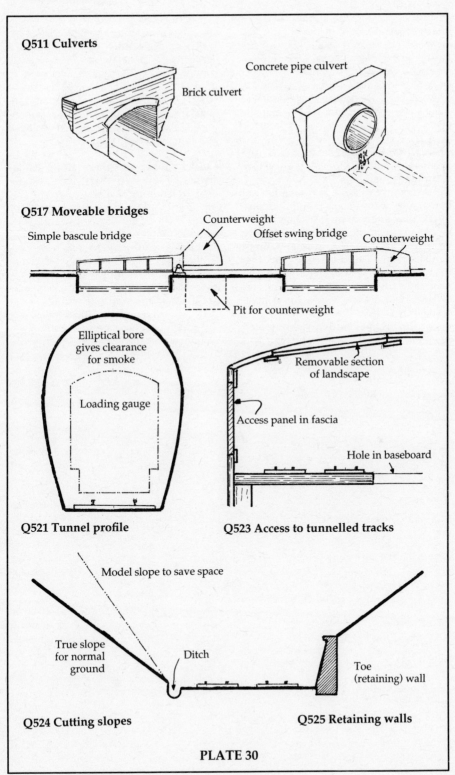

Q511 Culverts

Brick culvert

Concrete pipe culvert

Q517 Moveable bridges

Simple bascule bridge

Counterweight

Offset swing bridge

Counterweight

Pit for counterweight

Elliptical bore
gives clearance
for smoke

Loading gauge

Q521 Tunnel profile

Removable section
of landscape

Access panel in fascia

Hole in baseboard

Q523 Access to tunnelled tracks

Model slope to save space

True slope
for normal
ground

Ditch

Toe
(retaining) wall

Q524 Cutting slopes

Q525 Retaining walls

PLATE 30

fairly shallow and are usually twice as wide as they are high. In view of the lack of space on most models, liberties are taken under the general heading of 'modeller's licence'. It is more important to keep a reasonably even slope and to provide drainage ditches, as these are salient points that cannot fail to hit the eye.

525 Is it possible to avoid the problem of cutting slopes by providing retaining walls?

Up to a point this is so, but the high cost of retaining walls means that on the prototype they are only used as a last resort to avoid purchasing too much expensive land; they are therefore normally found only in urban locations. The exception to his rule is the 'toe wall'. This is a small retaining wall at the foot of a cutting and is provided either when an original double-track line was quadrupled or where the original cutting slope proved to be too optimistic and something had to be done to prevent repeated earth slips blocking the line. Localised toe walls are sometimes provided to give space for platelayer's huts, quite common close to tunnels where it is useful to have a store of tools close to the bore. On embankments, toe walls are normally associated with road widenings or are provided to allow room for a building on railway land.

526 Why are there often small arched openings perhaps half a metre deep in retaining walls?

These are refuges, provided to allow workmen to stand clear of trains. They are only found where the walls are close to running roads and are spaced at regular intervals. It will be noticed that not only are many occupied by relay boxes and other later fittings, but where telegraph and other railway wiring is carried in trunking or tubes along a retaining wall, these are frequently taken straight across the refuges!

PART 4
WIRING AND CONTROL

We come now to what is for many the most obscure part of the whole business, electrification. Whilst I have attempted to cover the principal problems, the following section is not a complete guide to model railway electrification and for a fuller understanding I would refer you to the books listed in the Bibliography.

Section 4:1
Power supply and control

527 **What sort of electrical supply is needed for a model railway?**
The majority of small-scale models operate on 12 V dc, and require up to 1.5 amp maximum current; larger-scale modules in gauges O and 1 require a 3 amp supply. Auxiliary supplies for point control are usually 16 V ac, and a similar supply is frequently used for lighting, although many people prefer to employ a lower voltage, usually between 6 and 9 V, to prolong the life of small lamps and give a more realistic effect (see Q478-9). On all but the simplest of layouts, more power is needed for auxiliaries than for the trains!

528 **What is the difference between dc and ac, and why is it important?**
Dc is direct current – one wire is always positive in relation to the other, or negative, wire. Ac is alternating current, where the leads are alternately positive and negative. The rate of change is termed the frequency and is measured in Hertz (Hz), the number of cycles per second. The small permanent magnet field motors used in most model locomotives will only work on dc.

529 **How do I get a 12 V dc supply from the 240 V ac mains?**
The best approach is to use a commercial power unit. This is a sealed box containing a transformer, rectifier, current limiting devices (cut-outs) and, in most cases,

a built-in controller for the trains. It is sometimes termed a transformer, but this is strictly a device to convert the voltage of ac supplies and does not have any rectifiers.

530 **As the motors are only rated to take under 1 amp, will it cause any damage if I use a 3 amp unit to power an OO gauge layout? Could I use this to run two OO gauge trains independently though two controllers?**
A unit with a large output won't affect the performance or do any damage to the model, as the locomotive will only take the current it requires. It may damage your pocket, since the higher the power output, the higher the price, but if you have such a unit to hand, by all means use it. The snag is that by using one source of power for the two controllers, common return wiring cannot be used and the more advanced systems of sectionalisation cannot be readily employed.

531 **Is it possible to use a car battery trickle charger to power a model railway?**
As the unit produces 12 V dc, it can power a train through a controller and if such a unit is surplus to requirements, it can be pressed into service. However, since such units are essentially low-powered, the idea being to bleed a very small current into the battery overnight, it is not a wholly satisfactory approach.

532 **Could I run my model railway from batteries?**

There is no real technical reason why you should not, though you will require eight 'D' cells in series to provide 12 V. The running cost, using alkaline cells, is going to be extremely high. As an alternative you can use rechargeable cells and reduce the running cost, but the capital outlay is likely to about the same as a standard model railway power unit and there will not be enough power to operate accessories like point motors and layout lighting. The advantages are small, unless you wish to build an ultra-compact small-scale or narrow gauge layout in an executive case.

533 **As a car starter battery can deliver 12 V at a considerable amperage, could I not use this to power my layout?**

Where no supply of mains voltage is available, the rechargeable lead-acid battery is a possible source of 12 V dc. However, the disadvantages are many. The most serious is that the battery can produce anything up to 60 A on full discharge, enough to wreak havoc, causing severe burns and even fire, so *all circuits must be protected by a low-current fuse alongside the battery* in addition to any normal circuit breakers. There is also the question of weight, a significant factor since the battery must be taken to a charging point. Although modern batteries are less prone to spillage, they do contain corrosive acid. It is also impossible to use common return wiring, though the split potential system can be provided with two batteries. Last, but by no means least, batteries are quite expensive items.

534 **I have an outbuilding some distance from the house which would be ideal for a layout were it not for the fact that it is difficult to provide, at reasonable cost, a supply of mains electricity. What do you advise?**

In theory the answer is to use rechargeable batteries. There are two alternatives, lead-acid starter batteries or Ni-cad 'D' cells. Of the two, the Ni-cad approach has a slight edge, since not only are the unit cells lighter and easily taken back to the house for recharging, but they are also clean and safe to handle. You do, however, need a very large number, and you will also need at least two four-cell recharging units, since eight cells are needed to provide the necessary 12 V dc. Similar cells can provide lighting through camping-type florescent lamps, but the operation of point motors is going to be difficult. On the whole, the cost of supplying a mains supply is going to be lower than the overall cost of a battery-powered system, and the convenience will be considerably greater.

535 **Could I build my own power unit?**

Certainly, if you know enough about electricity to handle mains voltages safely and are able to choose the correct transformers, rectifiers, etc, for the job. However, you will not save money by doing so. The reason for building one's own power supply is to meet a more detailed specification than the commercial units can provide – it is strictly for experts. It should moreover be noted that even experts use commercial units for convenience.

536 **What sort of power unit should one look for at the start?**

For OO, HO and N you really need a combined power unit/controller with a 1.5 amp rating on the controlled dc supply, and a 1.5 amp 16 V ac output from a separate winding on the transformer. This will provide ample power for a beginner's layout. However, if a simple unit, with only a controlled 12 V dc output rated at 9 va, is available, this will do for a start, but it will not work point motors or lighting, nor will it provide enough power for heavy trains, or double heading.

537 **I have a very small controller which came with a train set. It has only one output and only a couple of positions on the speed control. Can I use this on my layout?**

This unit is cheap and a 'rock bottom' device which is not only shorn of all refinements, but also has a very low power rating – usually 6 va. As a controller for a serious model railway it is useless; indeed it is tolerably useless for anything more than a very basic train set with a limited number of coaches in the train. However, as a supply of 12 V dc for auxiliary effects it can be of some value providing that the flimsy plastic casing is in good order.

538 My power unit has the outputs rated not only in volts but in va. What does this mean?

This is the power rating, and is arrived at by multiplying the voltage with the maximum current flow; va stands for volts multiplied by amps. This is similar to wattage but, where ac supply is concerned, va is a more meaningful term.

539 Could you explain the difference between a continuous rating and an hourly rating for a transformer?

The practical limit of loading for most electrical and electronic circuits is governed by the heating that takes place whenever current passes through wires or other components. The continuous rating is the output that can be sustained indefinitely without raising the temperature to dangerous levels, while the hourly rating is the current that can be taken for an hour at the most without causing damage through overheating. Transformers should have their normal loading restricted to the continuous rating; the hourly figure should be regarded as a safety factor for short overloads.

540 Will it hurt if I leave a power unit switched on overnight?

Providing that the layout itself is switched off and the power unit is in a reasonably well-ventilated place and not covered with anything, the only effect will be a rise in the next quarter's electricity bill, and even this will not be noticeable until you forget to switch off for a week!

541 My power unit gets warm after an operating session. Is there anything wrong?

All electrical equipment tends to heat up, as you will doubtless have found if you replace a failed electric lamp immediately after its failure. So long as your power unit is only warm and not too hot to touch with comfort, all is well. Should the casing get too hot to touch, then either you are seriously overloading the circuit or the unit is faulty.

542 The main lead from my power unit has only two wires. Surely it should be earthed for safety?

Modern power units are double insulated and are marked with a 'double square' symbol. There is therefore no need to earth the unit – in fact, it is safer not to do so. Second-hand units with a three-core lead should be regarded with extreme suspicion. Apart from their age, should they have a metal body it will be at earth potential and should you be touching this and come into contact with a live wire, the result will be very serious indeed.

543 How do I connect the two wires to a 13 amp three-pin plug?

Looking at the back of the plug, as one does when wiring (see Plate 31), the upper pin is earth (E) and is not connected when there are only two wires from the apparatus. This is the most important fact to keep in mind. The right-hand pin is connected via a cartridge fuse – this is the live pin (L) and is connected to the brown wire (brown, a warm colour, is live). The left-hand pin is neutral (N) and has no fuse – it is connected to the blue wire (blue, a cold colour, is neutral).

Most plugs are sold with a 13 amp fuse, but this must be changed for a 3 amp fuse. Earth wires, when fitted, are striped green/yellow – think of grass and corn. As mentioned previously, power units should not have earth wires.

544 The lead from the unit is too short to reach a socket. How should I extend it?

You don't extend it at all – instead you plug it into an extension lead, which must be long enough to reach from the socket to the operating position *without crossing any gangways* (see Plate 31). A four-way socket is required, as you will need to plug in a number of different devices such as soldering irons, drills, etc. Commercial leads are available, but may not be the required length. If you are making up your own lead, use three-core sheathed cable, preferably rated at 13 amp. The best four-way strip sockets have an integral fuse and neon indicator light, although providing that the plug is correctly rated, there is no need to worry about the omission of a fuse at the socket end. After all, each lead is also provided with a fused plug.

Never ever, under any circumstances whatsoever, attempt to extend a mains lead by means of a twiddle joint covered in insulating tape. Furthermore, do not make up extension leads from cheap twisted or flat flex. Shrouded cable, where the inner cores are encased in an outer plastic cover, is the best type of wire for all mains supply since it provides a warning of abrasion *before* the inner wire is exposed and the lead becomes dangerous. In addition, on a model railway, where low-voltage circuits abound, it provides an easy way of distinguishing those wires it is safe to cut from those which it most definitely is not!

545 Is it a good idea to use a RCD (residual current device) limiter in the main socket when connecting a model railway power supply?
Residual current devices are designed to cut off the power very rapidly should anything untoward occur and this greatly minimises any risk of electrocution. So far as the power supply side is concerned, the risk of accident is extremely small, providing that the leads are kept well out of the way of the feet and any sharp instruments. However, as it will be convenient to plug soldering irons and power tools into the circuit, where the risk of accident, whilst still very small, is nevertheless present, an RCD is a sound precaution.

546 I wish ultimately to control two trains. Would it not be better to buy a unit with twin controllers at the outset?
The snag with twin unit controllers is that the knobs are very close together, and cannot conveniently be used by two operators. Worse, should you wish to separate the controllers at some later date, for example to control two stations some distance apart, you will have problems. These controllers are really intended for simple train sets.

547 The lead to my power unit is damaged and I can see no way of get-

ting into the casing to replace it. What can I do?
If there is a reasonable length of undamaged lead on the unit side of the fault, cut the lead short and attach a fresh lead with a two-core connector, obtainable from electrical suppliers. Otherwise consult a qualified electrician. Regulations state that model railway power units, which can be used by young children, should be tamper-proof. Drilling out the rivets and replacing them after repair with self-tapping screws is therefore officially frowned upon.

548 The power unit is very heavy and has no means of fixing it to the baseboard. What should I do?
There is nothing you can do about the weight, but you could complain to the manufacturer about the lack of fixings! One solution is to fix a shelf below the baseboard proper and stand the unit on this. Another answer is to put the unit on the floor, close to the mains socket and well out of the way of feet. Then the power supplies can be taken to the layout with twin flexible leads.

549 How do I control trains if the unit is on the floor?
You use controller modules, either the panel-mounting pattern or hand-held, which are mounted in any convenient place on the layout. These are usually fed from a 16 V ac input, but 12 V dc will also work with a small loss of power. It is better to use shrouded transformers, which are supplied by specialist suppliers for powering hand-held and panel-mounting controllers, and reserve the original power unit for test purposes. The advantage of separating the mains transformer from the layout proper is that it keeps high- and low-voltage wiring apart.

550 Is there any risk in extending the low-voltage leads?
Electrically, the only risk occurs if you also run mains voltages, for lighting, etc, though similar wires, which is another reason why it is best always to use sheathed cable for mains supply. A greater hazard is tripping over the loose wires, so they should be carried neatly well out of the way of your feet.

However, they can cross gangways providing that they are covered, either by a plastic cover or even a length of carpet. Apart from the risk of tripping, walking over wires will damage the insulation, and while this will not be dangerous as such, it will mess up the supply. However, if the leads are longer than 4 m you may experience voltage drop unless you use heavy-duty wire. For this reason I would advise the use of twisted or flat twin *unsheathed* mains flex for main leads from a transformer, providing that all mains power is carried in *sheathed* cables and there is no risk of getting the two types of supply confused.

551 What is the difference between a standard controller and an electronic controller?

The traditional controller employs a variable resistance to vary the voltage, while an electronic controller employs transistors, either as separate units or, more commonly today, a combined solid state device (chip). The transistorised controller offers theoretically superior control, but its main advantage today is that it is, basically, slightly cheaper than the resistance controller. It also permits the introduction of feedback sensing circuits to further improve control. Most panel-mounting and hand-held controllers are electronic.

552 Can I make my own controller?

Certainly, but you won't necessarily save any money by doing so. In the case of the more advanced electronic devices, not only can you start by paying more for the parts, but unless you are well into electronic circuit construction, you may also end up with a lot of useless junk. A simple straight resistance controller requires a heavy-duty wire-wound 100 ohm potentiometer, and these are quite expensive.

553 Some electronic controllers have several control knobs. What is the purpose?

With electronic control it is possible to control the rate of increase and decrease of line voltage, so that there is a delay in the acceleration and deceleration of the train. This simulates the effect of inertia

on the prototype and adds to the realism of control. Provision can be made for adjustment of this delay period, as well as the effect of applying brakes, by means of additional knobs and switches. Like many such complications, these additions are generally neglected; one suspects they are put there because it seemed a good idea at the time.

554 What is the purpose of feedback in a controller?

A feedback controller senses the back EMF of the motor, which is roughly related to its speed, and adjusts the applied voltage accordingly. The result is that the train travels at a fairly constant speed regardless of conditions – including climbing or descending gradients, where the prototype would tend to slow down or accelerate. Good feedback controllers are also justly popular among serious operators because they give a more positive control. A good feedback controller will iron out quite a few cyclic faults in a poor mechanism, but in no way can any electronic device put mechanical faults right – at best it can only mask the symptoms.

555 Some controllers set speed and direction through a single knob, while others have a separate reversing switch. Which is preferable in practice?

This is very much a matter of personal taste. The 'centre off' single-knob controller in theory prevents one from reversing a locomotive at full speed, but as it takes roughly the same time to twist the knob from one extreme to the other as it does to throw a reversing switch, the advantage is more theoretical than practical. The separate reversing switch is simpler to build from standard components.

556 What are the advantages of hand-held controllers?

Providing that the lead is long enough, the operator can move about the layout with the train rather than remaining standing in one position. On the other hand, unless there is somewhere to deposit the hand-held controller, he has one hand permanently occupied. It is not difficult to provide both types of controller on a layout, getting the best of both worlds.

Section 4:2
Wiring

557 **What sort of wire should be used for a model railway?**
20 SWG plastic-covered wire is the general choice; this is often sold as bell wire or, more specifically, marked for low voltage only. This type of wire is frequently single core, and should not be used whenever the wires need to be bent or flexed in use. Flexible wire, which has a large number of extremely fine wires as its core, should be used for connecting cables and other places where the wires are frequently bent.

558 **Can I use ordinary flex as sold for lighting?**
This is perfectly satisfactory but needs to be carefully distinguished from wires carrying the full 240 V. The best way to do this is only to use shrouded cable (ie two-core or three-core in a larger plastic sheath) for 240 V, and to reserve twisted or flat flex for low voltage only. This is sound practice – the sheathed cable has a greater safety factor.

There are two advantages in using this type of wire – it is readily available and competitively priced, even when you don't have scrap lengths to hand. Because of its greater total cross section, the resistance is lower. Indeed, this wire is advisable for longer leads.

559 **I have a supply of flat twin flex. How can I split it into two separate wires?**
Usually, the wires can be pulled apart, but occasionally a wire is bared whilst this is being done. However, there is no reason why you need split it, for using twin flex makes cabling neater. Many items on the layout – point motors, for example – require a pair of leads.

560 **How do I tell which wire is which at the end of a long piece of twin flex?**
By trial and error! Link up, test and, if need be, reverse the connections. There is an even chance of being right first time. However, if you are buying twin flex, look for the type which has a mark on one side – this saves any bother.

561 **I have a number of spare three-core leads salvaged from old equipment. Can I use this for wiring the layout?**
Providing that you strip the outer sheathing from the cables, the wire is perfectly suitable. However, the braided pattern, commonly found on electric irons, is very difficult to strip. The twin + earth flat cable, used for permanent mains wiring, can be easily stripped by pulling the earth wire through the sheath with a pair of pliers.

562 **I have to run a long low-voltage lead to a control panel on my garden railway and experience a loss of power. What should I do?**
Use heavier wire. It is possible to obtain single-core wires in red, black and striped yellow/green from electrical suppliers; this heavier wire has a very low resistance and inhibits voltage drop. Alternatively, use two lengths of twin mains flex, with each pair of cores twisted and soldered together at the ends.

563 **I have on hand a quantity of multi-core telephone cable with very thin wires. Is it any use for a model railway?**
For very short runs, up to about 300 mm, the higher resistance of the wire is of little consequence. A simple answer is to connect pairs of wires together at each end and so double up the capacity of each circuit. The larger cables, which have the wires in pairs, one white, one coloured, are particularly susceptible to this treatment.

564 **Is the flat ribbon-pattern multi-core cable suitable for model railway connections?**
The normal type has single-core wires and is not suited for continuous flexing. There is a type which has a limited degree of flexibility, but for most purposes these cables are not really cost-effective since few cables have precisely the right number of wires. Furthermore, being intended for electronic circuits, where current levels are low, they cannot be used for long runs. It is simpler to build up the cables from single-core flexible wire.

565 I have had little success in tracking down multi-core cable with sufficient cores. Can you suggest where I should find it?

Most railway modellers make their own multi-core cables from individual wires. It is possible to obtain a braided sheath to slip over a loom of wires, but it is extremely difficult to gauge the final length of the covering when stretched over the wires. Spiral plastic strips are also produced for this purpose. An alternative is to stretch the cable out fairly straight and wind self-adhesive coloured tape around it.

566 Is it essential to colour code the wiring?

It is convenient, providing that ample supplies of each colour are to hand. However, there are not enough colours to allow each circuit to be individually distinguished, so marking is necessary, colour code or not. Most modellers are content to distinguish between 12 V feeds, 16 V ac and return wires, at most using the four principal colours, red, blue, green and brown. The main problem is gauging the quantities needed of each colour, since there is a tendency for one colour to run out rapidly whilst another is hardly used. At this point most modellers abandon colour coding in favour of wire labelling.

567 How does one label individual wires?

A popular method is to use small self-adhesive labels marked with ballpoint pen and wrapped around the wire, but it is better to use tag strips for terminating wiring and to label these (see Plate 31). A corresponding label at the point at which the wire passes through the baseboard identifies each end of the wire.

568 How does one prevent the wires beneath the baseboard becoming a terrible tangle?

By arranging the wires in a series of neat cables. It is necessary to think ahead whilst wiring and leave sufficient slack in the earlier runs to enable the most convenient route to be developed as you go along.

There are several methods of cabling wires. Proprietary plastic ties are often used, but the same results are achieved with wire twists, utilising short offcuts of wire (see Plate 31). A neat and professional touch is given by cabling with waxed thread; to prevent the thread from coming untied, it needs to be brought back inside the loop (see Plate 31). Waxed thread can be obtained from cobblers; it is used for sewing leather. However, you can make your own by passing carpet thread through a block of beeswax.

569 Is it possible to buy cable troughs for model railways?

For long runs, a good low-voltage cable trough is provided by the flat white plastic sheathing used to neaten surface mains wiring. The wires can be simply bundled inside and the cover snapped into place – this is, after all, the prototype method (see Plate 31).

570 How do you carry the current to the track unobtrusively?

If the last 5-8 mm of wire is stripped and the final 2 mm bent at right angles, it can be soldered into the web of the rail. Providing that the wider sheath is not visible, and the rail and wire are painted rust colour, the joint is unnoticeable.

571 There do not appear to be any wires to the rails on finescale layouts. How is this done?

Finescale workers arrange dropper wires from below the rail whilst tracklaying, and with a little forethought a similar arrangement could be devised with standard flexible track (see Plate 31). It does, however, add appreciably to the time taken to lay track and is only really justified if the rest of the permanent way will stand close scrutiny.

572 What are dropper wires?

Dropper wires are short lengths of bare copper wire, soldered to the rail at one end and passed through holes in the baseboard surface (see Plate 31). They should protrude at least 10 mm below the underside so that the main wire can be easily soldered in place. It is customary to identify the dropper wire underneath the baseboard.

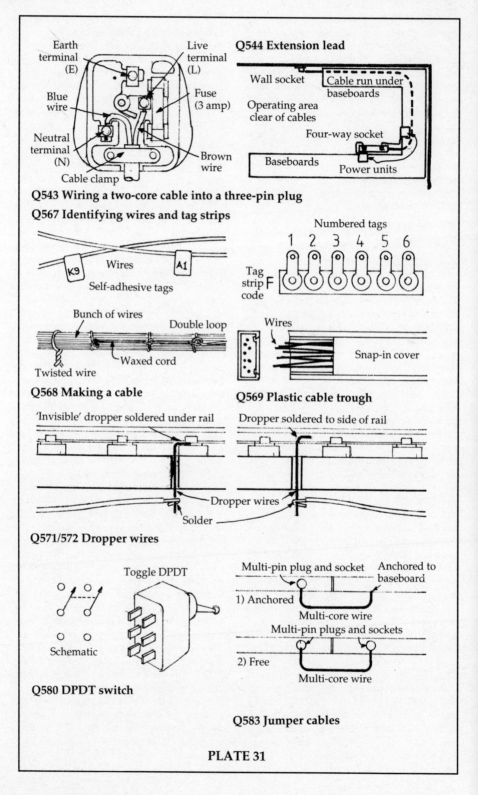

Earth terminal (E)

Live terminal (L)

Blue wire

Fuse (3 amp)

Neutral terminal (N)

Brown wire

Cable clamp

Q543 Wiring a two-core cable into a three-pin plug

Q544 Extension lead

Wall socket

Cable run under baseboards

Operating area clear of cables

Four-way socket

Baseboards

Power units

Q567 Identifying wires and tag strips

K9   Wires   A1

Self-adhesive tags

Numbered tags

1 2 3 4 5 6

Tag strip code F

Bunch of wires

Double loop

Waxed cord

Twisted wire

Q568 Making a cable

Wires

Snap-in cover

Q569 Plastic cable trough

'Invisible' dropper soldered under rail

Dropper soldered to side of rail

Dropper wires

Solder

Q571/572 Dropper wires

Toggle DPDT

Schematic

Q580 DPDT switch

Multi-pin plug and socket   Anchored to baseboard

1) Anchored

Multi-core wire

Multi-pin plugs and sockets

2) Free

Multi-core wire

Q583 Jumper cables

PLATE 31

573 If I turn the baseboard unit upside down for wiring, will I not damage the track?

You have two choices: fix temporary supports to the ends to hold the baseboard clear of the bench or, easier still, stand the board on its edge; a short batten clamped to one end will stabilise it.

574 I find wiring underneath a permanent baseboard very taxing. Have you any suggestions?

Provide some form of back support – an old cushion will often do the trick. The special boards on castors, provided for motor mechanics, also have their uses here.

575 Isn't it dangerous to solder from underneath?

There is certainly a risk, though you should not use so much solder that blobs fall off. It is advisable to wear safety goggles and, above all, not to get directly beneath the soldering iron, but work to one side. It is, however, better by far not to solder in such a position.

576 How can soldering from underneath the baseboard be avoided on a permanent layout?

As always, by pre-planning. Wires can be soldered from above or where, as in the case of point motors, the terminals are underneath, they should be put in place before the unit is installed. They can then be brought to a tag strip at the edge of the baseboard, and leads from the tag strip taken to the control panel.

577 What are tag strips?

Tag strips are a series of metal solder tags secured to a strip of insulating material. They are screwed in strategic positions and used to terminate leads. They should be numbered and the details noted in the wiring book (see also Q567).

578 What exactly is a wiring book?

It is a notebook in which you record every detail of the layout's wiring as you install it. It must be kept in a safe but readily accessible location so that, in the event of trouble, you can find out what you did all that time ago.

579 Is it essential to solder electrical circuits on a model railway?

In the sense that it is possible to wire a layout using screw and crimped connections, no. In the sense that these connections are not only costly, that you need a lot of them and they are less reliable than a good soldered joint, the answer is a very definite yes.

580 What is a DPDT switch?

DPDT stands for double-pole double-throw. The switches can be obtained in normal and centre off forms, and there are three main patterns: toggle, slider and rotary (see Plate 31).

581 Where can I get multi-pin plugs and sockets?

These can be found in most electronic stores. The DIN range of up to nine-pin sockets are extremely useful. The 'D' pattern connectors used in computers have proved very popular in recent years, particularly as the 25-pin version meets most needs. Ex-equipment suppliers (junk shops) and bring-and-buy stalls at exhibitions can often provide inexpensive second-hand multi-pin plugs and sockets.

582 Is it advisable to standardise on a single pattern of plug and socket?

There are advantages in having standardised jumper cables, but with the 'umbilical cord' system, it helps if each plug and socket is of a different pattern since this prevents cross-connection.

583 What exactly is a jumper cable?

This is a multi-core cable fitted with a suitable multi-pin plug connection for carrying electric circuits across a break. There are three approaches: pairs of cables with male and female connectors, a cable on one baseboard connecting with a socket on the other, and a loose jumper, with plugs at each end and sockets on each baseboard (see Plate 31). This last type avoids the hazard of dangling cables, but introduces a fresh hazard of its own, loss of jumper cables. A better solution to the tangling lead problem is to provide terry clips on the underside of the board to hold the leads securely in place whilst in transit.

Section 4:3
Two-rail circuits

584 What is meant by two-rail wiring?

With two-rail wiring, the rails are insulated from each other, and each is connected to the output terminals of the controller. All rolling-stock wheels are insulated and some means of collecting the current from the rails is provided. It is a convention that when the right-hand rail is positive, the train should move forward. It is also customary to wire the controller so that the directional control is natural; in other words, when moved to the right, the train moves to the right, and vice versa (see Plate 32). Whilst this is not compulsory, it is more comfortable.

585 How can I make sure that the controller is wired for natural movement when there is no indication on the output terminals which is positive and which is negative?

The reason why no indication of polarity is given is that the relative polarity of the output terminals depends on the way the controller is set! As there are only two possible ways of connecting the controller to the track, trial and error is the favoured method – there is an even chance that you will get it right first time. If not, simply swap the leads over.

586 Some writers talk of positive and negative rails, others of feed and return. Which is correct?

As the whole principle of model railway dc traction is that reversal of movement is effected by reversing the relative polarity of the rails, to talk of 'negative' and 'positive' only creates confusion – 'feed' and 'return' not only remove this confusion, but also make a very important practical distinction between the two wires. Section switches are placed in the feed; on the other hand, all returns are brought together to a common return wire. It is a convention to have the feeds on the far side – the edge of the baseboard facing the operator – and the returns on the near side. This is not vital, but the important point, particularly where the layout is built up in sections in

the workshop, is to establish your favoured convention *and adhere to it rigidly*. Any other course can only lead to chaos and a succession of short circuits.

587 How do you separate the various sections in the track?

Two-rail sections are separated by placing insulating gaps – generally made with insulated rail joiners – in both running rails (see Plate 32). Whilst, in theory, all return rails can be connected together, the introduction of pointwork makes it difficult to determine whether any rail end is *permanently* connected to either feed or return. The use of a double rail break saves a great deal of difficulty here, but there is a far more important consideration – the return circuit is taken though a proper low-resistance wire connection, rather than through the rails, which do have an appreciable resistance.

588 The running rails have a fairly large cross-section. How is it you speak of their having a high resistance?

For a start, most model railways use nickel silver rail and this metal, contrary to popular legend, has a fairly high resistance; indeed, nickel is a common alloying metal for resistance wire. As well as this, the standard rail joiner is not a particularly good electrical connection and tends to deteriorate over time. Hence there is not only some resistance in the rail, but there is also a small additional resistance at each joint. Although individually small, the various resistances do add up. So long as the section is not appreciably longer than 3 m, they can be ignored, but if all the return rails are linked into one and only connected to the power supply at one point, the total resistance will be enough to affect running. It should never be forgotten that although the nominal traction voltage is 12, most motors run on as low as 4 volts and some motors will turn over on 1.5 volts. Here the drop of only half a volt is serious.

589 Is there any way of reducing the resistance at rail joints?

The resistance of a rail joint can be reduced to a negligible amount by bonding the joint. This involves soldering a wire across the joint, and should be done where there is any possibility of the rail joiners not doing their job properly (see Plate 32). A good example of this is an outdoor layout, where joints should be bonded as a matter of course.

590 What happens at points, where one rail crosses over the other?

If nothing is done, there will obviously be a dead short. There are two ways of avoiding this: the live and dead frog systems. Needless to say, amphibians are not involved – the frog is the crossing point in the turnout.

With dead frogs, the crossing point is insulated, the exact size of the insulation depending on the design of the point (see Plate 32). Some manufacturers, notably Peco, have reduced this to a very small piece of plastic. A pair of jumpers carry current across the insulated section.

With a live frog the entire crossing is one electrical unit; this will be the case if the crossing is either a metal casting or if it has been built up from rail soldered or spot-welded together. The crossing is connected to the running rails through a changeover switch coupled to the tiebar or, more simply, by the contact between the point blades and the stock rails, aided in most cases by wiper contacts which compete the circuit.

591 Which is preferable, live or dead frogs?

As any environmentally-minded child will tell you, frogs are much better living than dead. However, in our field, the dead frog point is simpler to wire, and is preferred for train set and beginner's use. Live frogs must be accompanied by carefully located insulation breaks and, furthermore, the location of the feed point is critical. However, the advantage of a live frog is that it provides a continuous current supply to the train, and this is particularly important where short-wheelbase locomotives with correspondingly short pick-up spans are in use.

592 What is a self-isolating point?

Basically, it is a turnout where the road against which the point is set is isolated, so any locomotive standing on the siding will not move. This is automatically achieved with live frog points, as the siding has both rails at the same polarity. Therefore, although the locomotive is connected to the controller, the fact that both pick-ups are in contact with the same terminal means that the motor windings are bypassed and no current flows through them.

With dead frogs, the point blades and their continuation beyond the frog are only energised when they are in contact with a stock rail. With this arrangement one rail is electrically isolated (dead), so no current can pass through the motor windings either (see Plate 32). Most modern commercial dead frog points provide this facility, though some are provided with small spring wire links which bypass the point blade contact, rendering both rails permanently live. These links can be easily removed, but they are also easily lost unless immediately stored in a secure container which is suitably labelled.

593 What is the purpose of providing these links? Surely it is preferable to provide self-isolation in sidings?

The points in question are lightly sprung and can be passed over in the trailing direction, providing that the locomotive can receive power. In this case, self-isolation is definitely not wanted and the spring point is a fine example of a case where a dead frog is preferable. Spring points are very convenient at the exit of loops and, above all, in passing loops on an automatically controlled single-track system.

594 I have replaced my dead frog points with live frog points in the expectation of getting better running. All I get is a succession of short circuits. What has gone wrong?

With dead frog points, it is possible to hook the entire layout up as a single unit in a haphazard fashion, though this does not necessarily make best use of any self-isolating properties. With live frogs two rules must be followed: first and foremost all feeds must be located towards the toe end of the points; second, no feed must be directly connected to a frog, and to prevent this it will be necessary to introduce double rail breaks in every continuous circuit that includes point-work and between pairs of points placed

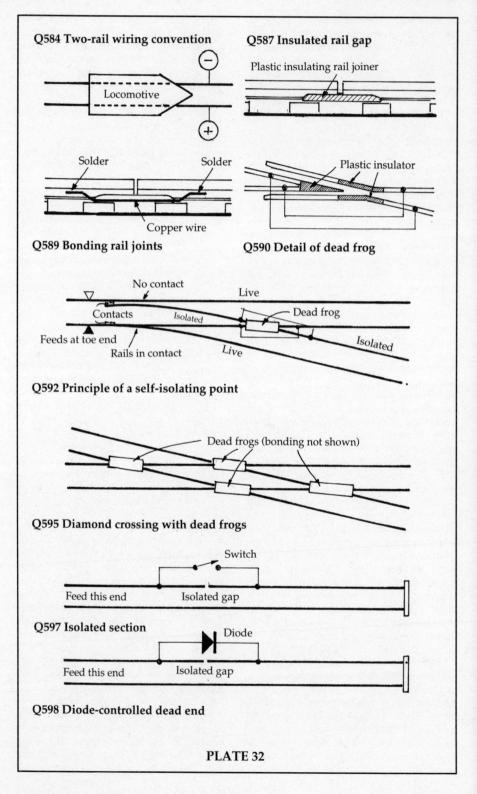

Q584 Two-rail wiring convention

Locomotive

Q587 Insulated rail gap

Plastic insulating rail joiner

Solder   Solder

Copper wire

Q589 Bonding rail joints

Plastic insulator

Q590 Detail of dead frog

No contact

Live

Contacts

Isolated

Dead frog

Feeds at toe end

Rails in contact

Live

Isolated

Q592 Principle of a self-isolating point

Dead frogs (bonding not shown)

Q595 Diamond crossing with dead frogs

Switch

Feed this end   Isolated gap

Q597 Isolated section

Diode

Feed this end   Isolated gap

Q598 Diode-controlled dead end

PLATE 32

back-to-back. Full details are to be found in my book *The PSL Book of Model Railway Wiring* (see the Bibliography).

595 What happens at a diamond crossing? How are the feeds and returns kept apart?

With dead frogs there is no problem – both tracks are completely insulated from each other (see Plate 32). Live frog diamonds, however, require no less than four changeover switches to connect each of the four crossing points to the appropriate feed or return. It is often suggested that this switch has to be manually operated, and this is true in the case of a toy train oriented figure-of-eight – here dead frogs are necessary. However, in a properly designed model railway, the majority of diamond crossings occur as part of a complex track formation, the simplest example being a double junction. In such cases it is a simple matter to determine which turnout controls the crossing movement; the changeover switches can then be coupled to this point.

596 I am considering including a scissors crossover on my layout and want to use live frogs. However, I cannot determine which point to couple the changeover switches to, since both crossovers control the crossing.

The scissors crossover is a very special case, but the problem can be resolved by looking at the end result – what happens when both crossovers are reversed and you then attempt to run two trains over the formation? The answer is a collision. Therefore, some form of interlocking can be introduced to prevent both levers being pulled off together, or else you can decide that one of the crossovers has priority and, when reversed, switches all circuits controlled by the other out of action.

597 How do you arrange an isolating section in a two-rail system?

An insulated break is placed in the feed rail and bridged by an on-off switch (see Plate 32). The power supply is therefore taken from the main section and controlled through the section switch. Isolating sections are commonly provided in locomotive yards, in locomotive

spurs and at the ends of terminal roads. However, they can also be located against stop signals, in which case they are frequently controlled by the signal; it is thus quite easy, on a model, to prevent a driver passing a signal at stop.

598 What is a diode-controlled dead end?

This circuit places a diode across the isolating break instead of the on-off switch (see Plate 32). The theory is that the locomotive will stop before reaching the buffers but move away when the controller is reversed. It is a very pretty idea and is to be found in every textbook dealing with model railway electronics. However, it is a tolerably useless device. The point of the isolated section in a terminal road is not to stop the train hitting the buffers – this is avoided by driving the train correctly. The purpose is to allow the train engine to remain isolated whilst another locomotive is attached to the other end of the train to haul it out leaving the original locomotive in position, ready to move on to shed or into a loco spur. The diode circuit prevents this happening.

Section 4:4
Cab control and common return

599 What is cab control?

Cab control is a system of switching controllers to any chosen section of the layout. The origin of the term lay in the fact that the operator was in the place of the driver in the cab of the locomotive rather than being confined to one location on the layout, in a position more analogous to the signalman. The term is of US origin, although the principles were developed independently on both sides of the Atlantic.

600 Does this involve any elaborate electronic devices fitted to the locomotive?

No electronics are involved – the system is operated by simple switched circuits which are incorporated into the layout itself and worked manually by the operator who selects those parts of the layout on which he intends to run his train. Although the principles are simple, there are a large number of circuits involved, so it can appear quite complicated if the full wiring diagram for even a modest layout is drawn out on a small sheet of paper. Apart from this, it is possible to incorporate a number of refinements such as linking the selection to the points.

601 What is the simplest form of cab control one can adopt?

The twin-cab system offers both relative simplicity and considerable flexibility and is generally adequate for the control of the majority of home layouts. Only two controllers are required, but whilst they can be combined in a single unit, it is more convenient to have separate units since it is usually advantageous to separate the control positions physically. Conventionally, they are referred to as the 'red' and 'blue' controllers, colour coding being very easy to apply. Each section is fed through a three-position changeover switch, allowing one to select 'off', 'red' or 'blue' at will (see Plate 33). Whilst it is not absolutely essential, cab control is more readily arranged where common return wiring is employed.

602 The twin-cab system seems fairly simple and trouble free, but will two controllers be enough for an ambitious layout?

It depends not so much on how ambitious the layout is, but on how many operators you can muster. The underlying principle of cab control is that instead of having an number of controllers connected to fixed sections of track, you have one controller per operator which can be switched into any section of track. Indeed, for testing or single-handed operation, the entire layout can be worked from one controller. The point is that if you set out to drive your trains, rather than let them run aimlessly under their own power, you soon realise that, no matter how elaborate your set-up, you can only *control* one train at once.

603 My layout involves a number of loops on which I want to have trains running independently, possibly under

some form of automatic control. Could I adopt cab control as well?

Basically, if you want to see a lot of trains in motion at once, all you need is a series of independent loops of track, each fed from its own controller. This is apparently the reverse of cab control where each train is driven over its route. However, given the necessary loops and sufficient controllers, there is no inherent difficulty in having a cab control system which allows the option of switching individual controllers on to specific loops. It is, however, going to get more than a little complicated, so it will probably be best to start with a simple direct hook-up and, when you get tired of watching the trains run past (if indeed you reach this point), start planning a more elaborate control system.

604 I have seen a reference to progressive cab control. What does this involve?

Progressive cab control is an arrangement whereby it is possible for a number of trains to be routed around a fairly elaborate system, each on its own controller throughout. Although the concept is quite straightforward, it goes without saying that it is a fairly complex arrangement, particularly if it is to be carried out automatically. On a purely manual arrangement, each cab is provided with a multi-pole rotary switch which is advanced step by step as the train travels around the system.

605 Can I have more than two controllers in a cab control system?

There is no theoretical upper limit, but in practice one is limited by the switchgear obtainable. Three controllers (red, blue and green) are quite common, four have been used with success, while only an elaborate system with many stations and a large length of main line really requires more than four controllers (see Plate 33). Where it is desired to have a large number of trains running at once, it is better to employ some form of automatic or semi-automatic control, with provision for switching in manual control at crucial points.

606 Is it necessary to have all the switches on one large panel?

There is every reason to locate smaller

groups of switches at strategic positions about the layout for ease of control. It is customary to have a controller near at hand, but if plug-in hand-held controllers are used, it is only necessary to have sockets at each panel; the operator merely plugs in to whichever location he finds most convenient. In many cases with twin-cab control, there are two panels at opposing points of the layout, each panel controlling the immediate area; in practice, the operator either sets a section to his own controller or to the other operator's unit. In this way one operator drives a train for the whole journey, and local control is only exercised after the train has come to a halt and shunting takes place.

607 What sort of switches are best for cab control?

There are three types of switch commonly used. The most readily available are centre-off changeover switches. Ex-telephone key switches are very popular, partly because of price, mainly because of the number of contacts provided, but they are not easily located. Rotary switches provide a wider range of options and can be built up in multiple banks to provide additional circuits.

608 Is it necessary to have a changeover switch on every section?

In many locations – locomotive yards are an obvious example – there is need for a large number of isolated sections, yet at any given moment only one locomotive will be moving. Here, the entire yard would be one cab section, with the local isolating sections then fed from this main input (see Plate 33).

609 I have several small yards scattered around the system. Obviously, it is best to operate these from a local panel, which would seem to involve a large number of controllers. Is there any way of keeping the relative simplicity of twin-cab control with this type of layout?

The answer is to have a 'king switch' at each local panel to allow the local operator to switch from the main feed from either the blue or red controller to the local controller. This allows you to shunt the yard locally, then pass control of the train over to the main panel when it is time to depart.

610 Is it possible to arrange matters so that when the key points are thrown, control is transferred to the appropriate controller?

This is not only possible, but could be regarded as highly desirable. The principle is quite straightforward – changeover switches are linked to the points to transfer certain section controls to the appropriate controller.

A typical case is that of a terminal bay in a through station (see Plate 33). Normally, when all points are set for through running, the bay would be isolated. When the points are set for the up road, power for the bay platform would be supplied through the up controller; when set to run into the down road, the power would be taken from the down controller. It will be seen that there is a section of the up line which would be thus switched to the down controller when the crossover is reversed, and that when the point leading to the bay is reversed, the bay road takes power from this section. Whilst we have talked of up and down controllers, in practice, with twin-cab control, these would be either the red or blue controller, depending upon which way the sections have been selected.

611 I have seen a reference to a system of cab control where each controller had a panel which allowed the operator to connect his controller to any section on the layout. How is this arranged?

This is an early US arrangement of cab control, where, as you say, every controller has a complete track panel and the operator selects the section he wishes to run into. It is fairly simple in concept and since all section switches are simple on-off toggles, the cost is fairly low at each stage. Indeed, the idea was to begin by providing only one panel and then add to this as you develop the layout. The only snag is that unless the operators work in a disciplined manner according to a carefully planned schedule, there is a considerable risk of two or more operators deciding to switch power into one key section. Whilst this

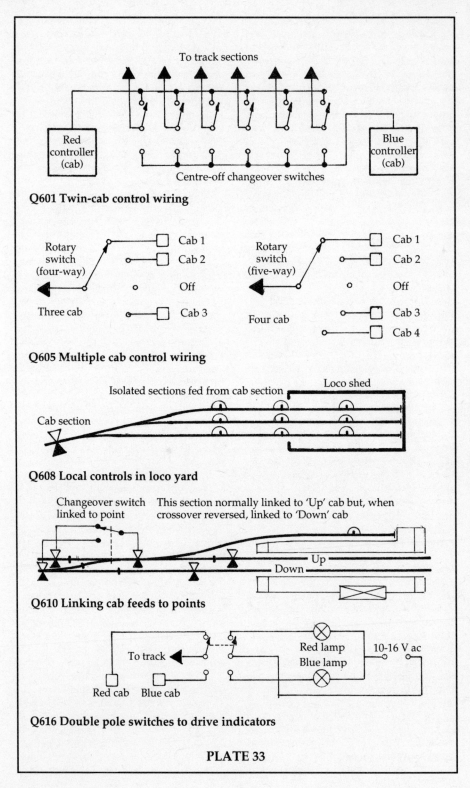

To track sections

Red controller (cab)

Blue controller (cab)

Centre-off changeover switches

Q601 Twin-cab control wiring

Rotary switch (four-way)

Three cab

Cab 1
Cab 2
Off
Cab 3

Rotary switch (five-way)

Four cab

Cab 1
Cab 2
Off
Cab 3
Cab 4

Q605 Multiple cab control wiring

Isolated sections fed from cab section

Loco shed

Cab section

Q608 Local controls in loco yard

Changeover switch linked to point

This section normally linked to 'Up' cab but, when crossover reversed, linked to 'Down' cab

Up

Down

Q610 Linking cab feeds to points

To track

Red lamp
Blue lamp

10-16 V ac

Red cab   Blue cab

Q616 Double pole switches to drive indicators

PLATE 33

might be thought to lead to a collision, the usual result is that at least one controller is set in reverse to the others and the cut-outs came into action. The system has fallen out of favour in the US and hardly gained ground in the UK, where the trend towards smaller layouts favoured the simple and relatively foolproof twin-cab system.

612 **I have seen reference to a system of cab control where 'wander leads' are plugged into sockets on a control panel. What are the advantages of this system?**

This arrangement is based on the obsolete telephone jack switchboard and has the apparent merit of simplicity, low cost and, above all, a means of avoiding getting two or more controllers hooked into one section. At the time, since the exequipment market was plentifully stocked with suitable plugs and sockets which were sold at ridiculous prices, the idea had considerable attractions. Unfortunately it was soon discovered that it was also an excellent method of getting a number of wires caught in a tangle, and it has not surprisingly fallen out of favour. Its demise has been hastened by the fact that plugs and sockets are no longer readily available at bargain prices.

613 **Must I install cab control at the outset or is it possible to provide this at a later stage of development?**

Although there are advantages in providing some form of cab control from the outset, it is by no means essential to do so. Indeed, it is probably best to begin with a fairly simple set-up and defer the construction of a final panel until not only have all the tracks been properly tested, but you also have a better understanding of the operating requirements of the layout. It is all too easy in the early stages of development to make the control panel over-elaborate in order to cater for possibilities which are either not needed, or, in some cases, quite impracticable.

614 **What is the best type of controller for a cab control system – panel-mounting or hand-held?**

A good deal depends on the type of layout. The hand-held controller allows the operator to move around and, to a considerable extent, keep pace with the train he is driving; on the face of it, this might seem more in tune with the underlying principles of the system. With plug-in hand-held controls, the operators can move freely around the system, providing that there are no obstructions to make this difficult. Many US designs follow this principle, and it is an idea worth copying where there is reasonable space available, as with an N gauge system in a garage. However, where several operators are involved, it is all too easy for them to get into each other's way and even to get the controller leads entangled.

615 **Which is the best arrangement for a cab control panel – a geographic layout, with section switches on the appropriate part of the panel, or uniform banks of switches?**

Both arrangements have their merits. However, as the more sophisticated forms of cab control are generally installed when the layout is in a fairly advanced stage of development, the geographic panel is greatly favoured. However, the design of the panel is not a key factor in cab control.

616 **I have only been able to obtain double pole centre-off changeover switches for my twin-cab system. As only one set of contacts is needed to control power to the various sections, what can I do with the other set?**

A very attractive arrangement is to use these contacts to energise indicator lights on a track diagram (see Plate 33). This can be particularly useful if there are two or more selector panels, as it is then possible to arrange a single display panel showing whether a section is energised or not and, if so, whether it is connected to the red or blue controller. If LEDs are used rather than lamps, it will be necessary to have red and green lights. The only snag is that it more than doubles the amount of wire required, much of which will be in the form of a massive multi-core lead to the indicator panel.

617 There seem to be innumerable ways of arranging a cab control system. Which do you think is the best to adopt?

Cab control is essentially a flexible system for connecting the controller to specific sections of track to enable the operator to drive his train where he wishes. The exact arrangement depends on the design of the layout and the favoured method of operation. For a modest layout, a twin-cab system is adequate for most needs and makes a good starting point.

618 What is common return wiring?

This is a system of model railway electrification where all return leads are connected to one common wire (see Plate 34). This reduces the amount of wiring involved and is basically a standard wiring system where a number of connections are made to a 'bus bar'. What this means, in effect, is that one lead from each controller is taken direct to the return wire and all switches are placed in the feed wires. *With common return wiring, each controller must be fed from a separate output from the transformer or transformers.*

619 What is a 'bus bar'?

Initially, it was – and occasionally still is – a strip of copper to which a number of leads were connected. It was called an omnibus circuit as it was for all wires, and the word was shortened in use.

620 If all controllers are connected together in this fashion, what happens when positive current from one controller meets negative current from the other. Doesn't that cause a short circuit?

Positive and negative are relative terms – in other words, a particular lead may be positive in relation to one wire and negative in relation to another. Where two separate power sources are concerned, no such relationship exists. It is normal practice to connect some part of an electrical circuit to earth, which is, in practice, a gigantic common return. However, the fact that you can connect positive to negative without difficulty is best demonstrated by any battery-powered device, where a number of cells are connected positive to negative to provide the necessary voltage.

621 I have a unit with two controllers. Can I use this with common return wiring?

All modern twin controller units are provided with transformers with two or more completely separate secondary windings on the transformer. These are completely independent of each other and may therefore be used with common return wiring (see Plate 34).

622 I have seen references to split potential wiring. What is this please?

You've been looking in an old textbook! Split potential wiring is an obsolete system of control, devised when it was customary to have one single power unit to supply the whole layout; indeed, it was largely based on the use of lead-acid secondary batteries (accumulators). The unit had a total output of 24 V with a centre tapping providing two 12 V outputs, one positive in relation to the common lead, and one negative (see Plate 34). The controllers took power from whichever side of the supply was needed, thus providing a common return wiring system. In practice, the full output of the unit could never be fully utilised for although the 3 amp split potential unit could actually deliver 6 amps at full power (3 amps on each side), because one cannot, on a normal layout, balance the two directions of running, this meant that a 3 amp unit could not guarantee to be able work more than three trains at once.

623 Would it not be more convenient and cheaper to have one single unit rather than several smaller units?

If one single unit is used, it is necessary, at the outset, to decide exactly how much power will ultimately be needed for the layout. This is not only rather difficult, but means that, at the outset, the modeller is faced with an extremely heavy outlay at a time when there are numerous other essential items needed. Furthermore, if the layout expands it is quite likely that what appeared to be a very powerful unit turns out to be rather inadequate. With the smaller units, one

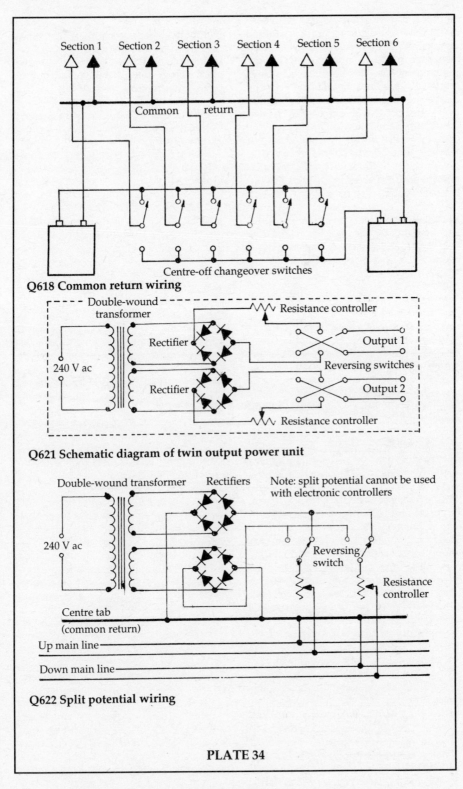

Q618 Common return wiring

Section 1 Section 2 Section 3 Section 4 Section 5 Section 6

Common return

Centre-off changeover switches

Q621 Schematic diagram of twin output power unit

Double-wound transformer

Resistance controller

240 V ac

Rectifier

Output 1

Reversing switches

Rectifier

Output 2

Resistance controller

Q622 Split potential wiring

Double-wound transformer   Rectifiers   Note: split potential cannot be used with electronic controllers

240 V ac

Reversing switch

Resistance controller

Centre tab
(common return)

Up main line

Down main line

PLATE 34

builds up power supplies as they are required. The smaller unit is also much better suited to mass production, and certainly a lot easier to stock in model shops. More to the point, large power packs need to be custom-built for the individual and are correspondingly more costly per amp supplied than the mass-produced standard units.

624 I happen to have two fairly powerful 12 V dc power units. Could I use these for split potential?
In theory, yes. In practice you would not be able to use any current commercial controller and therefore it would be necessary to build your own. As I said earlier (Q622), the system is obsolescent and is frankly not worth considering.

Section 4:5
Reverse loops and triangles

625 How do I wire a reverse loop to prevent setting up a permanent short circuit when opposing polarity rails meet around the loop?
The most straightforward approach is to isolate the entire loop completely with double isolation breaks in the rails near to the end of each leg of the loop, leaving approximately a train length minimum between the breaks. This section is now fed from the main output by means of a DPDT reversing switch (see Plate 35). It is necessary to stop the train on the loop and reverse both the main controller, so that the train can now proceed in the opposite direction, and the DPDT switch, so that the polarity of the rails now matches the other end of the loop.

626 The operation of the switches appears to be a trifle complicated. Can it be simplified in any fashion?
If the DPDT switch is replaced by a pair of changeover switches, preferably microswitches, wired for reversal and coupled to the junction turnout tiebar, the polarity of the rails can be automatically aligned. It will, however, still be necessary to bring the train to a halt.

627 I'm not sure that I care for the fact that the train has to be halted.

Is this a liability?
Not necessarily so. In many cases the reverse loop is partially in tunnel, and frequently the tunnelled section is provided with loops so that trains may be stored and brought out again in a different sequence. In such cases the train would normally stop in the tunnel. Where the loop is fully exposed, a simple halt platform can be provided to account for the stop. Alternatively, the provision of proper junction signals provides a rational reason for stopping the train – the signals can be set against it.

628 Is there a way of avoiding having to stop the train?
One straightforward method is to feed the reverse loop from a separate controller. Whilst the train is traversing the loop, the main controller is reversed, thus reversing the relative polarities of the loop and main line (see Plate 35). If this is single track then the junction points are reversed as soon as the last vehicle in the train has cleared the junction. Where the loop forms part of a double-track system, the junction can remain set. This arrangement is particularly suited for layouts where the loop forms a major part of the main line.

629 Is it possible to get continuous running around a reverse loop with just one controller?
If the controller has a separate reversing switch the auxiliary DPDT reversing switch can be wired across the input terminals of the original reversing switch (see Plate 35). This allows either section to be changed in relative polarity independently of each other, and is a very elegant solution for anyone with a modicum of electrical expertise. If you ignore the controller's switch altogether and then wire two reversing switches from the output, you will achieve the same end with only slightly increased cost.

630 Could this arrangement be used with a centre-off single-knob-type controller?
Not without some difficulty and confusion, since it would be difficult to avoid using the main controller for reversing. In a like manner, it would be difficult to apply to a combined power unit/con-

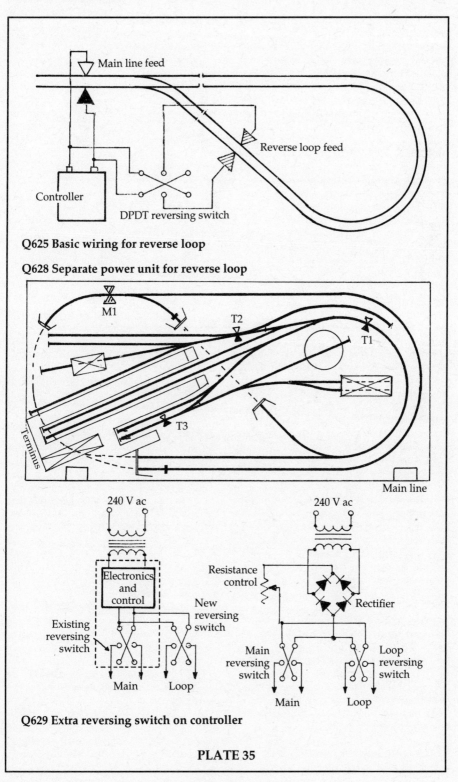

Q625 Basic wiring for reverse loop

Main line feed

Reverse loop feed

Controller

DPDT reversing switch

Q628 Separate power unit for reverse loop

M1

T2

T1

Terminus

T3

Main line

240 V ac

240 V ac

Electronics
and
control

Resistance
control

Rectifier

Existing
reversing
switch

New
reversing
switch

Main
reversing
switch

Loop
reversing
switch

Main

Loop

Main

Loop

Q629 Extra reversing switch on controller

PLATE 35

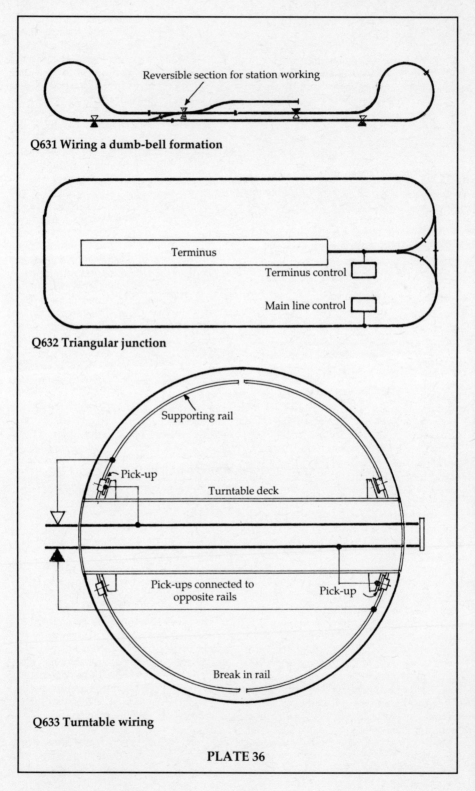

Q631 Wiring a dumb-bell formation

Reversible section for station working

Q632 Triangular junction

Terminus

Terminus control

Main line control

Q633 Turntable wiring

Supporting rail

Pick-up

Turntable deck

Pick-ups connected to
opposite rails

Pick-up

Break in rail

PLATE 36

troller since access to the control section is virtually ruled out.

631 I am considering building a 'dumb-bell' layout. Does this mean I must have two reverse loop feeds at each end of the layout?

Not necessarily. A dumb-bell can be regarded as an elongated oval, pinched in at the centre. As a result, the up and down tracks can be treated as part of one complete circuit and the only connections causing a conflict between feed and return rails would be crossovers and similar features linking the tracks. A simple way of getting round any difficulties is to arbitrarily allocate one side of the station to a reverse role. This can be switched manually or, with a little forethought in planning, the circuits can be transposed by changeover switches linked to the various turnouts and crossovers (see Plate 36). Whilst this would involve a fair amount of planning, the operational advantages would be well worth the effort.

632 How should one wire a triangular junction? I assume it would be very similar to a reverse loop.

The same solution can be applied to such a junction, but in practice the most common use for a triangular junction on a model is to link a terminus station to a continuous main line so that trains can depart and arrive in either direction. It is therefore quite logical to have one set of controls for the terminus and another set for the main line, since the basic pattern of operation will be to have trains trundling around the circuit whilst shunting and remarshalling takes place in the terminus (see Plate 36). When it is desired to bring a train from the terminus out on to the main line, or vice versa, the controllers would naturally be set in unison and, in practice, operators would not have to make any unusual manoeuvres.

633 Although this has nothing to do with loops and triangles, it does involve reversal. How do you wire a two-rail turntable?

There are two possible methods, depending very much on the arrangement of tracks radiating from the table,

and in both cases contacts are provided at each end of the turntable track to mate with similar contacts on the radial tracks. Where only one or two roads are involved it is probably best to feed the current to the table from the radial roads. In this way the table is only energised when the tracks are more or less in line. Where the turntable feeds a number of radial stub tracks, it is more convenient to use the table itself as the feed point, bringing the current in through a commutator-type split-ring pick-up, which provides automatic reversal of the table rails' polarity as it is moved through half a turn.

A popular method of arranging the ring pick-up is to lay the supporting track with standard bullhead rail, soldered to pins, then split this diametrically in two and arrange wipers on each end of the turntable connected to opposite rails. The feed to the circular rail is controlled by an on-off switch. The table contacts now serve to energise the tracks which are in line with the table rails (see Plate 36). This allows each radial road to be isolated and so able to hold a locomotive stationary without the need for numerous switches and, even more to the point, the vigilance of the operator to ensure that only the right locomotive moves.

Section 4:6
Three-rail and overhead wiring

634 Is three-rail wiring particularly difficult?

How times change – this used to be asked about two-rail when three-rail was in vogue! Except for the fact that in order to get self-isolation of sidings, a changeover switch has to be coupled to the tiebar of the turnout, the wiring is slightly simpler. All sectionalising takes place in the third rail – there are no complications with reverse loops or triangles and straightforward track circuits can be arranged if two-rail track is used. The mechanics are something else.

635 What are the problems with three-rail electrification?

For a start, as three-rail flexible track is

no longer manufactured there is the extra work of adding the conductor rail. A central third rail is normally arranged for all-level contact, necessitating special isolation of rails at turnouts and crossings; an outside third rail can foul bogie frames if set to scale spacing, and collectors are difficult to adjust effectively. The only purpose to be served by adopting three-rail electrification today is to be able to use vintage Hornby Dublo locomotives and stock.

636 Why did manufacturers adopt a centre third rail which is unknown on the prototype?

A centre third rail is the only really practical arrangement for a three-rail sectional track system, since it is difficult to devise a straightforward means of connecting the outer rails when they occur on opposite sides of the running rails. There is in addition the problem of arranging an outside conductor rail fixing that will not be damaged when the track is thrown into a box. It is worth noting that there *are* centre third prototypes: the Central Line of the London Underground before refurbishment in 1938-9 was one, whilst the pioneer tube railway, the City & South London, had an offset central third rail before reconstruction. The Volks Electric Railway in Brighton, which began life with two-rail traction, now has an offset central conductor rail.

637 Could a model based on the Southern Region be electrified from the third rail?

Providing there were no reversing loops or triangular junctions on the system, it is in theory practicable to have third rail pick-up for EMUs and electric locomotives combined with two rail for steam and diesel models, using the common return rail for both two- and three-rail supply (see Plate 37). This would permit independent operation of two trains on the same track without electronic complications. However, on most layouts with Southern electric stock, the third rail is purely cosmetic or else is used to provide a supply of current for train lighting. These comments also apply to models of London Transport four-rail systems.

638 Could you please explain the stud contact system?

Stud contact was introduced in Britain immediately after the war as a way of getting something close to the appearance of two-rail whilst retaining three-rail uninsulated wheels and track. The idea was based on early electric tramway practice, but the studs are raised slightly above sleeper level and the skate collector is generally arranged on parallelogram links to keep it as level as possible (see Plate 37). At turnouts and crossings the studs are slowly brought up above rail level to carry the skate clear above the running rails.

639 The Marklin system is electrified by stud contact. Why is this?

Marklin, who remained faithful to their pre-war electrification standards, developed this system to improve the appearance of their new tracks. As a locomotive fitted with a stud contact skate will also run on centre third rail track, this enabled them to maintain faith with established users. Similarly, Marklin alone retain ac supply, but many of their locomotives are now made available for 12 V dc two-rail working under the Hamo label.

640 Is it possible to use overhead catenary for electrical collection?

This is reasonably straightforward, since a high proportion of model overhead electric locomotives are provided with a switch to allow pick-up from two-rail or overhead. Providing care is taken to ensure that all locomotives have their earthed wheels the same way round, it is possible to work an overhead electric system on the twin system, but this precludes the use of reversing loops or triangles (see Plate 37). However, it must be admitted that few layouts equipped with overhead catenary use this as anything more than a cosmetic feature, preferring to leave tunnelled tracks without overhead.

641 How is it possible to persuade the pantographs of an overhead electric train to drop down to the catenary if they are allowed to spring up to their full height on the hidden sections?

A long inverted ramp, usually made of

stiff wire, is fitted at the entrance and exit of each tunnel mouth – on the hidden side, of course. This brings the pantograph down to the level of the catenary (see Plate 37).

642 How can you place stock on the track of an overhead electrified layout? The wires get in the way and I have the utmost trouble getting the wheels on the track.

It is almost always possible to arrange a stub siding without overhead wires where stock can be placed on the rails without any greater difficulty than is experienced on a normal two-rail system. However, the use of a re-railing system is well worthwhile, especially in N gauge.

643 Is it possible to make one's own overhead system?

It is certainly possible if you have a reasonable amount of skill in fine metalwork. Although the catenary appears difficult, it is readily built in sections on a simple wood and pin soldering fixture. The supports are another thing altogether, but once again a couple of suitable soldering jigs will speed production.

Section 4:7
Control panels

644 What is the best design for a control panel?

This is really a matter of personal preference. The main thing to bear in mind is that it should be convenient to use and that it should be possible for a fellow enthusiast to take over the controls without having to go through a long period of training. Excessive complication is not a good idea.

645 At what angle should the panel be set?

This is another matter for personal choice, unless it is wished to match the angle to your power unit/controllers. Clearly, the more vertical the board, the less space it occupies, but the nearer it gets to the vertical, the more difficult it is to see the switches.

646 What material is best for the front of a control panel?

For cost and convenience, good-quality 3 mm ply is preferable, but any stiff insulating material is quite sound. Metal panels preclude any chance of incorporating probe-type point operation.

647 Is it best to arrange the section switches on a miniature track plan or put then in ranks?

Once again, it is a matter of individual choice. The geographic-pattern panel is easier to understand but, should you alter the layout, a partial or full reconstruction is necessary. It also takes up more space. With ranks of switches, a simple annotated diagram provides the key, and alterations are easily accommodated (see Plate 37).

648 I need to keep the panel as compact as possible. Should I use subminiature toggle switches?

The minimum spacing between individual switches is governed by the size of a finger, and since the more robust standard miniature toggle switch is small enough for optimum spacing, there is nothing to be gained. However, the subminiature pattern looks more in keeping with a small geographic diagram. It is partly a matter of taste, but mainly a question of cost and availability, since either type of switch is equally good.

649 Do you recommend slider switches?

There are two snags with slider switches. The first is that they are less easy to fit into a panel – two holes and a slot have to be cut – whereas toggle switches fit into a single drilled hole. The second is that slider switches do not take kindly to being moved when passing high currents, and if this is done repeatedly their life will be shortened. On the other hand they are often appreciably cheaper than toggle switches and are normally supplied as changeover types, frequently with a centre-off position.

650 Where should a control panel be located?

The ideal location is as close to the main array of trackwork in the station as possible. This not only shortens the wiring

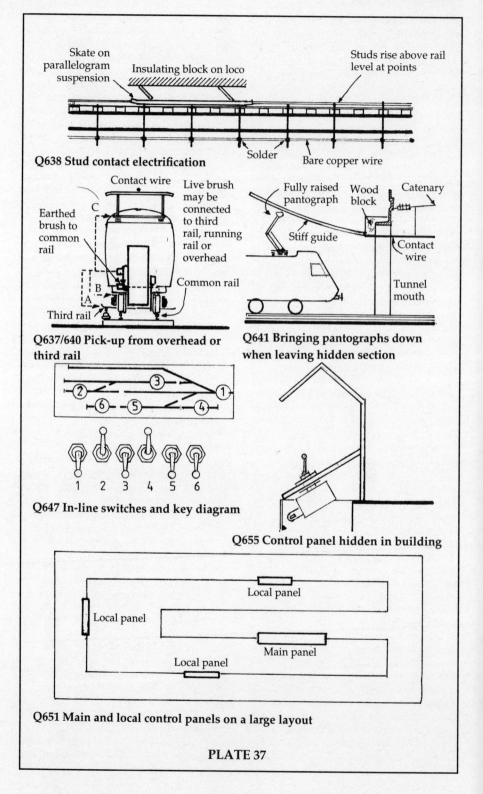

Skate on parallelogram suspension

Insulating block on loco

Studs rise above rail level at points

Solder

Bare copper wire

Q638 Stud contact electrification

Contact wire

C

Earthed brush to common rail

Live brush may be connected to third rail, running rail or overhead

Common rail

B

A

Third rail

Q637/640 Pick-up from overhead or third rail

Fully raised pantograph

Wood block

Catenary

Stiff guide

Contact wire

Tunnel mouth

Q641 Bringing pantographs down when leaving hidden section

1 2 3
6 5 4

1 2 3 4 5 6

Q647 In-line switches and key diagram

Q655 Control panel hidden in building

Local panel

Local panel

Local panel

Main panel

Local panel

Q651 Main and local control panels on a large layout

PLATE 37

involved, but also places the operator in the location where most movement takes place.

651 I am building a fairly large system with several stations. Should I have one large central panel or smaller panels situated at each principal station?

This is bound up with the method of operation envisaged. The central panel enables one operator to control the whole of the layout, although the difficulties of spotting trains accurately at a distance make it imperative to keep the main shunting and train formation work close to the panel. With several panels, a number of operators can run the model in a very realistic fashion and shunting can take place all over the system, but single-handed operation can get a little fraught (see Plate 37).

652 Is it possible to combine both approaches so that I can run the layout single-handed when my friends are not around?

There is nothing particularly difficult about this. The main panel is located beside the principal station, with smaller, relatively simple panels elsewhere. These are provided with a king switch which transfers control of the main running roads to the main panel. It is, however, a good idea to take this into consideration when designing the layout, since it is often possible to arrange two important stations, or a station and a large marshalling yard, on opposite sides of a reasonably large operating well. In this way one man can control both panels, or two can work back-to-back.

653 How is a king switch arranged and what sort of switch is needed?

A king switch is a multi-pole two-way changeover switch which transfers certain local circuits to the main panel. The most readily available form of switch is a two-position rotary switch with several banks of contacts, and is obtainable, usually to order, from major electrical suppliers.

654 Should the controllers be built into the panels?

Most people find this neater and more convenient, but it does mean that combined power unit/controllers cannot be readily used, and panel-mounting modules are to be preferred. This is particularly so where it is desired to build the panel into a portable layout, for the weight of the transformer and casing on a standard unit is quite appreciable. It is much simpler to keep the transformers on the floor and run a 16 V ac supply up to the layout.

655 How can one disguise the presence of a control panel on a scenic portable layout?

There are several tried and tested approaches. One is to build the panel into the side of the baseboard, and this is most readily done inside a hill or cutting projecting above the framing. Another is to build the panel inside a suitable building (see Plate 37). A signal box is a popular choice, but in the smaller scales this will limit the size of the panel; a long warehouse or factory is probably better. The building is built around a 3 mm ply carcase and the roof is arranged to lift off for operating purposes.

656 Many large exhibition layouts have a large and impressive control panel set some distance from the layout proper. Is this suitable for home use?

There is no reason not to have such a panel on a home layout, providing that you enjoy building such things. Whilst the main purpose of these panels is to enable one experienced operator to act as the controller, and oversee the working of the layout whilst other members drive the trains, they are equally effective in the home environment. Such panels indicate clearly that at least one member of the group is a keen electrician and is prepared to spend several months assembling the panel. Building elaborate control panels is a recognised facet of this complex hobby of ours. One point that should not be overlooked is that if there are 50 leads from the panel – and this is quite a modest figure – and the panel is only 1 metre from the layout, at least two 100 m spools of low-voltage flexible wire will be needed to make up the connecting cable. To this one must add the necessary multi-pin plugs and sockets, the switches and other equipment, as well as the timber needed for the panel housing. Such panels frequently cost more than a top-quality locomotive.

657 I would like to incorporate meters and indicators in my panel. How should I set about this?

With extreme caution. For a start, meters have little purpose on a layout control panel; their main value lies at the workbench, where locomotives are put under test. During normal operation the exact voltage and amperage drawn is of little importance. Indicators which merely repeat a condition that is visible to the operator are likewise of little real value, but when they show the condition of hidden tracks and remote turnouts they have some use.

The most important indicators, 'power on' and 'overload', are incorporated in most panel-mounting controllers and do not require special wiring. However, all indicators add to the complexity of a panel, and unless you have a fair idea how to set about wiring them it is probably best to avoid the additional work and concentrate on getting the essentials correctly wired.

658 My layout is developing nicely and I have gained confidence in my ability to carry out wiring. I rather regret having opted for a fairly simple control panel which I feel restricts the operating potential of the layout. Would you advise me to add extra features to the existing board, or would it be better to make a fresh start?

The best way to improve overall control is to spend a good deal of time thinking very carefully about the way you wish to operate the layout, in particular looking carefully at the sectionalisation to see if you need to modify this. Once your plans are made, it is better to construct an entirely new panel which can be fully wired and bench-tested away from the layout. Once you are satisfied that the new board is correct, it is a relatively simple matter to disconnect the old panel and install the new one. The task will be simplified if you have kept a record of the original wiring in a wiring book, whilst if you have used tag strips to terminate the layout wiring proper,

the installation of the new board will be largely a matter of cutting away the old panel leads, removing the old panel and setting the new one in place and then connecting wires from the panel to the layout tag strips.

Section 4:8
Automatic control and track detection

659 I intend to instal full automatic control on my layout, but I am having considerable difficulty designing the various circuits. Can you help?

It depends on what you mean by full automatic control. If you intend to have the entire layout running without attention, with points and signals being set automatically, locomotives uncoupling or shunting trains without a human hand on the controls, you are attempting a task that few experienced electricians would tackle. Our advice in this case is to set about the job in stages, starting with the straightforward business of applying automatic control to the main line so that you can have several trains in action at once. After this, develop circuits to carry out the various functions you require.

There are some simple ground rules to keep in mind. The first is that in order to have two or more trains in action on a single stretch of line you need a very long main line; it is no use considering this on a small continuous run. The second is that when locomotives are to stop and start without attention, and coaches and wagons are to be uncoupled, the performance of every unit must be absolutely impeccable. Full automatic control implies complete reliability of every part for if only one unit fails, the whole sequence goes awry.

660 How can I control two or more trains on a circuit so that they will operate automatically without collision?

The first requirement is sufficient track to enable the trains to be separated by an isolated section. For two trains on one circuit the minimum number of sections is three, but four are preferable. Each section should be at least 300 mm longer than the longest train, preferably as much as twice the length of the normal train you intend to use. As each train enters a section its presence is detected and a relay isolates the section behind. As an added refinement, the home signal controlling entry into the isolated section should be set at stop.

661 Is it possible to get a commercial device that will operate a section of main line automatically?

Many German manufacturers, notably Fleischmann and Marklin, produce automatic control kits. These are normally small bistable relays operated by detection triggers and provided with one set of changeover contacts, and are sold singly or in sets of three together with instructions. Peco supply a changeover switch to fit to their point motor, converting it into a bistable relay that can be used for the same purpose. Although relatively simple in concept and construction, bistable relays, used in sufficient numbers, can carry out quite complicated tasks, as many exhibition layouts by Marklin and Fleischmann have demonstrated in the past.

662 Is it possible to make a train slow down automatically when entering an isolated section?

This can be done electronically through a specialised controller, but a more generally adopted method is to have a slowing section immediately before the stop section. This consists of a relatively short length of isolated track fed through a small wire-round resistance, generally around 10 ohms value (see Plate 38). If the train is not to stop, then this resistance is bypassed by a relay contact. To get a more gradual start, once again one can resort to electronic control; alternatively, the stop section can be energised through another wire-wound resister.

663 Where does one get these wire-wound resistances?

The larger electrical suppliers can often provide them to order. They can also produce replacement coils for electric fires – these are made from resistance wire and by cutting short lengths from

the main coil, a small resistance capable of carrying well in excess of the 1.5 amp maximum of the average model railway traction circuit can be made. A multimeter is needed to find out the exact resistance, but the usual approach is to cut off a short length and proceed to fine tune the resistance by trial and error. The ends of the resistance coil should be connected to a pair of screws in a block of wood, and the wires – which are fairly stiff – should be bent so that no part of the coil is touching anything. These resistances can get fairly hot, but if suspended in air cool down quite rapidly; they are not in circuit long enough to cause any real problems.

664 How can I arrange for a train to stop for a short period in a station?

The simplest arrangement is to use a thermal delay switch. This consists of a bi-metallic strip which is surrounded by a small heating coil which, when current is passed through, makes the strip bend and change contacts (see Plate 38). It is fairly crude but quite effective, providing that the room temperature is not too high for it to cool down between trains. However, in recent years electronic delay circuits have grown in popularity. These can be made up around a suitable capacitor which is slowly charged through a ballast resistor until it is able to trigger a semi-conductor switch. It can take the form of an integral circuit which performs the same function. The advantage of the electronic circuit is that it is less temperamental and much easier to time with some degree of accuracy. Furthermore, by providing several values of bleed resistor, selected through a rotary switch or relay bank, a number of different stopping times can be arranged.

A totally different approach involves the interaction of a train on another track, which starts the first train when it passes a specific point on the layout.

665 How can I arrange for a branch train to shuttle back and forth along a single track?

Such circuits incorporate two elements: a flip-flop circuit or a bi-stable relay actuated by the arrival of the train at one end of the track to reverse the traction current, and a delay circuit to allow the train to pause for a predetermined time at each end.

666 I would like the shuttle train to wait in a tunnel for some considerable period to simulate its journey along and back a lengthy feeder branch. Most delay circuits seem to be of fairly short duration. What do you suggest?

The delay in an electronic circuit depends very much on the size of the capacitor: the bigger its value, the longer the wait. Advanced integrated circuits can be arranged for extensive delays – this is how the modern alarm radio works. However, this is something for the electronic specialist. A cam-operated microswitch, driven by a slow-running geared motor, can provide quite an appreciable wait, though usually at the expense of some noise. This is not necessarily a bad thing, as it does let you know that something is happening and that the train will ultimately reappear, whereas absolute silence could mean all is well or that the circuit has gone on the blink again.

667 I have seen models where a variety of devices are actuated in a predetermined order. How is this done?

In most cases the sequence is governed by a strowger or multi-selector switch. The contacts on the multi-selector are arranged to energise various circuits and some system of advancing the switch regularly is installed. This is frequently a geared motor fitted with a cam on the final drive shaft which actuates a microswitch.

668 Is it possible to automate level crossing gates?

The modern lifting barrier type gates are fairly simple to arrange. Indeed, there are versions which were lowered by the weight of the train passing over the crossing, but it is better to have a small motor lower the arms when a train is detected entering the section, with a further circuit to raise them again when the section is clear. The older pattern swing gates take an appreciable time to open and close and it is not so easy to arrange this automatically with the passage of trains. It is possible to link them to the signals so that they open when the signal lever is reversed but the signal arm itself is not set to clear until the gates are fully open. For added protection, the section itself would also be isolated until the gates were fully open. Automated level crossing gates are fairly advanced features and are a major task, comparable to the construction of a locomotive.

669 How is it possible to detect the presence of a train on a two-rail layout where track circuits are impractical?

There are two methods: the use of trigger devices, which are the equivalent of prototype treadles, and track circuits that are compatible with two-rail power supply. The former comprise simple contacts, which complete a circuit through some part of the locomotive, light-dependant devices, short trigger sections of track, and magnetically-operated reed switches. The latter either use relays in series with the power supply or an electronic detection circuit.

670 Which is preferable, a trigger device or a track circuit?

The balance of simplicity leans towards the trigger, but it will only detect the passage of a locomotive or a specially equipped vehicle past a specific point in the track. The track circuit will detect the presence of a locomotive in a specific section, and frequently will detect lighted coaches and vehicles fitted with ballast resistors as well. However, track circuits are not only more sophisticated, but the fact that they share the conductors with traction current creates problems, and the presence of high-frequency lighting or sound systems complicates matters to the point where track circuits, the most vulnerable part of an increasingly complex system, cease to be reliable.

Triggers are independent of traction current, so the circuits are basically more straightforward. The fact that they only detect the passage of a train might be regarded as a weakness in prototypical terms, where track circuits are largely used to prevent a signalman inadvertently admitting a train into an occupied section. This is of less importance on a model where not only are collisions little more than an embarrassing annoyance, but where the much shorter sections – a mere 2 metres as opposed to over 2 kilometres – mean that the possibility of losing of a train in a section is far less likely in practice.

671 Is it possible to instal track detection circuits in an existing layout?

It is not only possible, but is probably the best policy for the less experienced model railway electrician, since it allows one to defer the addition of a lot of extra wiring until the main system is up and running.

There is a further advantage, although it is good practice to determine the operating pattern before finalising the layout design; until a certain amount of hands-on operation has taken place, one cannot be absolutely sure of the full potential of the system or, for that matter, of any minor faults that may have crawled into the overall plan. It is thus possible to work out a much better operating schedule and hence a far better system of detection once you know, to take just one point, the best places on the layout for trains to stop.

672 I tried placing a relay in series with the power supply but it only served to stop the train. What went wrong?

Basically, you either used the wrong circuit or the wrong type of relay. For a simple series track circuit the extremely rare low-resistance relay, with a resistance under 5 ohms, must be used. The normal relay, with a coil resistance of anything from 500 to 3,000 ohms, is only suited for detection of trains held in hidden loops and sidings, or in conjunction with a more sophisticated circuit.

673 I would like to be able to detect which of my hidden loops holds a train. How can this be done without too many complications?

The simplest arrangement is to provide a holding circuit which can be isolated by a switch on the panel. If a standard 16 V miniature lamp, ideally in an indicator socket, is wired across the switch it will, when fully lit, have sufficient resistance to stop the locomotive (see Plate 38). A more sophisticated arrangement places a high-resistance relay in series with the holding circuit. This relay has a latching circuit, a circuit to interrupt supply to the holding section, and a further circuit to illuminate an indicator light on the panel. When a locomotive enters the section, the relay is energised and the latching circuit holds it in this condition. At the same time the section is isolated and the indicator lamp is lit. To release the train, a bypass circuit, controlled by a push-button, short circuits the relay coil, sending current direct to the locomotive and simultaneously releasing the latch on the relay which reverts to its normal state. The release circuit can be combined with some form of selector circuit to set the correct exit road.

674 Is it possible to arrange a normal track circuit using a high-resistance relay?

This can be done by having a completely separate power supply for the relay, which is so wired that, when the circuit is completed by the locomotive, the feed from the controller is substituted for the relay supply. This has one small snag, however – the relay circuit is now completed through the controller and so remains actuated even when the train has left the track circuited section, and will remain so until the supply is interrupted. This can be done by several means. One is to interrupt the supply to the track momentarily by means of a mechanical switch, so that when a section is clear, the relay drops out of circuit. Another is to switch the relay out by means of contacts on the next track circuit relay along the line; clearly this will only work when the trains are proceeding one direction only. The final relay in a series must be released by other means, possibly a treadle-type contact.

A third approach involves the use of diodes to block the reverse surge that occurs when the train leaves the section. This type of detection is falling into disfavour since the development of electronic sensing circuits such as the Twin T system.

675 What exactly is Twin T detection?

An electronic track detector developed

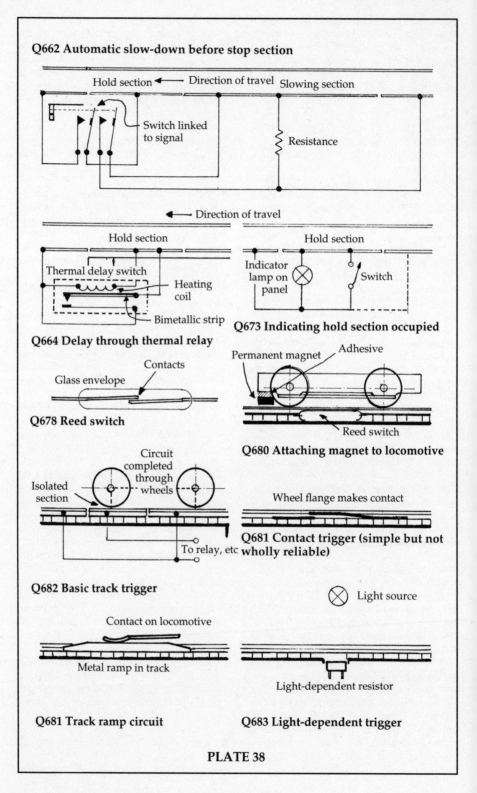

Q662 Automatic slow-down before stop section

Hold section ◄─── Direction of travel   Slowing section

Switch linked to signal

Resistance

◄─── Direction of travel

Hold section

Thermal delay switch

Heating coil

Bimetallic strip

Q664 Delay through thermal relay

Hold section

Indicator lamp on panel

Switch

Q673 Indicating hold section occupied

Contacts

Glass envelope

Q678 Reed switch

Permanent magnet   Adhesive

Reed switch

Q680 Attaching magnet to locomotive

Circuit completed through wheels

Isolated section

To relay, etc

Q682 Basic track trigger

Wheel flange makes contact

Q681 Contact trigger (simple but not wholly reliable)

⊗ Light source

Contact on locomotive

Metal ramp in track

Light-dependent resistor

Q681 Track ramp circuit

Q683 Light-dependent trigger

PLATE 38

by Linn Westcott of *Model Railroader*. It uses a pair of transistors and diodes to detect a current flow in either direction in a circuit and so energise an output circuit. This is normally used to energise a relay, but it could equally be employed to drive electronic circuitry.

676 Where can I get Twin T detectors?

We know of no manufacturer – the circuits are normally built in the home workshop. Information on electronic circuits for model railways is given in two excellent handbooks, *Model Railway Electronics* by Roger Amos, and *Practical Electronic Circuits for Model Railroaders* by Peter J.Thorne (see the Bibliography). At least one of these should be in the possession of anyone wishing to apply electronics to his layout. Clearly, in the space of a short answer we cannot cover the same ground as a large book on the subject.

677 What is the best type of trigger device?

Each system has its advantages and disadvantages. The reed switch and magnet is extremely versatile and, since it does not rely on physical contact, it is more reliable than the contact-pattern trigger, providing that the relatively delicate contacts inside the reed switch are not overloaded. In addition, it is necessary to fit magnets to locomotives and, on occasions, coaches.

The contact trigger is made in the home workshop, often from scrap metal, and is extremely cost-effective. The track trigger is a trifle crude in action but, when coupled with sensitive relays, remarkably effective.

Light-dependant systems are the only ones which will detect all vehicles and can unerringly pinpoint the front of the train – an important factor when dealing with storage sidings which are barely long enough to take the trains being run on the layout. They are, however, the most costly approach to the matter.

It should be pointed out that since the circuits involved remain the same no matter what type of trigger is used, there is no reason why two or more types should not be used on one layout.

678 What is a reed switch?

A set of contacts sealed in a glass capsule which make or break when in a magnetic field (see Plate 38). They will only switch relatively low currents but are extremely reliable and can be fitted in a number of different places in order to detect different types of train.

679 How can one prevent a reed switch from getting too heavy a discharge?

There are two lines of defence. One is to use a transistorised circuit – this opens a whole realm of possibilities. The other is to deal with the cause of the damage. When an inductive circuit is broken, a high-voltage reverse surge is fed into the circuit. If the circuit uses direct current, as is the case with standard relays, a reverse diode placed across the coil will effectively short-circuit the surge, preventing it from doing any damage.

680 How do you attach a permanent magnet to a locomotive?

The simplest method is to use double-sided self-adhesive tape, but for a more permanent fixing a little epoxy resin or cyanoacrylate glue can be used (see Plate 38). For visiting locomotives and/or stock, a little Blu-tak can be used to hold a spare magnet temporarily in place.

681 How is a contact trigger best arranged?

There are various schools of thought. One has a contact shoe on the locomotive which contacts a ramp in the track (the similarity to the old GWR Automatic Train Control system is very marked), while another places a contact near to a rail so that it is touched by the back of a wheel flange, thus completing the circuit (see Plate 38). The main snag with this is that the small gap between contact and rail can easily get smaller and so give a false indication. In the larger scales it is possible to fit a prototypical treadle mechanism that is depressed by the wheel flanges, making contact with a microswitch mounted below the baseboard.

682 What exactly is a track trigger and how does one make it?

A track trigger is a short isolated section

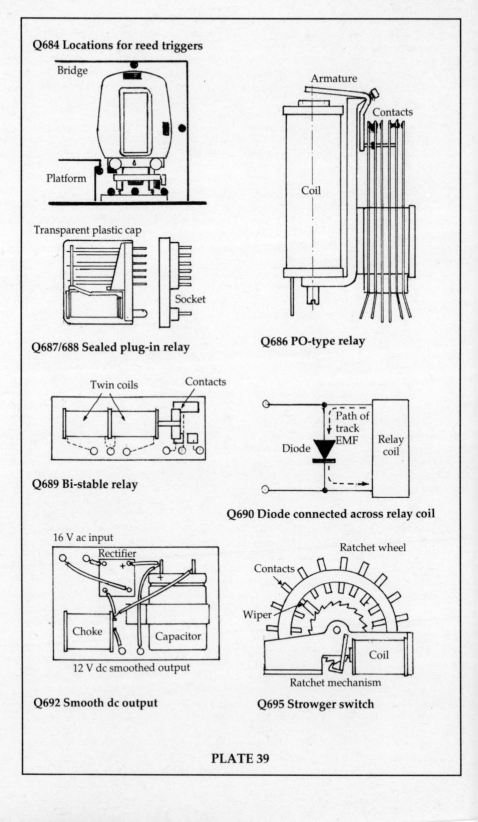

Q684 Locations for reed triggers

Bridge

Platform

Armature

Contacts

Coil

Q686 PO-type relay

Transparent plastic cap

Socket

Q687/688 Sealed plug-in relay

Twin coils   Contacts

Q689 Bi-stable relay

Path of track EMF

Diode

Relay coil

Q690 Diode connected across relay coil

16 V ac input

Rectifier

Choke   Capacitor

12 V dc smoothed output

Q692 Smooth dc output

Ratchet wheel

Contacts

Wiper

Coil

Ratchet mechanism

Q695 Strowger switch

PLATE 39

between 20 and 30 mm in length situated in the return rail. The traction circuit is carried around this section, which is connected to the return side of a relay coil. When a locomotive's wheels pass over this section the return circuit is completed and the relay actuated (see Plate 38). Providing that there are ample pick-ups on all locomotives and fast-acting relays are used, the system is surprisingly reliable. To make such a device the rail has to be cut – a small grinding disc in a low-voltage drill is best for this task. The gap is then filled with epoxy resin, although if the section is installed during tracklaying, insulated fishplates can be used with advantage. The running rail is bonded around the trigger section, which is connected to the relay coil.

683 What is a light-dependent device and how does one use it?

There are two basic types of light-sensitive devices used for detection purposes: the photo transistor and the light-dependant resistance. In each case the characteristics of the device are changed when light is shone upon its receptive spot. It is not wise to rely on room illumination – such devices need to be supplemented by a light source, which can be a lamp or an LED, placed so as to direct a beam on to the light-sensitive device. The interruption of this light beam by an item of rolling-stock triggers the detection circuit (see Plate 38). It is generally necessary to couple these devices to a small transistorised amplifier to drive a relay or other device requiring a fairly high current.

684 Is it possible to arrange matters so that only certain stock – a local or branch line train, for example – will be detected?

This is ridiculously simple. The main requirement is some form of fitting on the train, rather than the locomotive, which is detected by a special trigger device. An example of this would be a magnet fitted in the roof or side of a branch-line train, actuating a suitably-situated reed switch. A good place to locate this is in the signal gantry controlling the junction, or a conveniently located overbridge (see Plate 39). A mechanical contact on the underframe of the coach which contacts a lineside ramp is

another possibility. The possible variations are sufficient to allow one to have several such detectors on the layout to control a variety of train movements.

Section 4:9
Relays

685 What is a relay?

A relay is a switching device operated by an electrical circuit. Most relays contain a number of changeover switches, generally of the break-before-make pattern. Some, particularly ex-telephone patterns, also have make-before-break switches incorporated.

686 I have seen reference to PO 3000 relays. What is special about these?

The PO 3000 is a type of relay specified by the telecommunications section of the Post Office (now British Telecom) (see Plate 39). It is a standard telecommunications pattern relay, and its attraction to railway modellers lies in the fact that it is very rugged and, when bought ex-equipment, very cheap. They are now getting very scarce.

687 What is a sealed relay?

A relay with all the mechanism contained in a metal or plastic case; most modern relays are of this pattern (see Plate 39). They have the advantage that with the contacts encased there is little chance of their becoming dirty. In addition, the majority are of the readily replaced plug-in pattern.

688 What is a plug-in relay?

A relay mounted on a multi-pin plug so that it can be readily replaced if it proves faulty. This type is recommended for large exhibition layouts, since a suspect relay can be interchanged for one in stock so quickly that few members of the public even realise that there has been a fault.

689 What is a bi-stable relay?

A relay which is actuated by two coils and has its state changed by passing a momentary current through one or other of the coils (see Plate 39). A point motor fitted with contacts is a bi-stable relay, and since further contacts can be added – either from manufacturer's parts or with microswitches – this is a simple way for the modeller to make such devices. Commercial automatic control systems use this type of relay.

690 Why are diodes sometimes connected across relay coils?

A relay coil is an inductive device and, when switched off, sends a high-voltage reverse pulse through the wires. This can play havoc with any delicate devices in the circuit, but a diode placed across the terminals, biased against the relay dc supply, will effectively short-circuit the pulse (see Plate 39).

691 I have noticed that some circuits are operated by short- circuiting the relay coil. Isn't this undesirable?

Far from it, for although we normally associate short-circuits with a dangerous condition, this particular trick serves to bypass the relay coil and so prevent it from operating. If you check the circuit further you will discover that a resistance is also in circuit to prevent the power supply from being short-circuited as well.

692 I have a relay bank which produces a considerable amount of noise. What should I do to reduce this?

If you're using ac for the relay coils, they will act as buzzers. Normal model railway dc supplies are unsmoothed and generate a 50 Hz hum. Relays should be powered by a smoothed dc supply – a large-value electrolytic capacitor across the dc output and a choke in series does the trick (see Plate 39).

693 What is a capacitor?

A device for storing an electric charge; placed across an unsmoothed circuit it acts in a manner analogous to a flywheel. It is rated not only in microfarads but the working voltage is also given. For 12 V circuits use a 25 V capacitor, of not less than 50 microfarad capacity.

694 What is a choke?

In inductive device – in principle an electro-magnet – which has a high resistance when passing ac current but a negligible one when dc is passing. It thus acts as a filter. Smoothing chokes for relay circuits can be improvised by stuffing the core of one coil from a disused point motor full of iron or steel wire.

695 What is a strowger switch?

A large rotary switch, with at least ten sets of contacts – frequently more and often with more than one bank – actuated by an electro-magnetic ratchet mechanism so arranged that each impulse moves on the wipers one step (see Plate 39). It is named after its inventor and was the heart of the automatic telephone exchange before the development of solid state switchgear.

696 Is it possible to do the same work as a relay with solid state devices?

Many integrated circuits (chips) perform switching functions – logic gates are a case in point. However, their current-carrying capacity is low and they need, for our purposes, to be backed up by either high-power SCR devices or, more commonly, old-fashioned electro-magnetic relays where traction circuits are to be switched.

697 Which should I use, relays or chips?

That's up to you. Relays are very easy to understand, even for those disinterested in electrical matters, and in addition most switch several circuits at once. Chips are smaller, more versatile and in general cheaper, and once the supply of cheap ex-equipment relays dries up the move towards chips will become irresistible.

698 I understand that chips need to be powered by low-voltage stabilised current. Can they be used from a standard power unit?

It is possible to provide a stabilised low-voltage supply for the more sensitive devices from 16 V ac with suitable circuitry. However, as suitable power supplies are available, these are to be preferred. After all, one also needs a separate smoothed dc supply for relay power. For experimental purposes, batteries are recommended.

699 Could I use batteries for simplicity? I was thinking of employing the readily available Ni-cad rechargeable cells.

So long as you remember that a Ni-cad battery only delivers 1.2 V as opposed to the 1.5 of a standard disposable cell, and that you are prepared to recharge the cells systematically, this is quite acceptable.

700 What is a flip-flop circuit?

A configuration of two transistors which changes state according to which of two inputs has been momentarily energised. It is the electronic equivalent of the bistable relay.

Section 4:10
Command control and computers

701 What exactly is meant by command control?

Command control is a system of control where every operating unit on the layout is fitted with a module that responds to electronic commands from the central control unit. All tracks form a single circuit and a permanent traction supply is fed through them. Locomotives, points and any other accessory one cares to mention can be controlled from a single console.

702 Command control seems a wonderful idea. Why isn't it universally applied?

Primarily it is a matter of cost. The basic unit and the modules are based around microprocessors and although, for this relatively straightforward application, inexpensive 8-bit processors are perfectly adequate, they are only a part of a specialised electronic device. In addition, it is necessary to fit *everything* with modules at the outset – there is no halfway house. The system is at its best in a toy train approach, where sectional tracks are assembled and rearranged frequently and where a number of locomotives are likely to be left lying about in a random fashion. The closer the model approaches full-sized track design and,

above all, full-sized operating practicesa, the technical advantages of command control over a well-designed cab control system disappear rapidly. The cost advantages of cab control are overwhelming, although the snag is that, being hard wired, they only apply to a permanent layout.

703 On the demonstrations of command control that I have seen, all the main units of the system are grouped in one panel. Is it possible to have several control positions around the layout.

It is usually possible to arrange slave controllers at strategic positions around the layout where an operator can control a train from close quarters, but overall control must be vested in a central console unit. It does not appear possible to provide local control of points in a full command control system. However, where a centralised control panel is required for a large layout, the use of command control does reduce the amount of wire needed to link the panel to the layout very dramatically, anything up to 200 wires being reduced to just two!

704 What has happened to the Airfix and Hornby Zero 1 systems of command control which were described in the model press some years ago?

They have gone the way of Astrac, the abortive Jouef system, and some other attempts to market command control systems. Fundamentally, lack of support from the purchasing public led to the systems being withdrawn. These systems were soundly designed, and were shown to work reliably within their limits – I can vouch for that from personal experience. They were quite simple to use but there was always the question of cost which came, inevitably, at the outset of a project. As a result, a system which has its greatest appeal and value to a beginner was outside the initial budget, and by the time most people could consider the outlay, they had already installed a hard-wired control system that met their needs. As a result, the target market was missed; the actual market, established reasonably well-to-do enthusiasts about to begin a new system together with very wealthy new-comers, was too small and erratic to support the systems in an extremely difficult economic climate.

705 There appears to be a limit to the number of locomotives one can have independently controlled by this system. Is there any way around this?
You can install isolated sections on which duplicate locomotives can stand, but this vitiates the principle of command control and introduces complications into locomotive rostering; it is a fudge and produces more problems than if simple sectionalising were employed.

706 Why are the number of locomotives controlled 16 or 64 and not 20 or 50, which seem more rational numbers?
The number of channels is invariably a multiple of 8; this is an inherent characteristic of electronic control systems which are based on binary notation. In other words, to a microprocessor 8 is a rational number, but 10 is irrational. If you want to delve further, I can recommend a short course on number theory. Ten is only rational because we once counted on our fingers.

707 It seems that the number of channels is continually increasing. Would it be possible to upgrade an existing system?
The limit of controlled channels is set by the type of microprocessor employed. As this is the heart of the system, upgrading is impractical – one must refit all module-controlled equipment and invest in a new console and slave controllers.

708 Why does each make of command control use different standards? Would it not be helpful if they all adopted similar commands?
It takes many years work to produce a command control system and, not surprisingly, the manufacturer patents the novel parts of the system to prevent a rival making use of his pioneer work. Whilst in theory it would be possible for a manufacturer to licence others, in practice they apparently feel the market is too small to allow anyone else into their preserves. It is unfortunate that on two

occasions we have seen two manufacturers launch systems almost simultaneously, making the appearance of a market leader less probable. The difficulties are confounded by the rapid development of electronics which can transform the situation, if not overnight, certainly in a matter of two or three years.

709 Is it difficult to fit the modules into a locomotive?
Yes and no. The actual wiring is quite straightforward and, providing that there is space within the body to house the module, there is nothing difficult about installation, although it is not the sort of job one tackles in a casual manner, nor is it the sort of task one can confidently recommend to anyone with little interest in electrical matters. Unfortunately, not every locomotive has a lot of spare space inside for the modules and this is where the trouble begins; it can be necessary to cut part of the ballast weight away on many models. Some users have gone so far as to cut down and, in some cases, rearrange the disposition of the modules, a process which, whilst reasonably straightforward for anyone with a modicum of experience in electronics, completely invalidates the manufacturer's warranty.

Whilst the difficulties of fitting modules into small locomotives is often exaggerated, there is no doubt that the problems involved, the time required to carry out the modifications and the general hassle and trouble has a considerable negative influence. As mentioned in the first paragraph, it is not a job for anyone who dislikes wiring, and, far from reducing the practical problems of electrification, command control merely pushes them into a much more inconvenient position. Furthermore, it would appear that fitting a module into a locomotive built by another manufacturer invalidates that manufacturer's warranty. It certainly invalidates one's legal safeguards under consumer protection legislation.

710 If I fit modules to my locomotives, will they operate on ordinary controllers?
Unless you also fit a changeover switch

to restore the wiring to normal and isolate the module, they won't. There will be no deleterious effects if you stand them on a normal control layout, but they simply won't work in that environment. Unfortunately, in many, if not all, command control systems, should you place an unfitted locomotive on the layout, the motor windings will burn out in a few minutes.

711 I am rather attracted to the idea of only having two wires between the layout and the control panel, but I do not want to go to the trouble of fitting modules in my locomotives. Is there any other way I could tackle the problem?

Some experiments were carried out by feeding layout sections through locomotive control modules, using the Hornby Zero 1 system. This had the snag that one was limited to 16 sections which, whilst adequate for a small layout, created difficulties when applied to a larger system. The virtual demise of Zero 1 cut short what appeared to be a promising system for large club layouts. However, there are less involved ways of reducing the number of wires, using logic chips to sort out a series of commands sent down a pair of independent signal wires, with the actual switching being carried out on the baseboards. This would also appear to permit local panels to be used as well as the main master.

712 If I install command control and something goes wrong, what do I do?

Assuming you got it to work in the first instance and that no wires have become detached or broken, then the fault will lie either in the operating module or the main console. It is not difficult to discover which is at fault – if either nothing works, or a whole section of the system appears not to function (ie the points all throw but no loco will run), then the trouble is in the console, which will have to go back to the maker and may need replacement. A more likely cause is a failure of the operating module, in which case only one item, or a group of points or other auxiliaries controlled from one module, is malfunctioning. The solution is simple – the defective unit is scrapped

and a replacement fitted. Although in theory electronic modules can be repaired, the cost is considerably higher than replacement.

713 Isn't it worth all this bother and expense to be able to operate two locomotives under independent control on the same section of track?

If you wish to operate two locomotives independently within half a metre of each other on the same length of line then command control does provide a simple answer – though not the only one. However, the question then arises, is there any point in trying to control two locomotives independently in such a manner? Here, the answer is a very definite no. If the locomotives are under true independent control – in other words, there are two people involved – they then have to co-ordinate their movements. If one operator is trying to control both, the whole business becomes very fraught because the slightest lapse in concentration creates an awkward situation. The fact is that it has long been established that, because railway trains run on fixed paths and cannot swerve to avoid collisions, it is bad practice to try to run two trains close together. Whilst a collision on a model is not likely to lead to too much damage, it is still bad practice and should be avoided.

714 Is command control worth while?

This is something only you can answer, but in its present state of development I have my doubts. It is certainly not cost-effective for a normal layout, and the present size of locomotive modules and the difficulty of fitting them into many models is a serious handicap. The ideal module would be quite small and capable of sensing whether it was on a command control system or operating on a normal 12 V dc system, adjusting its circuits accordingly, and the channel could be blown into the module from the console and possibly changed in a similar manner. Whilst this is not feasible at present, it appears a distinct possibility some time in the 21st century. Providing, that is, that someone is prepared to invest enough in research to make it feasible. This is the key question.

715 Can I control my railway with my home computer?

Yes – if you can write the program and construct the necessary interfaces. Whether the effort is worth while is another matter – remember that a computer keyboard is not designed to make control of a model railway that easy.

716 What is involved in writing the program?

At the very least you will need a good grounding in Basic programming, and Basic is not regarded as the best medium for this type of programming. Then, when the program is complete, it will need extensive debugging – removal of errors which occur because, in the initial stages, you overlooked some small factor which succeeds in messing things up in the final analysis.

717 What is an interface?

A device to connect a computer I/O port to a mechanism. They are needed because:

a Computers work on low voltages and low current levels whereas model railways require relatively high currents and higher voltages.

b Most model railway equipment needing control puts out 'spikes' which, if leaked into a computer, confuse the controls more than a little.

Interfaces vary according to the requirements of the control system; for our purposes the computer would need to operate a relay to switch the fairly high currents used on model railways.

718 Isn't a computer ideally designed to control a model railway automatically?

If you like overkill, yes. However, the majority of effects can be readily achieved by the use of relays and other electro-mechanical controls, or by employing simple solid state devices in purpose-built control modules. Most of the essential functions of a computer are under-used in this type of application.

719 Has a computer any use on model railway?

Given a suitable program, a computer equipped with a printer can be set to prepare waybills and other documents for traffic control. The basic pattern of traffic can be stored data, with variables such as weather, changes in demand and even derailments, landslides, and other Acts of God determined by random seeds. A computer can throw dice to any required level of complexity and interpret the results in less time than the human eye takes to read the die. In addition, simple typesetting programs can print out documents for the line on a dot matrix printer. These uses do not require the computer to be linked with the layout, so they can be run on a machine used for other purposes.

720 Is it possible to compile timetables with a computer?

Computers are now being used to help compile prototype timetables, but as the programs have to be specially written for each system, and require several man years to write and almost as long to debug, railway modellers must stick to pencil-and-paper methods for the forseeable future.

721 I have seen VDU displays showing the layout timetable at exhibitions. How is this achieved?

The details are generally stored in data statements, then a simple reading program accesses the data in sequence and displays it on the VDU. This practice has gone out of favour of late, though with a slightly more sophisticated display program, which would mimic the VDUs seen on larger British Rail stations nowadays, a diesel era layout would be greatly enhanced. To get the most out of this type of program, the data should be held in a separate file which can be changed to present a different schedule. Although this normally demands a disk drive, the fact that one only requires sequential access to the data should allow the cheaper cassette filing system to be used, permitting one to employ a simple, possibly second-hand home computer coupled to an old black-and-white TV, thus cutting the cost of the hardware considerably. Colour is not necessary – BR gets on very well without it.

722 What makes of computer would you recommend for experimentation?

The BBC B and the Sinclair ZX Spectrum, for no other reason than that the only worthwhile book on computers for model railways, *Computer Projects for Railway Modellers* by Roger Amos and Martin Cook (Patrick Stephens Limited), deals with these two machines. The early Spectrums have one virtue in that their membrane keyboard is proof against accidental spillage, while the BBC B is a more versatile and robust machine, with superior Basic and good interface facilities. Both are frequently advertised in the For Sale columns of local newspapers.

723 What programs exist for model railway control?

There is a little support in the USA, but none worth speaking of in Europe. Whether this will grow is debatable; a more likely development is simulation programs to enable one to operate an extensive railway network or drive a train over an actual stretch of line on a PC compatible. Certainly such programs would have a better commercial value, though the initial offerings would probably be published as Shareware rather than normal commercial Games Software.

PART 5
LOCOMOTIVES AND ROLLING-STOCK

Strictly speaking, locomotives are also rolling-stock, but it has long been the case that, within the hobby, locomotives are locomotives and everything else on the track is rolling-stock. There is some logic in this, for model locomotives do not roll, whereas modern coaches and wagons are apt to take off at the slightest provocation. In fact, someone did once suggest that a free-running coach and a length of track was as good as a spirit-level any day!

As we are not considering either product-specific or detailed prototype queries – there are, after all, only 1,001 questions to begin with – this section might seem a trifle on the short side, but I feel that it covers the basics.

Section 5:1
Locomotives

724 Why do we use permanent magnet motors in small-scale model locomotives when it means that we must use rectified power supplies instead of taking the current direct from a transformer?

Unlike the wound field motor, a permanent magnet motor has the useful characteristic of being reversible, the direction of rotation being determined by the relative polarity of the motor brushes. This means that we can easily reverse the locomotive from a remote controller.

725 Marklin locomotives work on ac and yet they can be reversed from the track. How is this done?

The locomotive contains, in addition to the motor, a sequence reverser. In its simplest form, this consists of a small electro-magnet that changes the direction of a reversing switch every time the current is interrupted. This is extremely erratic in use, since a small interruption in the current through dirty track, etc, can cause the locomotive to go backwards, which to say the least is highly infuriating. Present ac models use the Marklin system, where an over-voltage pulse is sent through the track to actuate the sequence reverser. This system has limitations; it requires special controllers and limits one to locomotives from a handful of manufacturers.

726 Why was ac traction so popular in pre-war days?

Basically because although the theory of dc traction was understood and the virtues appreciated, the technology available was unable to provide the necessary equipment. There were two separate difficulties. Early copper-oxide metal rectifiers were unreliable; indeed, many dc power units used valve rectifiers, which were expensive, cumbersome and delicate – totally unsuited for the rough and tumble of a train set environment. Worse still, until the late 1930s most permanent magnets were made from high carbon steel and were not only bulky, but were prone to loose strength. Reliable transformers working off the standard ac mains supply could provide 16 or 20 V ac to power reasonably compact wound field motors, so this system was adopted for ready-to-run systems. Dc traction was available for amateur construction and was used in batch-produced commercial models.

The reasonably reliable selenium rectifier and nickel-cobalt magnet became available in the late 1930s, but only Meccano Ltd, with the Hornby Dublo system of 1938, was able to take advantage of this before the onset of war. Wartime radar research produced even more powerful magnetic materials, making a compact permanent magnet motor a commercial proposition, whilst the development of improved semi-conductor devices has made the supply of dc current a great deal easier.

727 I have noticed that there are a number of detailing kits on the market. Why are these necessary? Couldn't the manufacturers get the models correct at the start?

In fact, many current manufacturers do get the models correct, but as they usually work from a single preserved prototype, the resulting model is only correct for that one locomotive as it appeared after restoration. Locomotives are built in batches, but detail differences can appear within a batch and between batches, and significant design changes sometimes take place. Over the years, modifications and improvements occur during major overhauls. Hence there is some justification for a ready-to-run manufacturer producing a basic model which satisfies most people and allows the more demanding owner to add the necessary fittings to make the model a more accurate representation of a specific locomotive.

728 Which is easier – altering a ready-to-run model or building a kit?

This depends to a large extent on the type of modification envisaged. Where no modifications are required to the chassis, alterations to a ready-made body are more straightforward, particularly if they are carried out on a spare body moulding, leaving the original intact in case of a change of heart.

On this theme, there are some body-only kits which fit on to suitable commercial chassis, and in this instance it is often possible to obtain the necessary chassis parts from a specialist dealer.

Another good starting point for a conversion are second-hand models, which often have badly battered bodies and are ideal subjects for modification.

729 It is clear that I cannot obtain all the types of locomotive I want from ready-to-run sources and will have to use kits. Is it a difficult matter to construct these kits?

The honest answer is that not only does a lot depend on the kit chosen, but even more depends on the individual assembling the kit. Certainly one cannot sit down one evening and stick everything together in the sure and certain knowledge that, before you go to bed, you will have a working locomotive. A good deal of care has to go into assembly. For a start, the chassis has to be assembled with precision if the model is to have any hope of working; this can take anything from four hours upward, depending on the complexity of the design. Then the body must be put together accurately if it is to look good. Finally, the model has to be painted. This can take several weeks in many cases. There are today several books dealing with locomotive kit construction which are listed in the Bibliography, and it is advisable to purchase at least one of these before buying a kit.

It is also advisable to remember that inside-cylinder locomotives are easier to build than outside-cylinder types and that the best starting point is the basic 0-6-0, remembering that the rule on British railways in the steam era was 'When in doubt, make more 0-6-0s'.

730 Why do so many locomotive kits not contain wheels, motor and gears?

The usual explanation is that most builders prefer to make their own choice, but while this is an important consideration, there are other factors. For a start, the kit can then be sold at a lower price and the fact that, in order to complete the model, one must then lay out more money is neatly slid around. More significantly, the kit manufacturer avoids the need to obtain stocks of motors, wheels and gears, which in the case of the small cottage industry manufacturer is a very significant matter indeed. In addition, the retailer carries a smaller inventory, since it will only be necessary to hold motors in stock for a tenth of the stock of kits. The system would work more effectively were the kits to list, on the label, the recommended motor and the precise specification for wheels and gears; as it is, retailers frequently have to open the box to extract this information from the instructions. In view of the number of small parts in such kits, this is not a good idea, but there is little option as things stand.

731 What are can motors and what is so special about them?

Can motors are totally enclosed motors, generally of cylindrical form. In general they are more efficient, in that they require lower current to develop the same torque as the older open-frame motor. As a result, their control characteristics differ, which can lead to problems with control.

732 What is a ring field motor? Has it any special advantages?

This is a type of motor where the magnet is circular in section, completely enclosing the armature. It is mainly used for tender-drive and motor bogies for diesel and electric outline locomotives, though the later Hornby Dublo locomotives had this type of motor mounted in the cabs. The design has considerable virtues when incorporated into the chassis, as is the case with ready-to-run models, since the large, relatively slow running motor can drive the wheels through simple spur gear trains which are inherently more efficient than the worm drives commonly used with tunnel and can motors. Whilst the theoretical efficiency is a minor point, the simplicity of assembly on the production line has much to recommend the design. However, this type of construction is less suited for home assembly.

733 What is meant by a lean burn motor?

The term is a sales ploy, probably dreamed up by a marketing man who was deeply into cars. The term is correctly applied to a type of petrol engine which is claimed to be more economical and produce less pollution, and has no relevance to an electric motor. At a guess, one imagines that the intention is to imply that the motor in question requires lower current than the previous products of the manufacturer in question.

734 Why is the relatively inefficient worm drive preferred to spur gears for most amateur locomotive construction?

Although worm gears do absorb over half the power of the motor, they have one undeniable virtue – they are relatively easy to mesh correctly. With spur gears it is vital to be able to drill the bearings at precisely the correct centres; if this is not done, the efficiency of the drive falls off very rapidly. Furthermore, because the speed of most small motors is quite high, a large reduction is required; with worm and wheel this can be done in one stage, but with spur gears several trains are needed.

735 I am having a considerable amount of trouble getting my worm gear to mesh correctly. Can you offer any advice?

A simple way of getting the correct mesh is to place a piece of tissue paper between the worm and wormwheel, removing it when the motor is assembled. This will give the requisite clearance. It is important to have the motor shaft at right-angles to the axle centre-line and, if the wormwheel is dished, the worm must sit centrally. If the chassis design does not incorporate some simple adjusting device, the housing of the motor can be packed up with thin shims. Good-quality writing paper is very good for this purpose.

736 Some wormwheels are dished to take the worm, while some have flat teeth. Which is more efficient?

There is nothing to choose between the designs so far as efficiency goes. The dished wormwheel is the stronger of the two, which is why it is universally employed for large reduction gears used in industry, but its value for low-powered drives is less clear cut.

737 Is it better to have a high-ratio or low-ratio drive on a model locomotive?

There is a generally held belief that the

higher the gear ratio, the slower the locomotive will run. This is true if all other things are equal, but the finer pitch of the higher-gear-ratio worm sets makes the drive less efficient, and often this makes fine control more difficult. It is significant that ready-to-run locomotives often have quite low reduction drives and are still able to run at scale speeds.

738 Would you recommend the use of commercial gearboxes?

The only possible objection one can raise to these invaluable devices is the initial cost. They save an enormous amount of time and trouble and now that the majority of motors have completely exposed drive shafts there is no reason not to employ them. The fully enclosed pattern also helps retain a certain amount of oil around the gears.

739 Why are so many locomotive kits made from white metal? Why aren't they made from plastic? I'm sure they'd be much easier to assemble.

There are two reasons. One is that the weight is a considerable advantage, providing plenty of adhesive weight for the model. The other is that it lends itself to low-cost batch production. A cast white metal kit is produced by first making a set of masters, generally from brass, which comprise all the parts needed to build the locomotive. The kit can then be checked for accuracy of assembly by sticking the parts together with a low-strength glue, after which the parts are separated, cleaned and then used to produce rubber moulds from which the parts are cast in a centrifugal casting machine.

Plastic kits are produced in precision moulds and, since the parts are similarly precise, assembly of a properly-designed kit is a reasonably straightforward matter. However, the cost of such moulds is extremely high and can only be justified if the expected sales run into many thousands of kits, but the majority of locomotive kits have sales in the hundreds. There are in fact a few plastic loco kits, but they do not feature largely in the hobby.

740 Why are there so few 4 mm scale diesel locomotive kits?

Because there are so few diesel proto-types, and as most are available as ready-to-run models, the majority of diesel era modellers use these.

741 Are etched brass locomotive kits difficult to assemble?

As always, the degree of difficulty involved depends on the design of the prototype and on the actual kit. However, it is only fair to say that the majority of etched brass kit manufacturers today do take considerable pains with the design of the kits and in most cases provide adequate instructions. The main difficulties lie in the complexity of the models; many manufacturers have taken the opportunity of including a very great amount of detail into the models, and some of this is of necessity very small and accordingly difficult to handle without the proper tools. These should include fine-nosed pliers or good-quality tweezers plus, for preference, an illuminated magnifying viewer, since when dealing with fine parts it is always helpful to be able to see what you are doing.

742 A number of O gauge locomotive kits are now being made from a fibreglass-type plastic. What is your opinion of these?

The earliest products of this type were rather crude, but the recent models are extremely good. They are not conventional plastic kits, but resin mouldings that require a certain amount of fitting in order to allow the parts to bed down cleanly. They certainly seem to offer good value for money.

743 Is it difficult to scratchbuild locomotives?

Oddly enough, it can often be easier than assembling a kit. Although most scratchbuilders work in metal, there is absolutely no reason why one should build the bodies out of plastic sheet and tube. The main problem remains the chassis. However, it is often possible to do a lot using a standard commercial chassis, providing that the axle holes are in the right place. Since there was a remarkable degree of uniformity in locomotive coupled wheelbases, this is not as difficult as it might seem.

744 How should I set about scratchbuilding a diesel locomotive?

The first thing most modellers do is locate a commercial diesel bogie or chassis which has the wheels in the right place and, preferably, has roughly the right sort of bogie sides. This takes care of the motive power. The body is then built by any preferred method, although plastic card appears to be the most commonly used material. Some modellers prefer wood, in which case it is absolutely essential to use a good body filler to kill the grain. In order to get the correct body profile, not only is it helpful to make a female template to check the final shape, but it is also a good idea to build the body around a series of accurately shaped profiles. It is vital to make absolutely sure that the subtle curves of the body sides and, above all, the front ends, are accurately reproduced. The most important features after this are the body grilles – these need to be convincing if the look of the model is not to be ruined. Similar considerations apply to electric locomotives. Here it is customary to purchase the pantographs, as few modellers feel up to the task of making them.

745 I don't have a lathe. Is it possible to make boiler mountings without one?

For a start, a very large number of boiler mountings, chimneys, domes, safety valves, etc, are available from specialist manufacturers, although they do often take some tracking down. It is possible to modify commercial fittings by scraping, filing, cutting and sticking together, and it is also possible to make the main fittings out of tube, washers, solder, epoxy filler, etc. However, you may have a primitive lathe without realising it – a drill, held firmly in a vice, forms the business part of a lathe, and decorative items can be formed with a succession of files (see Plate 40). A lathe is a useful addition to the advanced scratchbuilder's workshop, but it should not be regarded as an essential feature, particularly in 4 mm scale.

746 I want certain locomotives which are not available as ready-to-run models, but I have neither the time nor the inclination to assemble a kit. Is there an alternative?

A number of concerns, usually one-man cottage industries, will build kits to order; some even provide a small selection of ready-built locomotives. However, such models are going to cost *at least four times* the price of the kit. It is often possible to obtain second-hand models of good quality from selected dealers and at exhibitions, whilst small advertisements can be a further source of supply. There is some initial risk, as one is dependant on the skill of the builder, so a few enquiries at exhibitions or through clubs would be advisable. A fair indication of the quality of the product is the length of the waiting list – only a relative newcomer of any quality can offer anything under six months to a year delivery for a special order.

Section 5:2
Coaches

747 British Rail coaches are described as being Mark I, Mark II etc. What is the meaning of this term?

There have been four main divisions of British Railways coach designs since the introduction of the Mark I standard coaches in 1951. The Mark II coaches are distinguished by being divided into four sub-groups, A, B, C and D. Types C and D are virtually indistinguishable externally, both being air- conditioned with fixed windows, and Type A is rather rare; they are really variants of the Mark 1 design. Mark III coaches were longer and had identical body shells for First and Standard Classes. Mark IV vehicles are an improvement on the Mark III for modern high-speed services and are suitable for push-pull working at very high speeds. The Mark I coach had the largest variety of types, was made in two lengths, the shorter bodies being mainly non-gangway compartment stock, and also embraced all types of passenger vans. In view of its relative longevity it is very popular with modellers, and most main varieties of corridor stock are now available as ready-to-run models.

748 What exactly is meant by the code letters applied to coaches?

The object of the code is to describe succinctly what the purpose of the vehicle happens to be. The BR system is the most comprehensive, each letter denoting a particular function, thus:

F   First Class
S   Second or Standard Class
T   Third Class (only used for pre-nationalisation stock)
C   Composite (ie First + Second)
K   Compartment stock
O   Open (saloon) stock
B- Brake (as prefix)
-B Buffet (as suffix)
R   Restaurant

Therefore a BSK is a Second Class compartment coach with van and guard's accommodation, an RB is a restaurant-buffet car, etc.

749 What is a composite coach?

This is a coach with more than one class of accommodation, generally First and Second (pre-nationalisation, Third). It is not, as was once suggested, a coach with guard's and van facilities – this is a brake vehicle.

750 Could you explain the difference between a three-arc roof and a plain arc?

The plain arc roof is formed from a single curve of reasonably large radius, usually struck fairly near track level. The result was a fairly low headroom which caused some problems in the days when all gentlemen (and any man wishing to rise in the world) wore a high (top) hat, adding some 6 to 9 inches to his height. As the plain arc roof didn't leave much clearance for lamps, the three-arc profile was developed – two smaller curves on each side of the main arc lifted the ceiling well clear for passenger stock. The final development was the modern elliptical profile roof, where the side curves are more generous and headroom – and ventilation space – duly increased (see Plate 40).

751 What is a clerestory coach?

A clerestory coach has a raised central portion to its roof which not only provided ample room for the oil and later gas lamps, but also, by means of side windows and ventilators, gave additional light and air (see Plate 40). Its heyday was the 1890s when many major companies in Britain adopted this style for their more important coaches. It was also very common in the USA and on the continent of Europe at the same time. However, it was expensive to construct and tended to weaken the roof, so was supplanted by the elliptical roof which provided more room and greater strength.

752 How do you pronounce clerestory?

The correct pronunciation is 'clear-story' with the accent on the first of two syllables; it is derived from the architectural term meaning a storey clear above the main structure, usually the nave of a church. However, many people say 'clerest-ory', and this is accepted.

753 Could you tell me something about slip coaches, and is it possible to reproduce slip coach working on a model railway?

A slip coach was a portion at the end of a non-stop express that could be detached from the train whilst it was in motion and so provide a service to an intermediate station without having to stop the main train, which could therefore remain a non-stop service, a useful commercial advantage. Whilst used by many major lines before the First World War, in subsequent years only the GWR and later the Western Region ran slip services. This was in no small way due to the fact that the GWR route to Plymouth featured continually increasing gradients, so it could be very useful to lose part of the load along the way. Some GWR expresses had no fewer than three slip portions.

A slip coach is easily recognised because not only does it have end windows to allow the slip guard to see what is happening in front, but it is also provided with a large number of reservoirs for the vacuum brake, since in order to control the run into the station, the brakes have to be applied and released several times.

It is not too difficult to arrange a slip coach on a model railway – special trip couplings are provided, almost invari-

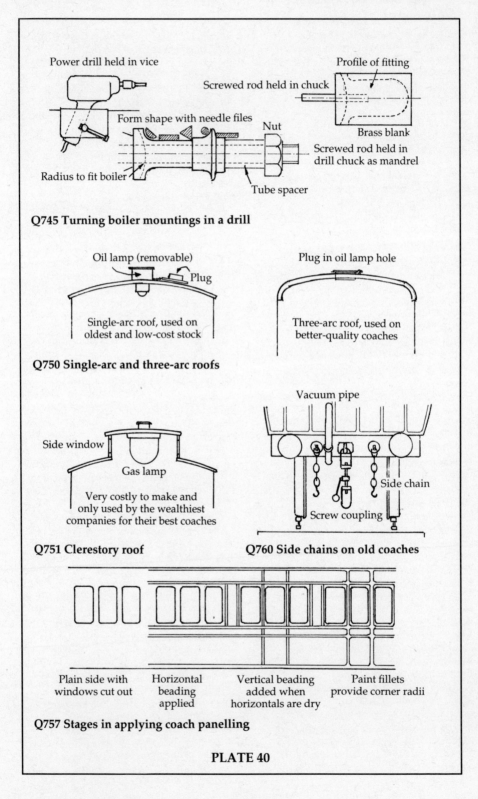

Power drill held in vice

Profile of fitting

Screwed rod held in chuck

Brass blank

Form shape with needle files

Nut

Screwed rod held in drill chuck as mandrel

Radius to fit boiler

Tube spacer

Q745 Turning boiler mountings in a drill

Oil lamp (removable)

Plug

Single-arc roof, used on oldest and low-cost stock

Plug in oil lamp hole

Three-arc roof, used on better-quality coaches

Q750 Single-arc and three-arc roofs

Side window

Gas lamp

Very costly to make and only used by the wealthiest companies for their best coaches

Q751 Clerestory roof

Vacuum pipe

Side chain

Screw coupling

Q760 Side chains on old coaches

Plain side with windows cut out

Horizontal beading applied

Vertical beading added when horizontals are dry

Paint fillets provide corner radii

Q757 Stages in applying coach panelling

PLATE 40

ably on the slip coach itself. These are operated by a trackside ramp and in most cases need to be manually reset. However, with much current emphasis directed towards branch and secondary line modelling, interests in model slip coach working has declined. The main difficulty is ensuring that the slip coach will coast to a stop in the platform, but it should be pointed out that even on the prototype this could be a problem.

754 What is so special about a Pullman coach?

A Pullman car (not coach) was a luxury vehicle owned and run by the Pullman Car Company, although hauled by the operating company's locomotives and, not infrequently, formed into a train with other company stock. A supplementary fare was charged to reimburse Pullman. In Britain, except in the earliest days, all Pullman cars were saloon stock, unlike their US counterparts which provided sleeping accommodation. In a full Pullman train a high proportion of the cars had kitchen or buffets provided; each car had an attendant and passengers were provided with meals, refreshments and a high standard of service. The company was taken over by the British Transport Commission on nationalisation and by 1960 the traditional Pullman car was phased out in favour of upgraded standard coach bodies. Worse still, the traditional Pullman livery was replaced by a version of the BR livery, the only remaining link being the supplementary fare and the loss of lower class accommodation. In short, the original Pullmans were *very* special; they provided better than First Class travel at very little above Second Class fares. They also make lovely models.

755 What exactly is a Wagon Lit?

This is a luxury coach owned and operated by the *Compagnie International des Wagon Lits et des Grande Expresses European*, the European equivalent of the Pullman Car Company. Although the main cars comprised convertible compartments for day and night use, restaurant and kitchen cars were provided, together with matching vans, or fourgons. As with Pullman cars, these vehicles were run in standard trains as well

as special luxury trains, the best known of which is the 'Orient Express'. The only Wagon Lits to run in Great Britain were the F Class cars of the 'Night Ferry' service. The current 'Orient Express' operations in Britain are carried out with Pullman stock, but in its original form the train started at Paris, and the connection to London was via the 'Golden Arrow'/'Flèche d'Or'. For more details of these coaches, the reader is referred to the many books by George Behrend on trains de luxe.

756 I have often seen exquisite models of old panelled coaches on finescale layouts at exhibitions. Where can I buy these lovely vehicles?

Most of the coaches you admire have been built from etched brass kits, but a few cottage industries build these kits, often to order. Expect to pay more for one of these hand-finished coaches than you would for a ready-to-run locomotive. Advertisements can be found in the model press, mainly in *Model Railway Journal*.

The assembly of an etched brass coach kit is not unduly difficult; in many respects it forms a good introduction to this aspect of the craft. The main problem remains painting the finished model, and the general consensus now has it that an air brush, whilst not absolutely essential, is a great help in this respect. Many enthusiasts have these models painted professionally.

757 How on earth is panelling applied to model coach bodies? It looks very difficult.

It is very difficult! Most panelled coaches today are made from etched brass kits, and anyone who has ever set out to produce panelling by hand tends to agree that they are wonderful value for money. There are two favoured methods. The simplest is to apply the beading in strips, exactly as it was done on the prototype. The only snag is that this leaves square corners, but in practice the paint usually forms a small curve (see Plate 40). Since the advent of plastic sheet, many modellers cut the entire panelled sides from a single sheet of material and apply this to the coach body shell. The reason why this is confined to plastic sheet is that the doiley, as the overlay is popularly known, is extremely fragile and most attempts to cut one from cartridge paper ended in disaster, usually about 80 per cent of the way through the delicate task of cutting it out.

758 What is passenger-rated stock?

The majority of special-purpose vans for perishable and similar traffic, together with both open and covered carriage trucks, were built with improved suspension, frequently fitted with the larger-diameter wheels of normal coaches and, above all, provided with continuous brakes so that they could travel safely at higher speeds. They could be marshalled in passenger trains, though this was restricted to semi-fast and local services and not principal expresses, where the only non-passenger vehicles were parcels/luggage vans. In many cases these vehicles were painted in the passenger livery and were fully lined out.

759 What is a mixed train?

A mixed train is one which contains both coaches and normal goods stock, and was only to be found on light railways and a few rural branches. The fact that the wagons were not fitted with continuous brakes meant not only that the speed was limited, but also that the Board of Trade, and in due course the Ministry of Transport, took a very dim view of such goings on.

760 What are side chains?

In the early days of railways metallurgy was one of the arcane arts and no great reliance was placed on highly stressed items such as couplings – with good reason. Accordingly, the more respectable railways provided, in addition to the central hook and coupling loop, two sets of chains, one on either side of the coach buffer beam (see Plate 40). The idea was that, in the event of the main coupling failing, these would keep the train together. By the 1880s the main couplings had become more reliable with the result that the side chains were rarely used, and by the 1890s the practice died out for new construction. They are a neat detailing point for models of 4- and

6-wheeled coaches of an early vintage, but few bogie coaches acquired them.

761 What is the exact meaning of 'rake' in connection with coaches?

Rake is the collective noun for coaches. However, it is normally used to refer to a set of two, three or more coaches which remain coupled together to form a train unit. Its extreme form is found in multiple unit stock, where sets of two, three or four coaches of different design are put together to form a unit and are only divided for maintenance purposes. Many suburban loco-hauled sets were designed as a unit and provided with special couplings within the unit; these, and other sets which remained coupled together for long periods, were referred to as a fixed rake. This term could also be applied to a long-distance express of fixed formation.

762 What are DMUs and EMUs?

The initials stand for Diesel Multiple Unit and Electrical Multiple Unit. As the acronyms are easily pronounced, the terms have gained wide currency.

763 What is a push-pull train?

A push-pull train (an auto-train on the GWR) is one where a modified or special-purpose driving trailer is coupled semi-permanently to a locomotive so that there is no need for the locomotive to run round the train at termini. It was widely used in the steam age for local and branch-line trains, but in general no more than four coaches were involved. The GWR and Southern made most use of this system, the former using a mechanical linkage which limited the number of coaches on each side of the locomotive to two. Other railways used a pneumatic system. In all cases the driver could only operate the regulator and apply the brakes or sound the whistle – the fireman dealt with everything else and, as a result, had to be a passed fireman (an experienced man, qualified to drive but awaiting a vacancy). Where diesel or electric locomotives are involved, the driver has full control. Modern push-pull trains are much longer and the driving trailer is specially built and much heavier than a normal coach. This is largely because of a case where an early push-pull train, with a modified Brake Second driving trailer, hit a herd of cows and disproved much of Stephenson's dictum; the train also came off badly and the Ministry of Transport took a jaundiced view of the proceedings.

764 **Why is there a dearth of ready-to-run electrical multiple unit stock?**
Because manufacturers believe that there is no demand for it. However, at one time they also believed that there was no demand for DMUs either, and the fact that the latest BR DMU models were brought out almost as quickly as the prototype offers some hope that BR EMUs will eventually appear on the market. In the meantime one must either build this stock from kits or adapt a suitable plastic body shell. A number of specialist concerns now offer cast white metal coach ends to assist this conversion and to cater for those gallant few who still scratchbuild coaches.

765 **I have seen some interesting varieties of coaches running on exhibition layouts. In particular I have seen electric multiple unit sets and other types of trains not listed in any catalogue I possess. Are these coaches scratchbuilt?**
A few coaches are scratchbuilt, but this is mainly done for older vehicles and then principally in 7 mm scale and larger. Many 4 mm coaches are kit-built – in most cases panelled coaches are made from etched brass kits. However, many modern coach models are produced by cutting and carving ready-to-run body shells. The standardised body profile and standardised window openings of modern British Railways coaching stock makes it a relatively straightforward matter to cut the body shells into sections with a razor saw and then cement the parts together. Plastic sheet can be used to fill in larger gaps, but in the main the favoured gap filler is either epoxy putty or plastic car body filler.

766 **Is it necessary to fit internal details to coaches?**
It is a good idea to provide internal and corridor partitions since their absence is fairly obvious, but there is no real need to do more than paint plain cut-outs in appropriate colours. The partitions also help to hold the glazing in position, which is a very good reason for their inclusion. Simplified seating can be added, but the provision of passengers is very much a matter of personal taste. Full internal detailing is really only of value in O gauge and larger, and in many cases the roofs are arranged to lift off so that visitors may admire the fittings. Restaurant cars are a favourite subject, but some imaginative detailing has also been carried out in model Wagon Lits. It is highly unlikely that any one coach ever carried so many nubile wenches at once!

767 **How does one arrange coach lighting that does not go out when the train stops?**
There are two favoured methods. One uses very high frequency ac to operate the lamps, with special filter circuits to prevent the dc traction current affecting it. The majority of locomotive motors are unaffected by this high-frequency supply, but some do require filters in the supply wires inside the locomotive. The other method has small Ni-cad rechargeable batteries in the vans, and is best used in conjunction with LEDs rather than lamps. The batteries are either recharged on specially equipped sidings or direct from the track current via specialised circuitry within the battery vehicle. This last system is only applicable to fixed train formations. In either case this arrangement should only be considered when the layout can be blacked out for night effects. It must be realised that under daylight conditions it is impossible to see from the lineside whether prototype coach lights are on or off.

Section 5:3
Wagons and their loads

768 **My interest in the steam age railway is increasing, for quite apart from the fascination of the steam locomotive, I am intrigued by the wide variety of goods vehicles that were used. Can you give me any guidance on the subject?**
This is so vast a subject that it is impossi-

ble to do more than outline the subject in a short answer. Fortunately, in recent years, a number of excellent books have been published, to which we refer you for full details. Most goods traffic was carried out in open wagons and covered vans owned by the company. Some specialised wagons could be found in most larger goods yards, such low-loading wagons for bulky loads, carriage wagons for the conveyance of road vehicles, cattle wagons, and a little-known but interesting vehicle, the ale wagon, a secure truck for the conveyance of beer in casks. Special-purpose wagons were uncommon visitors to the average goods yard. Indeed, one would be hard put to explain the presence of a propeller wagon at a country branch terminus, as these were built for the conveyance of large ships' propellers. For this reason it is inadvisable to buy a special-purpose wagon unless you have a reason for using it.

769 Why is it that all ready-to-run wagons of a particular type carry the same number? This doesn't help realism on the model.
Mainly because it is more convenient for the manufacturer to do this. It is, however, not impossible to provide a variety of numbers; the German firm Bemo does this as a matter of course and the trend is growing among the better manufacturers.

770 I am a little confused by the number and variety of private owner wagons offered by the trade. Some appear to be rather improbable, to say the least. Can you enlighten me?
The fact is that in recent years a large number of wagons have been produced which are alleged to be owned by well-known brand-name producers. Most of these are fun wagons, the companies concerned having never owned their own vehicles, but having said that there are some remarkable exceptions. To take one example alone, Cadburys not only owned a large fleet of vans, but also had steam locomotives at their plant at Bournville.

In pre-war days, the bulk of PO wagons were used in the coal trade; many were owned by small coal mer-

chants. One important characteristic of the majority of PO wagons was that they were confined to a single route, generally between one colliery and one coal merchant. One notable exception to this rule was the SC (Stephenson Clarke) wagon; this concern hired wagons to firms in need of this facility, so these vehicles turned up anywhere in southern England. This type of PO wagon became 'common user' in 1939 at the outbreak of war and never reverted to private ownership.

Tank wagons, whether for oil, chemicals or milk, have always been branded for specific users, although during the Second World War most oil tank wagons were labelled Pool.

Modern privately branded wagons for specific traffics are mostly found in block trains and, of course, containers are very frequently owned by large shipping businesses.

771 I would like to make sure that every PO wagon on my steam age layout is completely authentic for the location. Can you offer any suggestions as to how I should set about this?
If you are modelling an actual station, it will be necessary to find out what firms in the area owned their own wagons. A letter to the local newspaper will often put you in touch with a member of the family or former employees, though with time this source is literally dying out. A good deal of information can be acquired by close study of old photographs and, of course, the excellent detailed histories of specific railways usually provide a good deal of information on the subject. There are now a number of good books on the subject of PO wagons which give a good indication of the areas where they were to be found.

772 What exactly was an RCH wagon?
The Railway Clearing House (RCH) laid down a series of broad specifications for privately-owned goods wagons, which were used as a guide for private wagon construction. However, the major wagon manufacturers had their own versions of these standards, which were supplied to individual purchasers. It is now possible

to purchase 4 mm and 7 mm scale kits for some of these wagons.

773 I am a little worried about my ability to letter a wagon. Is there any easy way round this?

Transfers are obtainable not only for the grouped railways – LMS, LNER, GWR and SR – and British Railways in all its stages, but also, generally in alphabet form, for privately-owned wagons. It is also possible to use standard rub-down lettering, obtainable from most artist's suppliers and, in smaller sheets, from leading stationers and office suppliers.

774 How are tank wagons loaded and unloaded in goods yards? Are they connected by hose to a road tanker, or what?

Tank wagons have always been loaded at properly equipped sidings in a depot owned by the company producing the product. Whilst they have on occasions been unloaded by relatively primitive means, in the main the practice has been to provide proper facilities in the form of standpipes and storage tanks, since delivery in bulk is either to a wholesale distributor or directly to a large industrial user. Milk tanks were always loaded at milk factories, which received their supplies by road from the farms, and unloaded in large depots in the major cities.

775 Why is it that many stations in large cities had extensive cattle-handling facilities when there are no farms in the area? Is this merely a survival from the days before the city grew to its present size?

These facilities were provided for the unloading of cattle destined for the city's abattoirs. This particular traffic has changed its pattern and live cattle for slaughter now goes by road.

776 Why do wagons types have such odd names? I can understand how a well wagon might be a Crocodile, but some associations defeat me. Can you throw any light on this?

This practice originated in the 19th century when all day-to-day traffic organisation was carried out by telegram. Code names were devised so that, for example,

a station in need of a covered carriage truck could merely ask for a 'Damo'. Suffix letters distinguished between different types of the same general class. Wherever possible, the name had some relevance to the traffic concerned or the type of wagon, but how, to take a common case, a slatted van for the conveyance of milk churns became a 'Siphon' must forever remain a mystery.

777 I have tried my hand at building wagon kits but I don't seem to be able to get good running. Can you offer any advice?

Although a four-wheeled wagon appears a fairly simple object to build, it is essential that the underframe is properly assembled. Unless some form of equalisation is provided, the chassis must be checked for accuracy by placing the model on an absolutely flat surface. A length of track is not good enough, for it can be slightly uneven. The favoured surface is a glass mirror, since any distortion in the surface can be readily seen by the naked eye. A common cause of trouble with plastic kits is lack of weight; the answer is to add ballast. Lead sheet is probably the best, not from its density but from the ease with which it can be cut into small pieces, but any scrap metal may be used for the purpose (see Plate 41).

778 I am attracted to the very fascinating etched brass kits now on the market. Are they difficult to assemble?

There is nothing intrinsically difficult about etched brass kit assembly, providing that the etchings have been properly designed in the first place. Wagons make a good entry into this aspect of the hobby. Regrettably, one early manufacturer, now no longer trading, did not take sufficient pains with this and gave the whole genre a bad name. Some manufacturers provide very cryptic instructions which are barely adequate for the purpose and do not help a newcomer make a clean start. If you purchase your kits from a specialist model shop, staffed by enthusiasts, you can get advice on which kit they think best suited to the needs of a beginner. At an exhibition you can usually get advice from the organis-

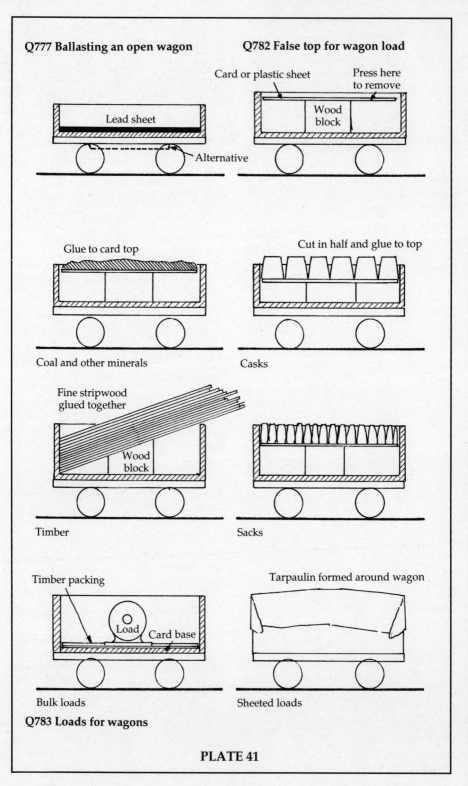

Q777 Ballasting an open wagon

Lead sheet

Alternative

Q782 False top for wagon load

Card or plastic sheet

Press here
to remove

Wood
block

Glue to card top

Coal and other minerals

Cut in half and glue to top

Casks

Fine stripwood
glued together

Wood
block

Timber

Sacks

Timber packing

Load   Card base

Bulk loads

Q783 Loads for wagons

Tarpaulin formed around wagon

Sheeted loads

PLATE 41

ers and, indeed, will often get a lot of useful help from fellow enthusiasts. Clearly, you will get better help at a major national show, or, better still, a show organised by one of the specialist societies, where not only will you find a large number of specialist suppliers, but an even larger collection of knowledgeable fellow enthusiasts.

779 Can you suggest the best way to begin scratchbuilding model wagons?

A growing number of exhibitions now include demonstration stands where experienced modelmakers show visitors how to make models. These demonstrators are always ready to stop what they are doing and explain to an interested visitor how to set about the task.

780 What is the correct colour for the inside of a wagon?

This depends very much on the age of the wagon and what type of traffic it has been used for. In general, the inside of wooden wagons was not painted.

781 I have noticed in one of Edward Beal's books a photograph of a model building lettered WAGON REPAIRS LTD. Was there such a firm, or was this a figment of his fertile imagination?

Privately-owned wagons did, from time to time, break down and require repairs. The railway companies were not prepared to do this and in most cases the builders were a long way off. Although the RCH design lent itself to easy overhaul by any intelligent craftsman, the work was generally carried out by specialist firms, and Wagon Repairs Ltd was the main concern.

782 I was fascinated to see, at an exhibition, a case where loaded wagons were run into a factory building, only to emerge empty. How is this done?

In all such cases the loads are mounted on a piece of stiff material, generally thin wood or plastic sheet, which fits snugly inside the wagon. This false top lies near the top of the wagon and is supported on a central wood block. It is a simple matter to press down on one side and so free the load, which is then lifted clear

(see Plate 41). For convenience, all wagons carrying a particular load, be it coal, timber, sacks or whatever, are of identical body size so that each type of load is interchangeable. Today, with ready-to-run and kit-built wagons, this is not a particularly difficult condition to meet. Although, on exhibition layouts, loading and unloading is usually performed 'offstage', the standard method on private layouts is to exchange loads at the end of each model day rather than to carry this out in a piecemeal fashion during a running session. This is not merely more convenient, but takes into account the fact that in full size a wagon takes some time to unload and is rarely freed until the following working day.

783 Where can I find out information on the types of loads carried in the steam age?

Most detailed histories of smaller railways give considerable information on the type of freight traffic on the line, and these can be taken as a good guide for wider application. Photos of old goods trains and goods yards also provide a wealth of information. Another source is the General Appendix to the Rule Book, which contains, amongst other information of considerable value to modelmakers, detailed information on the correct way to load wagons for various types of traffic. Whilst such books are not readily available, they are from time to time offered for sale by prototype-oriented societies, particularly at open days at various depots (see Plate 41).

Section 5:4
Wheels

784 What is the significance of wheel profile?

There are two factors concerned here: appearance – often referred to as scale accuracy – and running qualities. Most model wheels have to compromise between the desire to have a true-to-scale profile and the need to have wider treads and deeper flanges to ensure better running.

785 Why is this? Surely if the wheel profile works on the prototype, it should on the model when reduced to scale.

This is a common fallacy. It must be remembered that we are actually building full-sized railways with a gauge of anything from 6.5 to 45 mm. The laws of dynamics, in particular questions of inertia and the behaviour of springs and other forms of suspension, do not take scale into account, and whilst we think of a model as being a scale replica of a full-sized prototype, when it comes to running it is a very small but full-sized vehicle.

786 Why is there a difference between the wheel profiles on ready-to-run models and those used by finescale modellers?

The coarse profiles used by European ready-to-run manufacturers were primarily devised to give good running under less than optimum conditions. Remember that a fair proportion of train sets are put away by the simple process of throwing everything into a cardboard carton, which does somewhat affect the initial accuracy of the track gauge and wheel alignment. Finescale profiles were devised by highly skilled amateur modelmakers primarily interested in the appearance of their models, who not only treat their models with respect, but take pains to lay the track with extreme accuracy.

787 Surely it would be better to have one profile. Is this impossible?

Far from it. In the USA the NMRA (National Model Railroad Association) evolved the RP25 (Recommended Practice 25) profile, initially for HO gauge. Although it has a very good appearance, the major divergence from finescale being a wider tread and a very large root radius, it will hold the track well and is suitable for high-class ready-to-run models, where one hopes the owner, having paid good money for what is clearly a scale model, treats it with reasonable care. Unfortunately, a lot of British modellers believe that since it is an HO profile, it is not suited for OO. This is another fallacy, based on the mistaken concept that scale is real. It is in reality a very well-designed, general-purpose wheel profile for a 16.5 mm gauge railway and is slowly coming to be accepted as the best profile for ready-to-run models.

788 Some wagon wheels have spokes, while others are plain discs. Why is this?

Prototype wheels must have a certain degree of resilience, and in the early years all wheels were spoked to this end. Moreover, spokes came in a variety of patterns – bifurcated, bowed and straight. Some 50 years ago successful steel disc wheels were produced, and all modern freight stock is now so fitted (see Plate 42). It is interesting to record that quite a few four-wheeled wagons managed to acquire odd wheels; indeed, at least one BR official photograph of new goods stock showed this arrangement. Both types of wheel are obtainable in the popular scales.

789 What is a Mansell wheel?

The Mansell wheel was the earliest successful disc wheel for coaches. It comprised a steel rim and hub connected by hardwood segments which were secured by bolts (see Plate 42). It was more resilient than the older iron-spoked wheel and was in common use on coaches and certain vans until the development of the modern steel disc wheel, which supplanted it some 50 years ago. It is possible to get accurate models of Mansell wheels, but ready-to-run coaches are usually provided with plain discs.

790 Is there any point in changing wheels on commercial coaches and wagons?

First of all, quite a few mass-produced vehicles are fitted with wheels which have wide treads and deep flanges, so not only is an improvement in appearance achieved by changing them, but the stock will also then pass through finescale track. Indeed, in 4 mm scale, if you adopt EM or P4 the wheels must be changed. It is also possible to change to metal wheels, which are preferred by many enthusiasts.

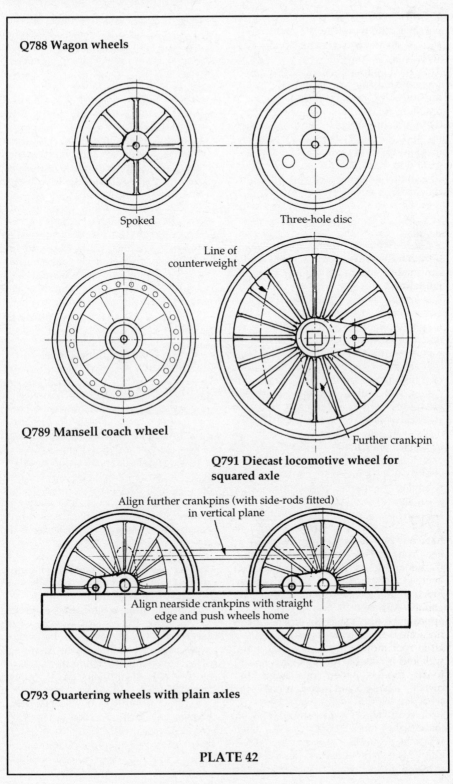

Q788 Wagon wheels

Spoked

Three-hole disc

Line of counterweight

Q789 Mansell coach wheel

Further crankpin

Q791 Diecast locomotive wheel for squared axle

Align further crankpins (with side-rods fitted) in vertical plane

Align nearside crankpins with straight edge and push wheels home

Q793 Quartering wheels with plain axles

PLATE 42

791 It appears that there are two main types of locomotive wheels in 4 mm scale – a rather restricted range of all-metal wheels and a much larger selection of much better-looking plastic-centred wheels. Which is best?

This is a case of horses for courses. The all-metal wheels were the original pattern; they are diecast and are provided with squared holes to make quartering a straightforward business (see Plate 42). The profile is to the old BRMSB standard and will run on both universal and NMRA standard track. Axles are made for OO (16.5 mm gauge) and EM (18.2 mm gauge). However, with a limited range of wheel diameters, fixed spokes and fixed crankpin throws, they are a compromise. The later finescale wheels are offered in an almost infinite range of diameters and numbers of spokes, with varying crankpin throws and positions suiting practically every type of steam locomotive built in Britain in the past century. They are naturally more expensive and, since they fit on to plain axles, must be quartered by the builder. They are intended for the more expert modeller and will only work satisfactorily on track laid to precise standards; they tend to fall off at universal points and will not run at all well on sharp-radius sectional track.

792 What is meant by quartering?

The crankpins on opposing sides of a coupled locomotive are set at 90° to each other, and this is known as quartering.

793 I can see how a wheel with a square-ended axle can be quartered, but how is this done with plain axles?

On a model, although it is not essential that the crankpins be precisely set to the right-angle, it is vital that all wheelsets are alike if the side-rods are not to bind. In small-scale work, the normal procedure is to fit one wheel to each axle, and then fit the side-rod. The axles are placed in the frames, the other wheels are lightly pushed on, and the fitted side-rod is placed in the bottom quarter. The other crankpins are lined up by placing a rule alongside, checking against the axle by eye, and putting the other side-rod in place (see Plate 42). The wheels are now rotated by hand and checked for possible binding. If this is found, it is corrected by wringing the offending wheel a fraction of a degree. Once the wheels rotate smoothly, they are pushed home to the correct back-to-back setting and, after a final check, the other side-rod is secured in place.

794 What is the back-to-back measurement and why is it important?

As the term implies, back-to-back is the distance between the backs of the wheel flanges. Unless all wheels are set to the same dimension, within close tolerance, and unless this measurement corresponds to the setting of the checkrails at turnouts, the vehicles will not pass through point formations without derailing. Strictly speaking, the critical measurement is the check gauge, the distance from the face of one flange to the back of the other, but as flanges are normally of the same thickness, the more readily measured back-to-back is employed.

Section 5:5
Couplings

795 Why are there so many different types of coupling? Wouldn't it be better if only one type were used?

It would be simpler if there were only one type for each gauge. However, to do this would not merely require the complete agreement of everyone concerned with the manufacture of model railway equipment, but it would also mean that further development would be ruled out. Since the ideal coupling does not exist, this would clearly be undesirable.

796 What is the ideal coupling?

Clearly, one that looks exactly like a prototype coupling. However, as there are several different types of coupling in use on the prototype, this immediately rules out any hope of getting one universal coupling.

797 What are the main types of prototype coupling?

There are two general types in use today: the hook and link, often called three-link, and the buckeye.

The three-link coupling is mainly used in Europe, it must be coupled by hand and is accordingly slow in use, but is extremely flexible and, for the past century, extremely reliable. It has the advantage that the coupling hooks on mating vehicles do not need to be at the same height.

Buckeye couplings are coming into increasing favour in Europe, particularly for coaching stock where their greater safety factor is appreciated. In the USA buckeye couplings are standardised. This took many years as agreement had to be reached on height and precise design.

In addition, narrow gauge railways usually use specialised couplings, whilst a good deal of multiple unit stock, which does not need to be universal in application, is equipped with specialised couplings.

798 What types of model coupling are available?

Couplings fall into five broad groups (see Plate 43):

Primitive pin and bar Used on cheap toys and as semi-permanent couplings in rakes of vehicles. Manual operation.

Hook and link Basically European three-link couplings. Manual operation.

Buckeye In model form, principally NMRA horn hook, Kaydee and Peco Simplex. Automatic operation.

Hook and bar Principally used by European manufacturers. Automatic operation.

Specialist Generally produced by small manufacturers to meet a specific need. In the UK, the Sprat & Winkle, an inverted version of the hook and bar, and the AFJ are the most favoured. Most are automatic.

799 All N gauge ready-to-run stock is fitted with compatible couplings. Why can't this be done in OO/HO?

When commercial N was introduced, most manufacturers had grasped the commercial virtues of a standard coupling, and followed the lead of the initial manufacturer. The convenience of a single type outweighs any technical difficulties with the unit and, by chance, the problem of patent protection did not arise.

800 Why can't other manufacturers standardise?

There are two obvious difficulties. The first is, who is going to decide on the standard? Second, if agreement were possible, what is to be done about the extensive collections in private hands which are fitted with non-standard couplings and thus could not be expanded with new stock. There are also more subtle objections. Some manufacturers prefer to be non-standard, which they believe means that anyone starting with their products must stick with them. Then the whole business is thrown into disarray by the user, who frequently insists on setting his or her own standards. Finally, an official as opposed to a de facto standard means that there can never be any improvements.

801 What is meant by an automatic coupling?

Primarily, that it will couple when vehicles are pushed together. It will also normally be possible to uncouple automatically by a ramp or magnet. Certain couplings also offer advance uncoupling.

802 What is advance uncoupling?

Advance uncoupling permits the couplings to be disengaged whilst the train is being pushed over the operating device and remain uncoupled until the detached vehicles are left in position on the siding. This means that only one operating device is needed for a fan of sidings and that wagons or coaches can be left anywhere on the siding.

803 What types of coupling offer advanced uncoupling?

The main commercial types are the Kaydee and Sprat & Winkle. Some specialised patterns, with limited distribution, and the AFJ pattern coupling also provide this feature. It is probable that more patterns will be introduced in the future, as its convenience for serious operation cannot be over-emphasised.

804 I have read about the AFJ coupling but have never seen it advertised. Where is it made?

The AFJ coupling was designed by Alex Jackson, a member of the Manchester Model Railway Society, in the late 1940s. It is made from spring wire in simple jigs in the home workshop; the Manchester MRS can provide an instruction leaflet. Whilst very effective with top-quality models, since it is unobtrusive and provides advance uncoupling, it demands precise workmanship and extreme accuracy of track, wheels and vehicle suspension if it is to work at all. Like the little girl in the poem, when it is good, it is very, very good, but when it is bad . . . A side effect of its near invisibility is that, when viewed at eye level, wagons fitted with AFJ couplings appear to be completely unconnected with each other!

805 I have a long siding where I have fitted two uncoupling ramps so that wagons can be left at two locations. Unfortunately, it is all too easy, with a long rake of wagons, to uncouple the wrong bit. What can I do?

It depends on the type of coupling. Where magnetic uncoupling is employed, the solution is to use electromagnets in the siding, only switching on the one you wish to use. With mechanical ramps, it is necessary to install a lever mechanism that pulls the ramp down and out of action (see Plate 43).

806 What is the best type of coupling for a model railway?

It depends on the operating requirements. If very little shunting is involved, then there is a slight weight in favour of non-automatic types, since these, in general, are less likely to become detached. Some operators like three-link couplings for intensive operation, since, providing that the uncoupling points are within easy reach of the operator, one can uncouple or couple anywhere on the layout, and stock can be pushed anywhere without re-coupling. Where coupling and uncoupling points are out of convenient reach, automatic coupling is essential.

807 Which is the best type of automatic coupling?

It depends on who you ask! For most people it is the type fitted to the majority of their stock, since this involves less conversion to a single pattern. All current types have limitations. Of the commercial patterns, the general consensus is that the Kaydee buckeye type is the most reliable and versatile, as well as being commendably small – not far off true scale size. It is, however, quite costly and rather fiddly to fit. At the other extreme, the European pattern of hook and bar coupling is very robust and whilst manufacturers have slightly different designs, most will hook together and stay coupled, but may need manual uncoupling. The hook and bar – or tension lock – coupling is particularly good when propelling stock around very tight curves.

808 I find it very difficult to uncouple hook and bar type couplings manually. Is there a better way than picking up the vehicles and juggling about?

There are two approaches. One is to use a flat strip of metal, bent at one end, to reach underneath and push up the droppers. Another, which only works where the hook is made from sheet steel, is to attach a small magnet to the end of a piece of dowel and lift the hooks with this (see Plate 43). Fortunately, the majority of hooks are made of steel.

809 Can I use two different types of coupling on my layout?

Certainly – this is only following prototype practice. However, it means that trains should generally be made up from stock fitted with the same pattern of coupling, and that shunting in goods yards, for example, is going to be very difficult. In general, it is best to standardise on one pattern for general use, but exceptions can be made in certain cases.

810 When is it a good idea to have different types of coupling?

There are two main areas. The first is where complete sets of vehicles, generally coaches, are coupled together with a semi-permanent coupling, with automatic couplings on the ends. A similar pattern can be employed with wagons, where short sets of specialised vehicles form a single unit. The primitive pin and

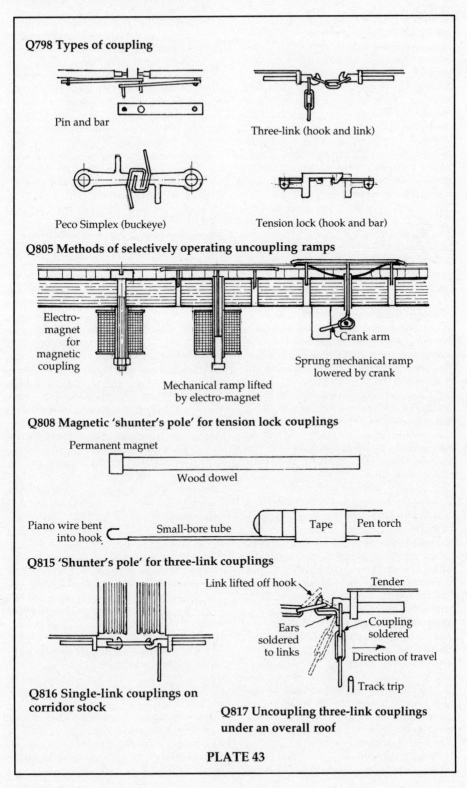

Q798 Types of coupling

Pin and bar

Three-link (hook and link)

Peco Simplex (buckeye)

Tension lock (hook and bar)

Q805 Methods of selectively operating uncoupling ramps

Electro-magnet for magnetic coupling

Mechanical ramp lifted by electro-magnet

Crank arm

Sprung mechanical ramp lowered by crank

Q808 Magnetic 'shunter's pole' for tension lock couplings

Permanent magnet

Wood dowel

Piano wire bent into hook

Small-bore tube

Tape

Pen torch

Q815 'Shunter's pole' for three-link couplings

Link lifted off hook

Tender

Ears soldered to links

Coupling soldered

Direction of travel

Track trip

Q816 Single-link couplings on corridor stock

Q817 Uncoupling three-link couplings under an overall roof

PLATE 43

bar coupling is frequently employed as a link in fixed rakes of coaches. Fixed rakes are greatly favoured where large numbers of vehicles are used on a layout intended for authentic train operation. The second reason for using different couplings involves multiple unit stock, railcars and HST and TGV sets, etc. Here the stock forms integral trains and is not coupled to other types of vehicle, so a different pattern of coupling can be used; most prototype multiple unit sets today are fitted with very complex couplings. It is possible to have three types of coupling in use on one layout without any operating difficulties, since never the three should meet!

811 Can I couple two different types of coupling together?

Yes, but with some difficulty! Quite a few differing patterns of coupling can be hooked together, but in such cases the chances of the stock becoming detached are fairly high. A simple but reliable arrangement is to use a bit of bent wire – a small paperclip is the traditional device, which works well as a stopgap. The most convenient method is to use a 'match vehicle', a van or wagon fitted with one pattern of coupling at one end and a different pattern at the other. In many cases, three-link hooks can be fitted to stock equipped with auto-couplers.

812 From time to time coaches get uncoupled from the train. Is there a cure?

The usual cause is slight misalignment of couplings, together with a bump in the track. The cure, whilst obvious, is not quite so easy to effect. Another cause is jerky running, caused by dirty track or poorly maintained locomotives. This is rather easier to cure. Involuntary uncoupling is more likely to occur when trains are driven flat out, so it is better to run at more realistic speeds.

813 My trains of ready-to-run vehicles are rather too far apart when coupled, yet I have seen similar stock at exhibitions which are much closer together. How is this done?

By resiting the couplings, or fitting a different pattern. However, this must be

done carefully, since the closer coaches are together, the larger the radius of curves needed.

814 I have seen European stock fitted with special couplings that open up on curves. Why are these not more widely used?

Mainly because they are protected by patents. Apart from this, other manufacturers would need to undertake extensive re-tooling of existing stock. Just be patient – 20 years should see this pattern in more widespread use.

815 I am having difficulty using three-link couplings. Is there an easy way of coupling?

A simple coupling hook can be made from a length of fine-bore tubing with a piece of piano wire passed through it, bent to form a hook. Another popular arrangement is to attach the piano wire hook to a pen torch, which gives good illumination of the working area (see Plate 43). An alternative method is to attach a small magnet to the end of a rod and ensure that the final link is made from steel wire. The coupling chain can then be lifted on the magnet. There is a type of swan-neck tweezers used by surgeons which is quite useful, particularly in O gauge. They are costly, but occasionally appear in surplus stores. In all cases, it's a matter of practice making perfect. However, it is notoriously difficult to couple three-link couplings more than 600 mm (2 ft) from the operator.

816 I am having particular trouble with three-link couplings under corridor connections. What should I do?

The favoured solution is a long single link; in addition one needs to have a bent coupling hook (see Plate 43). This is one reason why the idea of coupling coaches in fixed rakes is very popular with users of three-link couplings!

817 I am having problems uncoupling locomotives fitted with three-link couplings under an overall roof. What do you advise?

The simple solution is to lift off the roof whilst operating the layout. A slightly better arrangement is to provide a trip uncoupler on all locomotives. This is produced by fitting a pair of ears on the final link of the chain and soldering the other links together. A small spring wire stirrup in the track, set about 5 per cent further from the buffers than the longest locomotive in use, pushes the links off the hook and uncouples the coaches (see Plate 43). A side advantage of this is that the train will not recouple when a second engine backs on.

818 Where do I get pin and bar couplings?

They seem to have gone out of production, but are so easy to make in the home workshop that this is no snag. You need a supply of flat strip – brass, tinplate or nickel silver – two small drills, a supply of stiff wire which is a tight fit in the hole produced by the smaller drill, a soldering iron and solder, and a methodical approach. Dimensions are not critical, extreme precision is not required, and a couple of hours work will turn out enough couplings to fit out a fair number of vehicles and provide a stock for future use.

PART 6
BUILDING THE MODELS

Even when creating a model railway straight out of the box, a certain amount of construction work is inevitable. As one moves deeper into the hobby, modelmaking becomes a more and more important part of one's enjoyment of the craft. Whilst the kitchen table and, of late, the coffee table have been regarded as the traditional locations for craft work, a properly organised workshop makes life much easier.

In this section we also consider some basic techniques and have a look at suitable modelling materials.

Section 6:1
The workshop

819 Do I need a proper workshop in which to build my models?

In the sense that in order to work effectively you need an organised workspace and a selection of tools, yes. In the sense that you need a specific area set aside exclusively for modelling, no, though this is desirable.

820 How do I organise a working area in a small house?

The first thing to do is to find a place where you can store your tools and materials out of the way when not in use. You then need a working area. Whilst the traditional location was the kitchen table, the number of toxic substances used makes it undesirable to model directly on any surface used for handling or preparing food. The best answer is a portable worktop. This need not be elaborate – a large wooden tray is perfectly satisfactory in the initial stages.

821 I have used a tray in the past and found it a trifle awkward in use. Could you suggest an improvement?

A very good portable workshop can be built around a sheet of 12 mm blockboard measuring approximately 1 m x 0.5 m. Ply sides, 6 mm thick and 75 mm deep, are screwed and glued to three edges, with handholes being cut in the side pieces; the front ends of the side pieces can be bevelled. A twin 13 amp switched socket is fixed at the back; a shrouded three-core lead about 3 m long can be provided for lights, soldering irons, etc, the plug being fused 5 amp. If a small power unit can be incorporated, so much the better; a further refinement is a length of track for test purposes. Rubber feet should be screwed underneath to prevent damage to table tops, and a screw-on vice and saw table are useful refinements. The addition of an illuminated magnifying glass is well worthwhile (see Plate 44).

822 What is the best way of storing tools?

There are a number of multi-tier boxes on the market today which close securely and have a carrying handle; those sold for fishing have proved very popular amongst modellers, since the small divisions in the cantilevered trays are ideally suited for screws, pins and other small items. Alternatively, large flat multi-compartmented plastic boxes can hold an array of small tools. The all-metal toolbox proper is not really suited for indoor use, though the very elegant – and costly – wooden tool chests are clearly the Rolls-Royce approach, particularly as they are not wholly out of place in a living room.

823 **Have you any suggestions for a more permanent workshop?**

The garage is the traditional location for the home workshop. For the larger jobs, baseboard construction for example, it is ideal since the need to keep a space clear for the car ensures that there is ample space in which to work. For finer work such as modelling and electrical and electronic construction, the garage is not quite so convenient, but, with a little organisation in the form of large lidded tins, stout cardboard cartons and a variety of plastic containers, all labelled and arrayed on shelving, it is an excellent space for storage.

824 **I have a large cupboard under the stairs – is this suitable as a workshop?**

But for one snag it is ideal, particularly if there is a 13 amp socket in the hallway into which you can plug a lead feeding the lighting and power sockets in the workshop. The snag is that it is a small, closed, unventilated space, and model-making involves the use of fluids which give off unpleasant fumes. It is therefore absolutely essential to instal an extractor fan and to wire this permanently into the temporary circuits in the workshop so that a continuous flow of air is provided whenever the workshop is in use. Although the fact that the circuits are technically temporary, since they are fed through a fused plug at the end of a flexible lead, they must be wired in accordance with the current regulations.

825 **Is it possible to fit a small modelling workshop into a permanent railway room?**

It is more than possible – it is advisable. A workbench should be from 700 mm to 750 mm above the floor, whilst a layout can be 1.2 m high. This leaves room for the rear of the workbench to be situated below the layout, although some 300 mm of the working area must be clear. Thus it is best to arrange the workbench away from stations and yards and in front of scenic areas on the layout. Storage for tools and materials could be arranged under other sections of the layout (see Plate 44).

826 **What is the minimum equipment you recommend for a small workshop?**

Excluding tools, you require good lighting as the prime requirement, followed closely by a firm working surface – 19 mm chipboard is preferable, supported on 75 mm x 50 mm legs and offering a free working area at least 1 m x 0.5 m. You should have, clear of the working surface, storage for tools in drawers or racks. You also need storage for screws, nuts, pins and small parts – this in most conveniently provided by a number of nests of small plastic drawers. At least two 13 amp three-pin switched sockets are needed, and a low-voltage supply giving controlled 12 V dc and 16 V ac is desirable, though this can be in the form of a standard power unit plugged in as required. An illuminated magnifying glass on an adjustable holder is not absolutely essential, but should be an early acquisition.

827 **What tools are needed for modelmaking?**

If we exclude metalwork, the prime requirement is a steel rule measuring in millimetres and, for convenience, inches, a cutting board and a selection of knives. Some excellent craft knife sets are available, but many modellers prefer a scalpel for fine work. Other requirements are:

Heavy-duty knife
Small engineer's square
Small saw
Miniature mitre block
Fretsaw for more advanced work
Selection of small screwdrivers, pliers and tweezers (the type of tweezers that have to be pressed to open are particularly useful)
Drill brace and good range of small twist drills
Quantity of small files, including a set of needle files

828 **What tools are needed for metalworking?**

Basically you will metal-cutting saws and a good selection of top-quality files, both standard and needle pattern. The metal-cutting saws should include a jeweller's piercing saw, as there is much in common between model metalwork and

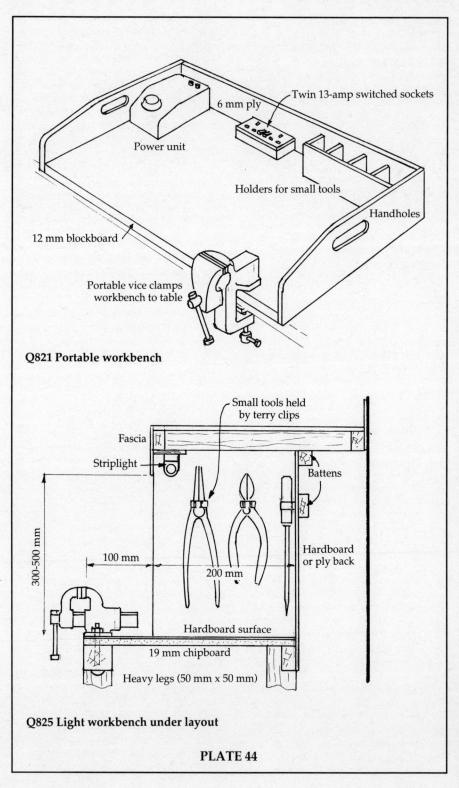

Q821 Portable workbench

Q825 Light workbench under layout

PLATE 44

jewellery. Other requirements are:

Jeweller's snips, for cutting sheet metal
Well-balanced hammer
Small centre punch
Good set of twist drills
Top-quality vice provided with protective jaws for fine metalwork
Small anvil (eg the soleplate of a discarded electric iron)

829 Is a power drill essential for scratchbuilding?

Far from it – enthusiasts built excellent models with nothing more elaborate than a geared drill brace. The normal domestic power drill, whilst excellent for general-purpose work, is a trifle heavy for much modelling, where a small low-voltage drill is much more useful.

830 What are number drills?

Small twist drills were manufactured in a series of somewhat arbitrary sizes and numbered from 0 to 80; there was a corresponding series of larger letter drills. These have been rendered obsolescent by the introduction in the UK of metric drills, but at the time of writing they are still available.

831 What is the advantage of a number drill? Surely it would be better to quote the size in inches.

The inch is a fairly large unit and, to complicate matters, standard workshop practice is to use fractions rather than decimals. The number range gave more readily remembered names.

832 Should I buy drills in sets, or just the sizes I need?

Sets of drills come in some form of container which keeps them in a neat and tidy manner. By getting a set you know that you will have all the sizes you will need when you discover you need them. However, individual drills break, become blunted and need replacing from time to time.

833 How does one sharpen a drill?

By hand, with considerable difficulty! Except for the smaller-sized drills, they should be sharpened on a proprietary drill grinder which fits on to an electric drill. Smaller drills can be resharpened on an oilstone slip. It should be noted that once a drill has been sharpened, it is even less likely to drill a hole of the correct size.

834 Why should a drill produce an incorrectly sized hole? Surely the diameter is not affected by sharpening.

It is virtually impossible to ensure that the point of the drill is exactly in the centre of the bit when regrinding. As a result, the outer fraction of the bore is cut by just one side of the drill (see Plate 45).

835 Can anything be done to ensure an accurate bore with a twist drill?

There are two possibilities. The first is to keep a complete set of best drills for precision work, using older, resharpened drills for jobs where extreme precision is not needed. The second is to begin by drilling a smaller pilot hole. The main drill will then tend to cut a more accurate hole which will be good enough for most work (see Plate 45).

836 How does one get a precise bore?

This is best done in a machine tool, where both workpiece and cutting tool can be precisely controlled. However, for most railway modelling purposes a very accurate bore can be achieved by drilling fractionally undersize and finishing with a reamer.

837 What is a reamer?

A precision-ground hardened-steel tool which looks rather like a twist drill with a number of flutes but no point; the shank generally has a squared end to fit into a tap wrench (see Plate 45). For our purposes, the main use of a reamer is for getting accurate bearing holes for model locomotives; 1/8 in and 2 mm diameter reamers are needed for 4 mm scale loco construction.

838 How do you produce screw threads in metal?

You require a set of taps – these have threaded ends provided with cutting edges and are simply twisted into a suitable-sized hole (see Plate 45). The diameter of drill needed to produce a tapping hole can be found in tables of taps and dies. Screw threads can be cut on rods with dies, which are held in a diestock. The principles are simple; however, hardened taps are very brittle and the smaller sizes break very easily. Hence it is best to start with the larger sizes – 4 mm or more.

839 What are BA threads?

The BA series of screw threads was introduced to provide a sensible range of small sizes within the imperial (inch) system of measurement. Paradoxically, the standards adopted were metric! The system is obsolescent, having been replaced by ISO standard threads. However, plenty of BA screws are around. In practice, only the even sizes were used.

840 Is there any way of simplifying the business of screw threads and screw cutting?

Certainly – the self-tapping screw. This looks rather like a wood screw, but is much harder, has a shallower, closer-pitched thread and cuts its own thread in all but the hardest metals. Alternatively, a captive nut can be used. This is a normal nut, usually brass, soldered in place on a piece of metal to take a screw (see Plate 45). It should also be pointed out that standard metal screws will cut their own thread in most plastics.

841 What is a power tool?

At one time the term was confined to fixed machines, such as lathes, bench drills, milling machines, shapers, planers, boring machines, grinding machines, etc, hence the term machine shop for that part of the factory where these tools were housed. These tools allow parts to be produced to precise sizes. In the last 50 years, an ever-increasing range of hand-held electrically powered tools have become available. Unlike the machine tool, such tools have no greater inherent accuracy than normal hand tools – their purpose is to cut out hard work and, in general, make life easier.

842 What hand power tools are needed to build a model railway?

An electric drill is the most obvious first choice, followed closely by the powered jigsaw or, to give it its US name, sabre saw. This will cut sheet material into curved shapes for track bases in a fraction of the time needed to do the job by hand and, with a little care, will cut straight lines as well. These tools are also very useful for household maintenance. A cordless drill and an electric screwdriver, whilst less essential, will be found to be extremely useful for layout construction.

843 Is a circular saw of any use for railway modelling?

A circular saw, *mounted in a sawbench*, is a useful tool for advanced baseboard construction, but is by no means essential. A bandsaw is also a useful tool, but both this and the circular saw need to be treated with due respect – they are potentially dangerous.

844 What machine tools proper are required?

Unless you intend to scratchbuild locomotives, machine tools are not needed. For locomotive construction, the first priority should be a bench drill; this allows holes to be drilled square with the material, a prime essential for frame construction. However, a power drill held in a suitable cradle also meets this requirement. As boiler mountings can be produced in a primitive lathe made by gripping a hand drill in the vice, a lathe is by no means essential. The multi-purpose machines, of which the Unimat is the best known, which can be adapted to work as milling machines, are ideally suited for our purpose.

Section 6:2 Materials

845 Where do I get suitable wood, insulation board, etc, for layout construction?

Timber merchants carry good stocks of standard softwood sections, and a reasonable range of man-made boards of all description. The larger DIY supermarkets generally carry stocks of most requirements for baseboards. 9 mm Sundeala, in nominal 4 ft x 2 ft sheets, is sold by some well-stocked model shops.

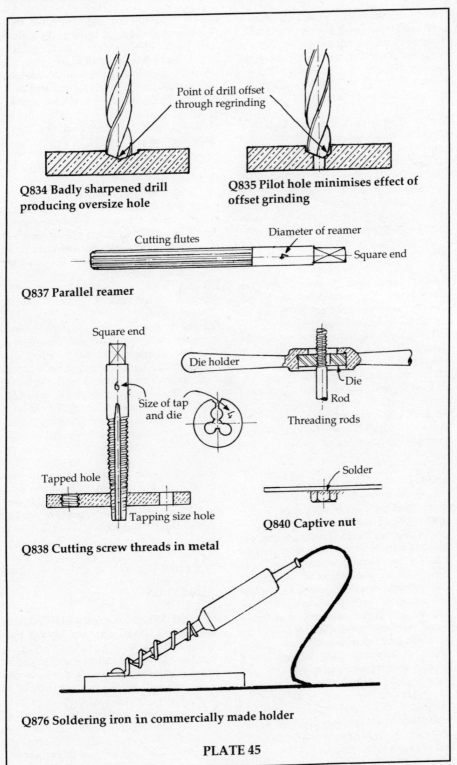

Q834 Badly sharpened drill producing oversize hole

Q835 Pilot hole minimises effect of offset grinding

Point of drill offset through regrinding

Cutting flutes

Diameter of reamer

Square end

Q837 Parallel reamer

Square end

Die holder

Die

Rod

Threading rods

Size of tap and die

Tapped hole

Tapping size hole

Solder

Q840 Captive nut

Q838 Cutting screw threads in metal

Q876 Soldering iron in commercially made holder

PLATE 45

846 **My local DIY store only stocks small sizes of plywood. Where can I go?**
A timber merchant normally carries nominal 8 ft x 4 ft sheets of ply and blockboard in various grades and thicknesses. They also carry stocks of insulation board and other man-made boards.

847 **The local timber yard is closed when I'm not working. How do I get along?**
You can order by phone, but delivery will be made in working hours, so you will need to make your own arrangements. There are large builders merchants who open on Saturdays for the DIY market – check your Yellow Pages.

848 **How would you recommend getting 8 ft x 4 ft sheets home from the stockist? They're too large to fit into the car**
It is possible, by prior arrangement in most cases, to have a timber merchant cut boards and timber to your preferred sizes; the larger DIY stores may offer this service. Whilst a hatchback or estate car is preferable, 6-foot long boards can be got into most saloons, but need to be secured with the seat belt for safety. A roof-rack is a better solution – these can be hired from DIY stores for this very purpose.

849 **Where can I get very thin plywood?**
A good timber yard usually stocks 3 mm ply and can often get 2 mm ply to order. 1 mm ply is more difficult – model shops, particularly those catering for ship modellers, are a more reliable source.

850 **Where do I get stripwood?**
If your usual model shop cannot help, try one catering for aeromodelling. The material is stocked in 3 ft or 1 m lengths. It's advisable to buy in bulk as it is very easy to break a single length in transit.

851 **Where can I get supplies of sheet metal?**
The better model shops carry stocks of brass and nickel silver sheet cut into handy sizes, together with small sections (angle, channel, 'I'-section and flat strip) and tubes. Such stockists attend the larger exhibitions.

852 **I have seen metal stockists advertise a small part service. Are they any good?**
They are excellent if you want a quantity, but as most operate a minimum order system, they are costly or even impracticable for small quantities.

853 **Where can I get tinplate?**
You probably throw a fair amount away, as it is the main constituent of tin cans. Probably the best source is a 5-litre oil can, for it has fairly large flat sides and the metal is nicely protected against rust. Cut the can into four flat sheets, but wear stout leather gardening gloves or risk lacerated hands. A little white spirit will remove the oil, and the printed side makes marking out much easier.

854 **Where can I get steel rods and bars?**
If there is a small engineering works close to hand, enquire there – they may have offcuts at scrap prices. The advertisement columns of *Model Engineer* list stockists of bar and rod metals, and many attend model engineering exhibitions. The best source is the annual Model Engineer Exhibition, currently held at Alexandra Palace, London, in the New Year; enthusiasts come there from Europe to get stocks.

855 **Where does one get plastic sheet?**
Small-sized sheets are sold by the better model shops. Larger sheets can be bought from main stockists; they do, however, insist on a minimum order of at least £50, but generally offer really thick sheets as well. Two of three enthusiasts can make up an order.

856 **Where can I get piano wire? Do I have to go to a music shop?**
Piano wire is sold by most model shops, although in general it is the concerns catering for aeromodellers which carry the best stocks. It comes in a variety of gauges.

857 **Where is it possible to obtain good-quality card?**
Artist's suppliers carry quite good stocks of quality card. In the past Bristol Board was highly recommended, but its place

has largely been taken by plastic sheet. Mounting boards are particularly useful for model building construction; they are 2 mm to 3 mm thick with at least one good working surface. One cheap source for good quality thin card is cereal packets.

858 I understand that the strength of card can be considerably increased by soaking it in shellac. Is this true and, if so, where does one get shellac?

There is no doubt at all that shellac strengthens both paper and card, and creates a smooth, hard surface which can be sanded if desired. It also makes an excellent filler for wood. It is sold in the form of fine flakes which have to be dissolved in methylated spirit. Button polish, intended for French polishing, is actually shellac varnish, and this is probably the easiest form to obtain. If too thick, it can be let down with some methylated spirit. One point to bear in mind – after card or paper has been filled with shellac it can no longer take watercolours and, of course, applying the material over a pre-printed or painted card changes the colour drastically.

859 Where can I get suitable wire, switches and small lamps?

The majority of model shops catering for railway modellers can supply them, and they are advertised in the model press. They can also often be bought at specialist electrical suppliers; electronics suppliers are also stockists.

860 Who supplies transformers?

The majority of firms offering model railway controllers can also supply transformers. The larger electrical and electronic suppliers list them in their catalogues and most electrical suppliers can obtain your requirements to order.

861 Where can I buy small supplies of electronic components?

The Tandy chain of electronic stockists can supply most requirements, carded, but at a price. Larger quantities can be bought from suppliers advertising in the electronic press. Maplins sell a comprehensive catalogue of electrical and electronic parts through major newsagents. A few model shops carry some electronic bits, mainly LEDs.

862 What are ex-equipment suppliers? I understand they offer bargains.

These are scrap dealers who sell suitable components to the public often in well-conducted shops. The well-established firms are scrupulously accurate in their descriptions, but goods carry no guarantee and the usual rules of merchandisable quality do not apply. Technically, everything is taken from used machinery – ex-equipment – but in practice a fair amount of stock is unused surplus components. You must use your own judgement.

863 Where can I get Perspex?

Perspex is the trade name of a transparent acrylic plastic sheet which is mainly sold in large sheets through trade channels. Large DIY stores stock sheets of acrylic plastic primarily for secondary double glazing. Perspex offcuts can frequently be purchased from signmakers. Model shops generally stock thin transparent sheet for modelmaking.

Section 6:3
Soldering

864 Is it necessary to be able to solder?

Soft soldering is essential for electrical work and for much scratchbuilding, but is not a difficult technique to master. Silver soldering, a more difficult technique, is not necessary, although it has its value in advanced scratchbuilding.

865 What equipment is needed for soldering?

An electric soldering iron, a supply of solder, flux and some means of cleaning the work before soldering. The favoured clean-up tool is wet-and-dry paper.

866 How does solder work?

The process is quite complex – in broad outline, solder forms a surface molecular bond with the metals being soldered, making for a fairly strong joint. When a soldered joint is broken, it is the solder itself that shears.

867 What is the secret of successful soldering?

Use a very hot iron, have the work cleaned of oxide film and well fluxed, apply the solder sparingly and work rapidly. Ideally, the parts should be tinned first. Above all, remember that practice makes perfect.

868 What is meant by tinning?

Tinning is coating the surface to be soldered with a thin film of solder. This is done by first cleaning the metal with an abrasive paper or scraper, coating with flux and then applying the hot tinned bit to the workpiece.

869 Why must the parts be cleaned before soldering?

If there is any appreciable oxide or other chemical film on the metal, the solder cannot bond with the part; in fact, it will roll around in small globules instead. However, freshly stripped insulated wire and plated solder tags on new switches, etc, will usually take solder without cleaning.

870 My soldered joints are very weak and won't conduct electricity. Why is this?

These are dry joints. The reason is that the solder was not sufficiently heated and has not bonded properly. It should have a bright silvery sheen when molten, rather like mercury, and flow freely. If it is dull grey and behaves like putty it is not hot enough. To avoid this, allow the iron ample time to heat up initially and between jobs. If this doesn't work – when, for example, you are soldering larger items – either fit a larger bit, or use a more powerful iron.

871 What sort of soldering iron is best?

For electrical wiring, a 15 watt instrument iron is ample, while a 25 watt iron covers most needs; however, for serious scratchbuilding, particularly in the larger scales, a 60 watt iron is needed.

872 Is it worth while getting an iron with interchangeable bits

This depends on the work you are doing. If you are only using it for wiring you will only need one type of bit, a rela-

tively slender one. If interchangeable bits are left in place for a long time, they tend to get stuck and cease to be interchangeable.

873 What is a temperature-controlled soldering iron and is it useful?

A temperature-controlled iron contains a thermostat which shuts off power when the working temperature is reached. It is of most use when the iron is left on continuously, as is the practice with many modelmakers.

874 Are 12 V soldering irons of any value?

The main difficulty is that most power units – in particular transistorised units – do not provide quite enough punch. Their main attraction is the ease with which they can be run off lower voltages for soldering white metal castings.

875 Can a soldering iron cause a fire?

If used carelessly it can bring volatile or flammable materials close to danger point. It needs to be kept in a holder and not left lying about the workbench. It is a good idea to clear flammable material away before beginning a soldering session. Obviously, it should not be laid down on a bench whilst switched on – this will char the surface and could start a fire if it is forgotten.

876 Do you need a holder for the soldering iron?

You need somewhere to keep the very hot tool safe out of harm's way (see Plate 45). Commercial holders do this admirably, while home-made gadgets can be a trifle unstable; a holder that could fall over at a touch is a serious accident looking for a suitable time to occur.

877 Is it dangerous to leave the soldering iron switched on for a long time?

So long as the iron is in a holder there is little risk of damage, but if left on for long periods, for instance overnight after the working session is finished, the copper bit will be severely eroded. You will also waste a considerable amount of electricity.

878 My soldering iron is a little battered. Where can I get it repaired?

Don't bother – throw it away (after salvaging the plug) and get another. Damaged electric soldering irons can easily become live and dangerous.

879 What is the easiest material to solder?

Tinplate, since it is already coated with a solder-like alloy. Brass and nickel silver are also easy to work with, but sheet steel is tricky and zinc very difficult, although we rarely meet it. Copper is straightforward, but needs a very hot iron. Gold and silver can also be soldered. Lead, and lead-based alloys, require special techniques.

880 Is it possible to solder aluminium?

There are special solders and fluxes available, but they are very tricky to use. In fact, aluminium is widely used for soldering fixtures because it is so difficult to bond with solder. It is also virtually impossible to solder mazak diecastings.

881 Can I solder cast white metal parts?

If you have enough experience, using low-melt solder and, ideally, a soldering iron that works at a lower temperature, then larger castings can be successfully soldered. However, the finer details should be stuck in place with epoxy or cyanoacrylate adhesives.

882 Are there any tricks in soldering lead?

Lead oxidises rapidly, but is easily scraped clean. You need a very hot bit indeed – most lead soldering is done with a flame, active flux and high-melting-point tinman's or plumber's solder.

883 Where can I get a low-temperature soldering iron?

Specialist firms, such as Brewsters and Carrs, can advise. However, many modellers either use a 12 V iron on 10 V, using a suitable transformer, or power a mains soldering iron though a dimmer switch.

884 What is the purpose of a flux?

As the name suggests, it helps the solder to flow. It also inhibits the formation of an oxide film on the metal.

885 What sort of flux is best?

For electrical work, a paste flux is preferred. For other work, particularly on white metal castings and etched brass kits, the more active phosphoric acid-based fluxes are preferred. These fluxes must be washed off before painting.

886 Will a flux be needed when using cored solder?

For electrical work, probably not, but a fine smear of paste flux is a sensible first step.

887 I can only get cored solder. Does this matter?

In theory it is slightly wasteful for a good deal of scratchbuilding, but in practice the fact that plain solder is not that easy to locate outweighs this point.

888 What is low-melt solder?

Solder with a lower melting point than the usual solder. It is used not only for soldering low-melting-point lead-based alloys (white metal) but is also employed for soldering etched brass kits.

889 I have been told that it is not advisable to solder etched brass kits. Is this true?

The relatively large area of many etched brass kits makes the parts very effective cooling fins, so it is difficult to raise the temperature sufficiently for the solder to stick without distorting the metal by local expansion. However, the use of low-melt solder obviates many problems.

890 How can I unsolder a complex kit that has gone wrong in the assembly?

Providing that there are no white metal parts that can't be readily replaced, lay a sheet of aluminium over a low flame on the domestic cooker. Place the kit on the hot plate and poke about with a screwdriver and pliers until the whole thing comes apart.

891 I have seen reference to miniature butane powered blowlamps for soft soldering. Do you advise them?

Many advanced model locomotive

builders swear by them, but even they agree that they do create a fire hazard and should only be used in a well-laid-out workshop. Whilst, in safe hands, they are excellent for brass kit assembly, they are a very quick way of reducing a white metal kit into a rough paper-weight. They are also fairly expensive, since cheap versions are potential firebombs. If you need to ask, you aren't experienced enough to handle one.

892 What is the most important point to remember whilst soldering?

That not only is the business end of the iron very hot, but that anything it has been in contact with for even a second or so will also be too hot to touch. As a corollary, a pot of soothing cream for the treatment of minor burns can be very welcome, but the best first aid for a minor burn is to place the affected part in cold water.

Section 6:4
Adhesives

893 What is the right adhesive for wood?

White PVA general-purpose adhesive, obtainable in large containers at any DIY store and in smaller quantities at most stationers, is the preferred adhesive. Use generously and wipe any surplus away with a damp cloth as soon as practicable.

894 What can be used to stick paper and card?

A great deal depends on the amount to be stuck. PVA adhesive is excellent for large surfaces where speed is not of the essence. For smaller joints, particularly where a quick setting is required, acetate cements are to be preferred. Stationers sell a wide variety of office glues which stick paper and card, but in general they are not too convenient for fine model work. Wallpaper adhesive is cheap and, since it does not stain, very useful for scenic work.

895 What is acetate cement?

A general-purpose adhesive made by dissolving acetate plastics in acetone. It is often sold as balsa cement and has a very pungent odour. It is ideal for use with wood and card, but will not stick the majority of plastics.

896 I have considerable trouble using plastic cement. How do the experts avoid unsightly blobs and strings?

By the simple process of not using plastic cement in the first place! There are a wide selection of plastic solvents on the market; some work with all plastics, while others will not touch ABS plastics. The solvents are applied with a brush, generally to the inside of the joint, after the parts are placed together. Capillary action carries the solvent into the joint and the bond is self-supporting within half a minute, although several hours should be allowed for the joint to harden fully.

897 Is there any point in using plastic cement?

It is invaluable for reinforcing large joints; a fillet run inside a wall will strengthen the building, although setting time is likely to be several hours. It is particularly useful for fitting roofs in place and will help fill the small gaps that can occur when modifying a kit. It can also be used to produce small puddles and will simulate dripping water or even icicles. In fact, it is an extremely useful addition to the modeller's armoury.

898 How does one stick brickpaper to buildings?

The most suitable adhesive is Cow Gum or wallpaper paste, both of which provide a degree of slip and allow the paper to be properly positioned. Cow Gum is the trade name for a rubber-based adhesive, produced by a company of that name. It is principally used by illustrators and layout artists, not to mention magazine editors who do their own make-up, and is an excellent way of sticking paper and card together. There may be other brands of rubber adhesive, but if so they are very elusive. Good stationers and artist's suppliers stock Cow Gum in tubes and pots.

899 I am thinking about getting a hot glue gun. Is it difficult to use and what sort of work is it best suited for?

Hot glue guns are quite easy to use, but

one needs to work fast if the plastic is not to solidify before the joint is brought together. As it is difficult to gauge the right amount of gunge put out, it is not much use for fine modelmaking – the solidified plastic is very hard to shift – but it has considerable use for framing work and as a means of securing larger scenic items in place.

900 Can one stick metal parts together?

Two-part epoxy resins are excellent for this purpose. Indeed, when properly heat-cured under pressure they have immense strength and are widely used in the aircraft industry – it's not only plastic aeroplane kits that have their wings stuck together! Even without heat setting – a difficult process in the home workshop and definitely not advised where white metal parts are involved – they possess considerable strength. The quick-setting types are not as strong as the original 24-hour pattern, but for most modelling purposes they are excellent. They also make excellent fillers and are good electrical insulators, with the result that they are extensively used for encapsulating small parts that might touch a metal body and create a false earth circuit.

901 Are 'superglues' as good as they are claimed to be?

When correctly used, a cyanoacrylate adhesive ('superglue') gives a very strong, almost instantaneous bond. They are particularly useful as a means of assembling etched brass and other metal kits, but are not without their faults. Of these, the most serious is the short working life of a tube of superglue. Although more recent formulations are less prone to this problem, the moment they are exposed to air they begin to harden. Whilst other glues also exhibit this fault, it is impossible to apply the usual solution to a tube of superglue since, once put back, a screw cap would be cemented firmly in place! An annoying quirk is extreme sensitivity to contaminants – a small trace of grease will prevent bonding.

902 I have heard that it is possible to stick one's fingers together with superglue and not be able to get them apart. Is this so?

Their ability to stick flesh together is well known, but what is not so well known is that immediate washing in hot water will frequently break the bond. However, it is dangerous to get the glue into the eyes – this calls for immediate hospital treatment but can be avoided by keeping the nozzle pointing away from your body, and from anyone else in the vicinity. Superglues are not for the careless or haphazard worker for, quite apart from any risk to oneself, they have an annoying habit of sticking things where you don't want them stuck.

903 I have stuck two parts together with superglue and want to break the bond. How can I do this?

Providing that the parts will stand up to heat, placing a hot soldering iron near the joint will usually do the trick. Otherwise, be more careful in future.

904 Are joint compounds such as 'Loctite' of use in the hobby?

These materials are widely used by experienced modellers to fix wheels and gears on axles; the popular versions make a permanent bond, which is not necessarily a Good Thing. There is, however, a type with a lower bond ('Lock'n'Seal') primarily intended for sealing small nuts on their screws, which can be more readily broken.

905 I want to stick two pieces of Perspex together inconspicuously, but everything I have tried fails to work. What is the right adhesive to use?

The only known solvent for Perspex is chloroform. It can be obtained, with considerable difficulty, from a pharmacist and then only after signing the Poison Register. For obvious reasons, work in a well-ventilated workroom and keep the bottle well out of reach.

It is as well to point out that although other solvents are not restricted in this fashion, they are all potentially toxic and need to be stored safely, away from heat and direct sunlight. Many are now only sold to persons over 18 – younger readers must enlist the help of their parents.

906 I find the various claims on adhesive packages a little hard to swallow. Are they justified, and what can I believe?

Probably the prize for claims was made by one firm which said that there was a stronger glue than theirs, but it had a serious fault – you couldn't get it out of the tube! The main slogans on the packaging are very carefully worded, or else a caveat appears in small type providing a get-out. In particular the adjective 'Universal' has been so overworked that it has lost any clear-cut meaning. However, reputable makers always provide, in small but readable type, detailed instructions for use and a clear indication of the type of work for which the adhesive is intended. This is also repeated on the tube or bottle, but often this needs a magnifying glass to decipher, so take care to hang on to the backing card. If you can't see any instructions on an new product, leave it on the hook. There are plenty of alternatives which do tell you what you need to know.

Section 6:5
Painting and finishing

907 How can I obtain a smooth, even paint finish on my models?

Mainly by painstaking practice, coupled with the use of quality tools and materials. The main error of most beginners is to apply the paint too thickly – it is better to put on two thin coats than one thick one.

908 Could you recommend a particular brand of paint?

Any paint from a reputable firm will perform well in careful hands. There is a widespread belief that paints by foreign manufacturers perform better, yet a video made in the USA extolled the virtues of a British brand that many British modellers affect to despise.

909 What is the difference between cellulose and oil paint?

Paint consists of pigment – today almost invariably synthetic – and a medium, which ultimately evaporates, together with certain binders to hold the grains of pigment together. The medium determines the rate of drying and what type of thinner is used to let down the paint and clean the tools after use.

910 Are cellulose paints preferable to oil-based paints?

Cellulose-based paints dry quickly but are not so easy to apply with brushes and do attack many plastics. Oil-based paints are more widely applicable, being suitable for brush or spray use. Moreover, they are readily available in small tinlets in hues closely matched to prototype liveries.

911 What is the best way to begin in order to achieve a good paint finish?

A very fine exponent of the craft did suggest putting Rose Murphy on the gramophone, which is another way of saying that one needs to be comfortable and relaxed. The model itself must be clean and free from grease. Use the best-quality brushes, apply the paint sparingly, leave the model overnight in a dust-free location, and clean the brushes carefully after use.

912 Where can I find a dust-free location?

The traditional arrangement was an inverted shoe-box, but a transparent plastic container is better as there is little chance of a helpful member of the family damaging the model by tidying up after you if it can be seen (see Plate 46).

913 How do you get grease off a model? Come to that, how does it get there in the first place?

Our fingers are slightly greasy to begin with, and since it is a good idea to test a loco before painting it, oil gets on some parts. Metal is easily cleaned with white spirit, applied with a soft brush. Allow to dry naturally in a dust-free atmosphere and don't touch it afterwards.

914 Where do I get good brushes?

Top-quality brushes are to be found in artist's suppliers, but cost about twice as much as the run-of-the-mill types. Having said that, it must be admitted that excellent results can be achieved with the less costly ones sold by better model shops, and that cheap brushes can come in useful for rough work (see Plate 46).

915 How do you clean a brush?

A simple procedure is to have a small bottle with a little thinner or proprietary brush cleaner in it to swill out the brush after each application of a particular colour. The wet brush is then wiped on a piece of cloth before a fresh swirl and wipe. At the end, give a couple of final swirls in clean thinners or brush cleaner before carefully drying with a clean rag.

916 What are thinners?

Basically, they are the medium used to suspend the pigment in the paint. For oil-based paints, professionals maintain that the best thinner is pure turpentine, mainly sold in artist's suppliers but occasionally to be found, at much lower prices for larger quantities, in DIY stores. White spirit is a fair substitute and is ideal for washing models and brushes. Acrylic paints, very popular for scenic work, can be thinned with water from the tap. Cellulose and other specialised paints have their own thinners supplied by the manufacturers.

917 Whatever I do I seem to get a very high gloss on my models. How is this avoided?

There are two methods of losing gloss from model paints. One is to pour away most of the medium, leaving a moist residue of pigment. This can then be placed on a pallet and let down with turpentine, thus thinning the bulk of the paint; two or three coats may well be needed. The other is to add some talcum powder to the paint – this breaks up the surface and kills a lot of the gloss.

918 What is dry brush painting?

This is a technique, mainly used on plastic models, where almost dry paint is brushed across the model (see Plate 46). It is particularly suited to model buildings, where one wishes to get uneven shades of the base colour.

919 I have seen some plastic buildings where individual bricks are slightly different in colour. How is this done?

Initially, the wall is painted by dry brushing in the base colour. Then, with a small pointed brush, individual bricks are lightly touched in with different colours (see Plate 46). It is nowhere near as difficult as it sounds since it is not necessary to paint the whole of any one brick or stone to change its apparent colour.

920 How can one paint window frames without either getting paint on the glazing or on the surrounding walls?

The answer is obvious – window frames and other small details are best painted before they are put in place.

921 Are aerosols available for simple spray painting?

Yes – you will find them in car accessory shops for retouching the family saloon. Although the colours are given exotic names, one can usually find a close match to any railway livery. However, it is by no means easy to spray a model with an aerosol.

922 Is there any other way of spray painting a model?

The airbrush, a miniature spray gun with an adjustable spray pattern, widely used by commercial artists, is an excellent tool, and most professional model painters use one. It is invaluable for locomotive and coach painting, and a considerable boon for scenic work as well. Airbrushes are normally powered by a small compressor.

923 Are there are alternatives to a compressor?

There are aerosol cans, but as one can is barely sufficient to spray a locomotive, it doesn't take long for the cost to exceed that of a compressor. The best alternative is a spare tyre, which can be over-inflated at the garage, or replenished with a footpump.

924 How do you clean an airbrush?

By squirting a quantity of thinners through the nozzle. This is where the compressor is so useful – you do not feel constrained to stint on the cleaning.

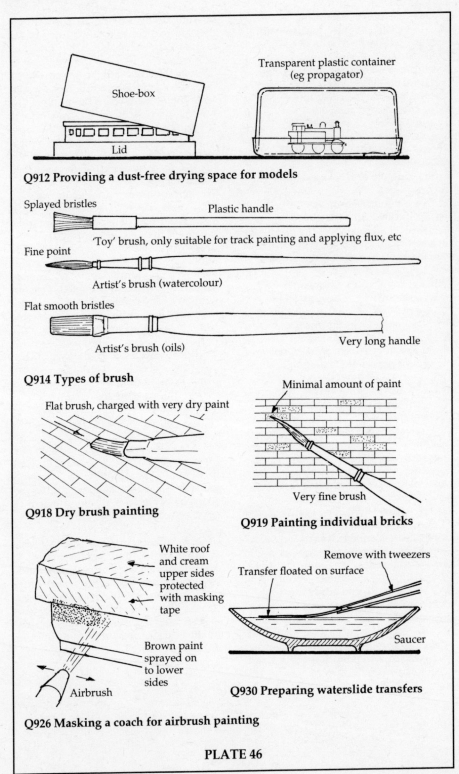

Q912 Providing a dust-free drying space for models

Splayed bristles   Plastic handle

'Toy' brush, only suitable for track painting and applying flux, etc

Fine point

Artist's brush (watercolour)

Flat smooth bristles

Very long handle

Artist's brush (oils)

Q914 Types of brush

Flat brush, charged with very dry paint

Minimal amount of paint

Q918 Dry brush painting

Very fine brush

Q919 Painting individual bricks

White roof
and cream
upper sides
protected
with masking
tape

Remove with tweezers

Transfer floated on surface

Saucer

Brown paint
sprayed on
to lower
sides

Q930 Preparing waterslide transfers

Airbrush

Q926 Masking a coach for airbrush painting

PLATE 46

925 **Is airbrush painting difficult?**
It is essential to apply the paint thinly with the nozzle held at an even distance from the model. It is largely a matter of practice to discover just how best to hold the instrument. Once the knack is learned, it is a lot simpler for large areas than brush painting.

926 **How do you apply two colours alongside each other with an airbrush?**
By masking the first colour, either with a masking fluid or with light adhesive tape; normal adhesive tape tends to be too sticky and lifts the first paint coat (see Plate 46). Frisk sheet, used by commercial artists, is also very good. It is as well to spray the lighter colour first.

927 **How does one avoid getting paint everywhere when using an airbrush?**
A paint booth is an essential accessory. Initially, a cardboard carton will do nicely, but for serious work a purpose-built booth makes life easier.

928 **Airbrushing leaves a dreadful smell of turps around the house. What should I do?**
If at all possible, work in an outdoor location. The garage is ideal; with the door fully open there is ample ventilation. Of course, spraying with a water-based paint leaves no smell.

929 **How does one get accurate lettering on a model?**
Transfers are available from good model shops. They are normally sold as sheets of associated styles.

930 **How do you apply transfers?**
The common waterslide type should be cut out and floated face down on water held in an old saucer (see Plate 46). When sufficiently moist, the transfer is lifted with tweezers and applied to the model. Surplus water is mopped off and the backing paper lifted gently off the transfer film.

931 **Is there anything that can be done about the backing film on water-slide transfers? It looks rather ugly.**
It is possible to trim the film very close to the lettering or insignia, using a scalpel on a firm base.

932 **Are there transfers without backing film?**
The varnish-type transfer has no backing film, and is applied directly on to a thin film of varnish or gold size applied to the model and allowed to dry. The backing paper is then moistened and removed. It is generally regarded as slightly more difficult to apply. Another version is bonded by methylated spirits, but this type (Methfix) is a little difficult to track down, although it is very popular with advanced workers.

933 **Is rub-on lettering available?**
These have been available in the past but aren't quite as easy to apply to a model as they might seem.

934 **Where does one get hold of transfers?**
Most model shops stock a selection, but the main showcase is at exhibitions. One problem is that model railway transfers are mostly produced by small firms and supplies are erratic. It is advisable to build up a stock for future use.

935 **Where can I get suitable transfers for locomotive nameplates?**
Apart from some stick-on alternatives for ready-to-run models, locomotive name and numberplates are made by etching brass sheet. Whilst a few specialised model shops carry stocks, it is usually necessary to order directly from the manufacturers, who advertise regularly in the model press.

PART 7
ODDS AND ENDS

This final section is something of a rag-bag of miscellaneous items mainly covering operation, clubs, exhibitions, troubleshooting and purchasing, with a few definitions to round matters off neatly.

Section 7:1
Operation

936 Is it necessary to operate a model railway in strict accordance with full-sized practice?

There is absolutely no reason why you should do anything more than play trains on your model if that is your pleasure. It's your railway – you run it as you like and if anyone objects you can treat him with contempt, always providing that you don't in turn try to lay down the law to him. However, it is generally agreed that it is more interesting to work the railway according to some form of schedule which mimics such facets of full-size operation as can be carried out within your necessarily limited resources of tracks and trains. If nothing else, it does ensure that the stock ends up in a convenient spot at the end of a session.

937 I have heard that some people are so obsessed with their timetables that they have been known to get up from the table in the middle of a meal to run a train. Is this so?

This appears to be one of those plausible tales which is vouched for by a friend of a friend but which cannot be pinned down to actual instances. However, the author has been told of a good friend who was reputed to have done just that. But as he has a very impish sense of humour, it is far more likely that he was quietly sending up a rather pompous individual.

938 I understand that some people have incorporated full-size signalling equipment into their layouts. Is it really necessary to go to such lengths?

Whenever two operators are out of direct contact, some system of communication becomes imperative, and prototype block instruments are a tried and tested method of passing trains safely from one section to another. In addition, the devices are lovely examples of the brass-and-mahogany technology of a century ago, and to keep them at work is a labour of love. Indeed, the only reason more are not so used is that the few remaining specimens are now cherished collectors' items and accordingly too expensive to use in this fashion.

939 How does one set about creating a timetable?

Creating a timetable from the ground up is not easy; one's mind usually blanks out. A simple solution is to look for a prototype line with a strong resemblance to your own and use that table as a basis for development. As you will probably be working from a public timetable, you will only have the passenger trains shown; goods trains can be fitted into the gaps. Once you have laid out your timetable on paper, you can set about testing it on the layout. It's quite likely that you will find that a fair proportion of your initial proposals call for more stock than you possess, or may even exceed the capacity of the line, but a little trial and error will enable you to iron out these difficulties.

940 Isn't there a more scientific approach to the subject than trial and error?

Prototype timetables are prepared by highly-skilled specialists using train graphs and complicated tables who, in the event of a major timetable revision, expend several hundred man-hours, backed up today by the use of powerful computers, in order to do this. One reason why timetables remain static for long periods is the sheer volume of work involved in making alterations. At the same time the fact that the tables are published and have to be circulated to the operating staff in the form of working timetables means that it is difficult to make anything other than minor alterations to train schedules. Railway modellers have no such restraints. Far from publishing timetables, few layouts owned more than the one master copy of the operating schedule until photocopiers became widely available; the only reason it might be difficult to effect a change is that it's too much bother to rewrite the schedule, which is a good reason for using pencil. Anyone with a home computer, printer and wordprocessing program can put the schedule on disk in a form that is not only readily modified, but which can be printed out fairly quickly should the need arise.

941 What is a train graph?

This is a graph with the various stations on the route represented vertically, and time represented horizontally. The departure and arrival times are plotted first, then joined with coloured lines, up and down trains being a different colour for easy distinction. The slope of the graph represents the speed of the train, the time spent standing in a station is represented by a horizontal line, and the train number is written alongside the line (see Plate 47). On single-line systems, trains have to pass each other at stations provided with loops. The train graph gives a very clear picture of what is going on.

942 How does a working timetable differ from the public schedules?

The working timetable (WTT) is a fully detailed document giving every scheduled train movement, including light engine movements. It details arrival and departure times for all stations and additionally gives the train number and other relevant information needed by the operating staff. Special trains and revised schedules to deal with public holidays, engineering works, etc, are notified in supplements, whilst appendices contain general operating details such as station sizes, permanent speed restrictions, etc, which are not in the main subject to change. WTTs were not supposed to be handed to members of the public, but BR now make spare copies of out-of-date tables available through Collectors Corner, near Euston station, and a fair number of older tables were passed to enthusiasts by friendly signalmen in the past. Many detailed line histories include extracts from the working timetables of various periods.

943 Must I lay out my timetable in the same way as is done in the British Railways timetable book?

There is no compulsion to do this, but the tabular form adopted seems to be the most easily read. It is, however, very unlikely that you will need quite so many footnotes.

944 I have seen operators at exhibitions flipping over cards and consulting them before moving a train. Why is this?

The layout is being operated on the flip card system. Each train movement is written out on a sheet of thin card which has two holes punched in it. Cards are arranged in a stack on two metal guides, and at the end of each movement the card is flipped over to reveal the next movement, hence the name of the system (see Plate 47). Many exhibition layouts arrange matters so that the discarded card hangs vertically and shows the details of the next train; this, however, makes it difficult to modify the schedule. The favoured source of the metal guides is either a worn-out ring-binder or a discarded arch file; the holes are produced with an office punch and the cards are standard index cards.

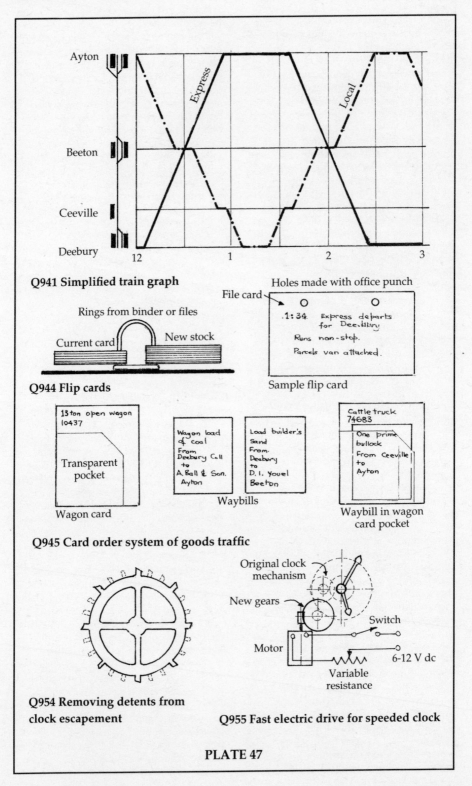

Ayton

Express

Local

Beeton

Ceeville

Deebury

12   1   2   3

Q941 Simplified train graph

Holes made with office punch

File card

.1:34   Express departs
        for Deebury
Runs non-stop.
Parcels van attached.

Rings from binder or files

Current card   New stock

Q944 Flip cards

Sample flip card

13 ton open wagon
10437

Transparent
pocket

Wagon card

Wagon load
of coal
From
Deebury Coll
to
A. Ball & Son.
Ayton

Load builder's
sand
From.
Deebury
to
D. I. Youel
Beeton

Waybills

Cattle truck
74683

One prime
bullock
From Ceeville
to
Ayton

Waybill in wagon
card pocket

Q945 Card order system of goods traffic

Original clock
mechanism

New gears

Switch

Motor

6-12 V dc

Variable
resistance

**Q954 Removing detents from
clock escapement**

Q955 Fast electric drive for speeded clock

PLATE 47

945 Can you explain the principles of the card order system of operation?

The card order system is a method, devised originally in the US, for adding realism to the operation of goods trains. There are three basic items involved: a pocketed card for every wagon in the fleet; a series of waybills; and a series of holders alongside every station and the fiddle yard to hold the wagon cards. A dice or other system of determining chance is usually employed.

The wagon card carries full details of the vehicle, owner, number, type of vehicle and traffic it can handle. The waybills describe loads, with point of origin and destination, and slip into the pockets of the wagon cards (see Plate 47). Initially the wagon cards are placed in a holder adjacent to their location. A number of waybills are then dealt out and the loads matched to wagons. In the case of open wagons, suitable dummy loads can be provided. The wagons are then deemed loaded and have to be routed to their ultimate destinations. It can occur that a special load is offered but no suitable wagon is available; in this case it has to be worked empty to the station. When the train is assembled, the wagon cards are placed in a different holder and any waybills that cannot be allocated are placed in a third. When the train leaves, the cards for the wagons are handed over to the next operator who finds out if any wagons are for him and then adds his own vehicles to the train. It is usual to set a limit to the number of wagons each locomotive can haul, leading to the position of an operator having to decide which wagons have priority.

This is only a bare outline of a system which is capable of considerable refinement to suit the special nature of the layout concerned.

946 I am now able to have my previously portable layout permanently erected. I now find that my timetable, which was previously very satisfactory, ends up with a lot of the stock in the wrong place, and I have to shuffle it by hand to start the day. Could you explain this?

The timetable is not satisfactory – it fails in what is sometimes said to be the whole purpose of the timetable, to ensure that everything is back in its starting place at the end of the working day. Because your layout was portable and you had to take all the stock off at the end of the session, the fault was masked. It looks as though you've another planning session ahead to get the stock where it should be, but now you don't have to dismantle the layout you can easily find time to run some extra trains.

947 If the running session is not long enough to run through the complete timetable, how do I keep track of where I have got to?

A very simple memory aid is a broken wristwatch – simply set the hands to the model time you reached, so that on your return you will know where you must restart. When a speeded electric-drive clock is used to govern the operating session, switch it off as soon as the last train of the session has run.

Part 7:2
Time and scale

948 I have seen a mathematical proof of the fact one cannot scale time. Could you explain this?

The so-called proof starts by assuming that a specific factor on the model, generally the revolutions-per-minute of the wheels, remains constant. This is then expressed as a mathematical formula. Unfortunately, it also means that one has the same factors on both sides of the equation, with the result that you end up, in effect, 'proving' that $1 = 1$! In short, the mathematics lack rigour as anyone with A level maths should know.

949 Is it possible then to scale time?

Certainly – this is done when using test tanks and wind tunnels. Froude's Law gives the mathematical relationship between scale time and real time, which explains why OO gauge toy trains can take 400 mm radius curves at scale speeds in excess of 200 kmph! A very convincing demonstration of this effect can be produced by making a pendulum, say, 1 m long, then making a scale model of it to hang alongside. When set in motion, the scale model oscillates very much faster, beating out one version of scale time. This apparent anomaly is commonly known as the scale effect.

950 Could you define what is meant by scale speed?

The generally accepted definition is that the wheels of the model should revolve at the same speed as the prototype. In addition, if a synchronised steam sound generator is fitted, the exhaust beats would sound the same. If these conditions are met, the model train appears to travel at a realistic speed past any nearby fixed item. Under these conditions we are working in real time, that is to say time as understood by both the operator and observer. Indeed, it is very difficult to see how any other concept of time can be used to create a pleasing visual effect on a working model, since the observer cannot alter his or her perception of time in the same manner that one can accept the concept of linear scale.

951 I have seen finescale layouts at exhibitions where the trains seem to take an inordinate time to get round the circuit, yet the operators insist that they are running at the correct speed. Could you explain this please?

This effect arises because, in scale terms, you are high up in a tower block some considerable distance from the railway. Were you to observe a full-sized train from such a viewpoint, it too would appear to be crawling. However, because you are in reality only a metre from the model, you believe that you are standing by the lineside. This is a neat demonstration of the abstract nature of scale and the way our senses can confuse us.

952 If we accept that our conception of time cannot be scaled, why do people use speeded clocks? Do these not show a scaled-down time?

Speeded clocks are normally used for timetable operation on a system where there is more than one operator; their function is to provide a common point of reference for timetable purposes. As inter-station distances are grossly under-scale, trains take very little time to travel between stations and so, in order to make the timetable appear rational, schedule time is adjusted accordingly. Station movements, however, have to be carried out in real time.

953 I have seen reference to reversing the hands of a clock to create a speeded clock. How is this done?

References to this appeared in early copies of *Model Railway News* and old textbooks, but no details of precisely how it was achieved were ever given and regrettably all concerned have taken the secret to their graves. The implications were that one changed round the hands and then reversed the gear drive so that the hour hand was on the minute spindle and the minute hand on the hour sleeve which now rotated 12 times faster instead of 12 times slower. In theory, this will work. However, inspection of the component parts of a broken clock will reveal that something more than a simple swap is needed, as the relative bores of the gears also need to be altered. This is a job for a skilled engineer with access to a lathe.

954 Are there other ways of speeding a clock?

A very effective system of speeding a clock is to remove a proportion of the detents on the escapement wheel (see Plate 47). This is best done with a worn-out alarm clock, where the wheel is a fair size in diameter and pressed from thin brass which is easily snipped away with a pair of angle cutters. This has the added advantage of rejuvenating the mechanism – the more rapid movement of the gears overcomes the wear in the simple bearings. A side effect is that the tick becomes even louder, which is not altogether a disadvantage since it provides an audible time signal to the operators. However, electric drive is the favoured method today.

955 How is an electric drive arranged for a speeded clock?

A redundant clock has its normal drive and escapement removed. A small low-voltage motor is then connected to a convenient spindle through whatever method seems most appropriate – spare clock gears, pulleys and even redundant worm and wheel gears from an old locomotive have been used (see Plate 47). The motor is controlled by a some form of variable resistance and an on-off switch is provided, since although it takes power from the layout's main supply, it is clearly necessary to switch this on at least a few minutes before operation begins in earnest. The resulting timepiece is somewhat erratic in performance, owing more to W. Heath Robinson than Thomas Tompion, but this is of no real consequence.

956 Is it necessary to have a speeded clock to operate a timetable?

If time is of the essence, then some form of clock is needed. However, for a simple home layout a sequence schedule, set out as if it were a timetable, is enough. Here the rule is that when the 08:15 local for Little Snoring departs, it *is* 08:15!

957 Some time ago I saw a layout at an exhibition where, from time to time, the hands of a prominent clock would move rapidly round, then slow down to normal time. Why was this and how was it done?

At many prototype junction stations the operating pattern consists of roughly a quarter of an hour when trains appear from every direction and concentrate on the station, and three-quarters of an hour where nothing much happens. An excellent way of operating such a line is to edit out the dull part of the schedule. The layout you saw uses the clock to tell visitors where operation has got in the timetable, which is prominently displayed alongside the clock so that viewers can identify the trains. The system of operation is simple – a normal mains electric clock drive is used, and the hands are advanced manually between the bursts of activity.

Section 7:3
Troubleshooting

958 The other day I switched on the layout, only to find that nothing would work. Could you suggest where I should start looking?

It may sound rather obvious, but is the power unit connected to the mains? It

has been known for the main plug to be removed from the socket in order to run the vacuum cleaner over the railway room. If it is plugged in, is the fuse OK? Fuses do fail from time to time, and whilst this is usually a case of having the fuse very close to the normal current rating (ie a 3 amp fuse on a circuit loaded to 2.5 amps), it can be that the fuse has been hit by a surge of current.

The next place to check is on the output side of the unit. Often a lead will have come loose, but in any case if you check whether there is an output, you will know that the power unit is performing correctly. It is then just a matter of slowly working along until you find where the break has occurred.

If the power unit appears to be inactive, remove the leads and check again. A permanent short circuit on the layout will actuate the internal cut-outs; removal of the load will let the power come on again. This could be caused by something as obvious as a metal object lying across the rails, but it is more likely to be a small pin that has fallen into a gap.

959 How does one check that current is flowing in a circuit?

The simplest method is to use a light tester, a small lamp with two trailing leads which are held across the circuit; if the lamp lights, all is well. A similar rig, including a battery, can be used to check the continuity of circuits (see Plate 48). However, the most convenient test equipment is a multi-meter. A cheap pattern, giving readings for dc and ac volts and ohms, is all that is required.

960 I'm a little confused by the number of options on my multi-meter. How does one use it to check model railway circuits?

To check if current is flowing, set the meter to read ac volts at 15 volts setting. This will allow you to apply the probes randomly, whereas the more obvious dc setting will not necessarily show a reading since you could have the leads in opposition.

To check the continuity of a circuit, set the reading to ohms. Check that the meter is correctly adjusted to give a full scale deflection when the probes are brought together, then clip one probe to the far end of the circuit and touch the other end with the other probe. If the needle doesn't flicker, the wire is broken.

It is useful to have a length of flexible wire, at least 2 m long, with a crocodile clip at each end. One clip can be connected to the circuit and the other to the probe, leaving one hand to hold the other probe and one to hold the meter.

961 If the meter suggests that a wire is broken, how can I find out where to repair it?

Ninety-nine times out of a hundred the wire is not broken, but is just not making proper contact at one end. Often it has simply fallen off the terminal. Check the ends first – if these are OK, cut the wire out of circuit and run another in its place.

Should you find that you are getting a lot of breaks in circuit, consider rewiring or at least relocating the cable run, since this is an indication that the cable is getting undue strain at one point. Should the cable have to twist, check that all wires are flexible; that is to say that they are made from a large number of very fine wires. Solid-core wire should only be used where the cable run can remain virtually undisturbed.

962 What is the best way of finding out where, on the layout, a persistent short circuit has occurred?

We assume that you have checked that no rolling-stock is derailed – this is a very common cause of short circuits, particularly where metal wheels and metal-bodied stock is concerned.

Begin by switching all sections off. If the fault persists, it is either in the control panel or in the leads to the control panel. Now switch on each circuit in turn – if the fault occurs, you know where it is. If the circuit is OK, *switch off* and check another. If, having done this, no fault appears, the cause is interaction between two circuits, a rare but infuriating fault, which is why you need to test each section alone.

Interactive short circuits are frequently caused by an item of rolling-stock bridging a section break. Whilst this is less likely with fully-insulated two-rail stock and common return wiring, it can happen.

963 What happens when something goes wrong in an electronic circuit?

You have problems! However, providing that the equipment is not subjected to extremes of heat, excessive voltage or current or – as often happens – is doused in coffee, chips carry on working for decades. The only cure is complete replacement of the faulty component, if this can be traced. Usually one has to replace the entire circuit board.

964 What is the best way of keeping the track clean so that pick-up is reliable?

Providing regular operation takes place, there is no need to do more than to burnish the top of the rails with a proprietary track cleaner, a hard rubber-based abrasive block. Heavy oxidisation will need something more drastic like fine wet-and-dry abrasive paper, either applied with the fingers or wrapped around a rubber block. It is also helpful from time to time to clean the rails of oily muck, and this is most readily done with a proprietary spot remover of the 'Dabitoff' type, sold to remove stains from clothes; the pad provided is just as effective for removing grease from rails as it is from cloth.

Commercial track-cleaning vehicles, used according to the maker's instructions, are very effective, and for larger layouts often prove invaluable.

965 All my trains slow down alarmingly at one point on the track. What is causing this and how can I rectify it?

This is almost certainly a case of voltage drop, caused by the fact that either you are feeding current at only one end of a very long section, or that the rail joiners are not making good contact. The simple cure is to put in an additional feed to the place where the speed is lowest (see Plate 48).

966 One of my locomotives is travelling more and more slowly. What is wrong?

It is almost certain that the locomotive is overdue for a check. It may be lack of oil, but more likely it is the result of over-oiling which has led to a build-up of muck in the mechanism. You need to

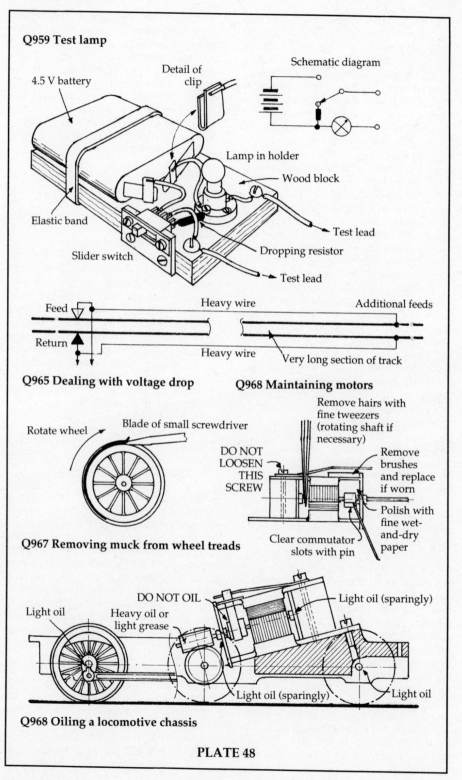

Q959 Test lamp

4.5 V battery

Detail of clip

Schematic diagram

Lamp in holder

Wood block

Elastic band

Test lead

Slider switch

Dropping resistor

Test lead

Feed

Heavy wire

Additional feeds

Return

Heavy wire

Very long section of track

Q965 Dealing with voltage drop

Q968 Maintaining motors

Rotate wheel

Blade of small screwdriver

Remove hairs with fine tweezers (rotating shaft if necessary)

DO NOT LOOSEN THIS SCREW

Remove brushes and replace if worn

Polish with fine wet-and-dry paper

Q967 Removing muck from wheel treads

Clear commutator slots with pin

DO NOT OIL

Light oil (sparingly)

Light oil

Heavy oil or light grease

Light oil (sparingly)

Light oil

Q968 Oiling a locomotive chassis

PLATE 48

remove the mechanism from the body and to clean every working part. Then apply a few drops of light oil to the bearings and a smear of heavier oil to the gears. If you haven't lost the maker's instruction sheet, check this for details. Some manufacturers provide basic maintenance instructions in their catalogues; it is a pity that they do not all do this.

967 A considerable amount of muck has built up on the wheels. What should I do about it?

About the only reliable way of removing muck from wheels is to invert the model and gently scrape the gunge from the treads; the most popular tool is a small screwdriver (see Plate 48). To avoid damaging the model itself, use a foam plastic cradle. By applying power to the pick-ups, locomotive driving wheels can be readily cleaned, though this should not be done if there are rubber tyres; special wire brushes are available for this purpose. In general, metal wheels are less prone to collect muck than plastic.

968 There is muck inside the motor. What should I do to get it out without doing damage?

This depends on the type of muck. Fine hairs, which have a habit of getting wound round the shaft close to the bearings, are best removed by gently pulling them out with tweezers. The gummy mixture of oil and dust can be winkled out with a toothpick, or washed away with cotton buds soaked in white spirit. Prevention is better than cure, so try to keep dust and dirt off the layout. Do not over-oil – this is the commonest cause of trouble; a single drop is enough at each bearing (see Plate 48).

969 How does one apply just a single drop of oil to a bearing?

Although some people use a hypodermic syringe filled with light oil, I prefer to apply the oil with a piece of thin wire. This not only makes it far too tedious to put too much oil into the motor, but wire has a further advantage – it is cheap and you can always find a suitable length in the scrapbox. For larger quantities of oil, bend the end of the wire into a tiny loop, which will carry quite a lot of oil over to the bearing.

970 I keep on getting derailments. How can I reduce these?

First and foremost you have to find out why the derailments are happening. One cause is excessive speed at curves, and here the cure is so obvious that few operators should have this particular problem – but they do! One reason why it is a good idea to run at 'scale' speed is that stock is far less likely to derail when running steadily than when it is dashing about at high speeds.

Next is faulty track. If the derailments occur in one place, check the track alignment and gauge; frequently it is not too difficult to see what is happening. If one vehicle derails all over the place, there is something wrong with it. Often a bearing has become misplaced, or a wheel has moved on the axle. Steam locomotive bogies and trailing wheels are very sensitive and can easily be accidentally bent when taking the locomotive off the track for storage. Occasionally the trouble is intermittent, the cause being one or two vehicles which are at one extreme of the working tolerances meeting a section or sections of track which are at the other extreme. This problem is exacerbated by excessive speed.

Finally, misaligned couplings can cause problems, particularly when reversing.

971 How do I retrieve a train that has derailed inside an inaccessible tunnel?

It is usually possible to fish the model out using a long length of wire with a small hook at one end – another use for wire coat-hangers! However, this should be regarded as an emergency procedure, for if it is a common occurrence you should set about making the tunnelled track accessible so that you can repair or, better still, relay it completely. Then work out how to make that section permanently accessible, either by the provision of some lift-off facility or by a strategically located handhole.

972 How does one reach stock that has derailed on the far side of the layout?

The only consolation when this happens is that it is a little easier to use the bent wire to fish the stock off the track than it is when the derailment has occurred in a tunnel. It is possible to use a pair of remote tongs, as used by street cleaners to pick up rubbish; this approach is employed on large permanent exhibition layouts. Basically, this is the sort of problem that should have been anticipated and a suitable access hatch provided.

973 **I have an old but cherished Hornby Dublo loco which I have had since I was a boy. It is no longer in working order. What can I do to get it back in running order as the manufacturer has gone out of business and spare parts are no longer available?**

Although Meccano Ltd are no longer in business, G. & R. Wrenn took over the Hornby Dublo tools and dies and are still making the locomotives, so it is probable that they can provide spares. This is an exception – in general, discontinued models do pose a spare part problem, the more so since, with reputable makes, parts rarely wear out in ten years of normal use and not infrequently are still in good order after a quarter of a century. Collectors often buy broken models to cannibalise for spares. Sometimes the only answer is to fabricate the broken part in the home workshop, but this almost always implies the use of a lathe. However, with the all-round improvement in the standard of railway models, the most satisfactory solution would be to buy a new model and retire your cherished locomotive to a display case.

Section 7:4
Purchasing

974 **A nearby toy retailer has a good range of model railway equipment. Should I go there in preference to a more distant model shop?**

It is your privilege to shop where you please, and your right to expect good service. Assuming that both concerns have knowledgeable staff, it is clear that the nearer store has one obvious advantage, though clearly a general toy shop will not carry the more specialised model kits and components that you will need sooner or later. Furthermore, at the model shop you are more likely to get advice on modelling problems.

975 **I live a long way from a regular model shop. How can I obtain the specialised kits and components that I need?**

The obvious answer is to make use of mail order, through the advertisement pages of your favourite magazine. This is fine, providing that you know exactly what you want and take pains to set this out clearly in your letter. Remember that with mail order, you buy sight unseen and that if things go awry, it is very difficult to rectify matters.

976 **What should I do to avoid difficulties with mail order?**

Make sure that everything is clear – print or type your name and address, and give a clear the description of the goods required, together with any specific requirements you wish to make. Do not try to write an essay – short, clear instructions are needed. Enclose a crossed cheque, postal or money order, or, if applicable, your credit card number. Do not under any circumstances send cash. State the amount sent with your order and indicate what the payment is for. Date the letter, take a copy and keep it safely. Allow 14 days for delivery unless otherwise stated – most model dealers offer far better service, and the main delays are in the post. In the event of non-delivery or other cause for complaint, refer to your original order, giving the date of the letter and using the same name.

All this may seem obvious, but the great majority of problems with mail order arise because the customer has failed to be crystal clear. You should never forget that, to a mail order firm, you are just another piece of paper with a remittance attached, not an individual with a recognisable face.

977 **Isn't there a Mail Order Protection Scheme to cover one in case of trouble?**

There is, but if you read the conditions carefully you will find that you are only covered if the firm concerned goes out of business and you make an application within a short time of this happening.

Fortunately, most magazines do their best to sort out difficulties, usually with considerable success.

978 Why don't the magazines bar the dodgy firms?

It is very difficult to prove beyond reasonable doubt that a firm is acting dishonestly; the normal reason that a transaction goes wrong is that a mistake has been made by one or other of the parties concerned. Certainly it would not be proper to take drastic action on the basis of one unsubstantiated complaint, as some indignant writers think should happen. Fortunately a dishonest or incompetent advertiser also fails to pay for the advertising, which gives the magazine proprietors an unassailable reason for withdrawing the offending insertions.

979 Is there an alternative to mail order for people living a long way from model shops?

Most model railway exhibitions are supported by one or more model shops and a selection of manufacturers. Two in particular, IMREX in London and the Bristol exhibition over the Spring Bank Holiday, are very well provided with trade stands. The specialist societies' shows also have excellent support from small manufacturers. To many enthusiasts, exhibitions offer a wonderful opportunity of not only seeing a wide range of products at first hand, but also of stocking up for the following year's modelmaking. Many regard the traders as personal friends.

980 My funds are limited. Where can I get the best bargains?

If we define a bargain as a wanted item at well below list price, then you require a good deal of persistence, infinite patience, an encyclopaedic knowledge of the products available and their value, together with a good deal of luck. You also need something few people with limited funds have, a supply of ready cash to snap up the bargains when you see them. The best place to find bargains is at an exhibition; generally you will need to be near the front of the queue on opening day as well.

Section 7:5
Clubs, societies and exhibitions

981 Need I join a model railway club?

No. Thousands of railway modellers enjoy their hobby without being a member of any body or organisation connected with the hobby. Benefits of membership only accrue from active participation; merely joining, paying a subscription and then sitting back waiting for someone to do something for you is futile. Hence you can only benefit if the meetings are held at a time and place you can attend, and if you are prepared to work as a member of a team.

982 If I join my local club, can I help operate the club layout?

The majority of British model railway clubs build layouts primarily for exhibition purposes; during the rest of the year the layouts are usually undergoing reconstruction or refurbishment. You can help build the club layout, you can help transport it to a show and help erect it. You can then help operate it.

983 Where can I find details of clubs and societies?

Your local public library should have details of your local club, which will probably hold some form of annual exhibition or open day. This will be advertised in the local press and, in all probability, by handbills and banners. Most magazines maintain a register of societies; it is probable that the one held by *Railway Modeller* is the most comprehensive. A letter to the Editor, accompanied by a stamped, self addressed envelope will bring an answer. To join, contact the Hon Secretary, enclosing a SSAE, or apply for membership at the club's exhibition.

984 There is no club near to my home or place of work. What can I do?

You can always start a club yourself. Write to the model press asking for interested individuals to contact you, then arrange a meeting. If numbers are small, meetings can be arranged in members' homes on a rota basis. A permanent club-room is not necessary at the outset – schools, church halls and community centres will hire rooms to amateur societies; your local public library can help with addresses. But be warned – you are likely to be the first Hon Secretary, which is hard work. On the other hand, if the club is a success, you will be The Founder, a rare and cherished distinction.

985 Why is there no national society in Britain?

The probable answer is that the existing local societies, even the worst-run groups, offer a better return for individuals than any overall body. Furthermore, these groups absorb most of the organising talent in the hobby. In addition, the large number of specialist societies catering for specific scales and gauges, which are national in character, siphon off most of the potential members of a national body, and again provide a service more attuned to the needs of the individual. There are in addition a number of specialised prototype societies covering the interests of former railway companies and overseas railways. All these bodies publish regular magazines, which are generally worth the subscription.

986 Isn't the Model Railway Club a national body?

In so far as membership is spread thinly over the whole of Britain, it can be considered as such, but since all its activities are based in London, this is merely a matter of semantics. The MRC – or to give it its full legal title, The Model Railway Club Ltd (by Guarantee) – is the oldest body in the hobby, having been founded in 1910. It owns the freehold of its clubrooms in Islington (Keen House) and organises the International Model Railway Exhibition (IMREX) through its wholly-owned subsidiary, Model Publicity Ltd. This is also the longest-running show in the world, dating back to member's displays held regularly before the First World War. Membership is open to any enthusiast and the clubroom contains one of the most comprehensive reference libraries in the country, but unless you can visit London regularly on Thursday evenings, you will only get the bi-monthly club Bulletin for your subscription.

987 There are several nearby societies which organise one-day shows. Is it worth while visiting these as they are quite small and don't attract any well-known layouts.

These unpretentious shows often offer better value than the larger, more popular affairs, simply because they are less crowded and you can therefore spend more time looking at the layouts without being jostled by other visitors anxious to see a slice of the action. The fact that the layouts are unknown doesn't mean that they are inferior. Above all, the more relaxed atmosphere affords a better opportunity to get to meet fellow enthusiasts in your immediate vicinity; many good friendships have been started at these local exhibitions.

988 How can I get my layout into an exhibition?

The best way is to join a club running a small weekend show and provide the exhibition organiser with a set of good photographs and a detailed sketch plan of the layout, giving its size. Allow at least 9 months lead time before a show, but most major exhibitions are set up anything from 18 months to two years ahead. If you have produced an interesting, reliable model, then your spare time will be curtailed for the foreseeable future as other exhibition organisers will ask you to attend their shows. You will meet a lot of interesting people and suffer a good deal of ill-informed criticism. You will learn a great deal about the hobby. Above all you will get the satisfaction that comes from doing a good job in a worthy cause, promoting a fine hobby.

989 I feel that a lot of exhibitions have too many trade stands. Do you agree?

Not at all. It is worth pointing out that two long-established specialist exhibitions, those organised by the Gauge O Guild and the EM Gauge Society, both have a high proportion of sales stands because their members wish it so. Indeed, it can be argued that no show can have too much trade for more than two years at the outside, for unless visitors to the exhibition patronise these stands, the traders concerned do not come again. Apart from the fact that the trade forms an integral part of the hobby, a large number of enthusiasts look on the major shows as a painless way of getting the more specialised kits and components that they need. Furthermore, the revenue from the trade stands covers a good deal of the cost of the show. Many critics fail to realise that if there were fewer trade stands at the larger shows, there would be fewer layouts, not more.

Section 7:6
Terminology

990 What is meant by a prototype? My dictionary defines it as the first example of a series.
You have a very basic dictionary. The term once meant the example from which copies were made, hence it has come to mean the full-sized original on which a model is based, and most modern dictionaries give this modelling usage. In railway modelling, it also refers to the full-sized railway system on which all our modelling is based.

991 What is the NMRA?
The National Model Railway Association, a body based in the USA, with flourishing branches wherever enough modellers following the US railroads are to be found. It has set standards for wheels and track which are universally applied throughout the USA and are gaining greater support throughout the world.

992 What is MOROP?
The Continental European equivalent of the NMRA. It too has set standards, but these are aligned to those employed by the major European ready-to-run manufacturers whose products form the backbone of Continental European railway modelling.

993 I have seen reference in old journals to the BRMSB. What is it?
The BRMSB was an ad hoc committee set up in the immediate post-war period to attempt to establish wheel and track standards for British manufacturers. It had a limited success, but lacking any positive support from the amateur side of the hobby, and only a limited compliance on the part of a small number of far-sighted firms, it gently faded away as members of the committee lost heart. The standards were in the main so close to the NMRA equivalents that most British firms aiming at the serious market for OO/HO have adopted these instead.

994 What is, or was, META?
The Model Engineering Trade Association, a body set up at the same time as the BRMSB in a laudable attempt to regularise the retail and manufacturing side of the hobby. It remained in existence until the early 1980s but faded away through sheer apathy on the part of both the public and the trade in general.

995 What is finescale and what scale does it represent?
Finescale, paradoxically, has nothing directly to do with the scale of the models, but refers mainly to their quality. In the main it involves the use of correctly proportioned components, in particular track parts and wheels, but in its fullest sense it also includes the detail fittings on the models themselves. Finescale modelling also demands close attention to prototype accuracy and, in most cases, involves a fixed timescale for the models. The standard modelling scales, 4 mm and 7 mm to the foot, are maintained.

996 Who or what were the 'Big Four'?
The four British main-line railway companies formed by compulsory amalgamation in 1923 were known collectively as the 'Big Four', since there were a number of small railways, mainly the electrified lines of the London Electric Railway and the Metropolitan Railway, plus a number of small light and narrow gauge railways, which remained independent. The main companies in order of size were the LMS (London, Midland and Scottish Railway), the LNER

(London & North Eastern Railway), the GWR (Great Western Railway) and the SR (Southern Railway). They were nationalised in 1948 to form British Railways, a name, incidentally, used in the 1930s by the 'Big Four' for joint publicity.

997 What was the Grouping and when did it take place?

After the First World War many of the independent railways of Great Britain were financially insolvent, so Parliament decided that the best policy was to amalgamate them into five larger systems. This was reduced to four when it was realised that the proposed Scottish group would be insolvent from the start! The amalgamation took place on 1 January 1923. For further details, and listings of the pre-Group railway companies, consult a general history of the British railway system.

998 What is meant by interlocking?

Interlocking is a means of linking a number of manual controls so that it is impossible to set up an unwanted, generally a dangerous, condition. In the context of railways it usually implies the linking of point and signal controls so that incorrect indications cannot be given.

999 What is meant by a 'block'? It sounds like an obstruction on the track.

This is a signalling term and a slight case of loose terminology – the correct term is block section, a length of railway between two home (stop) signals. In absolute block signalling, only one train is allowed into a block section at a time. Block signalling is so called because the line is assumed to be blocked by a train until shown to be clear. In US model railroad parlance, a block is an electrical section, and here there is an analogy to the signalling.

1000 Why is the term 'motive power depot' used instead of engine shed, and what is a sub-shed?

An engine shed is just that, a large building to stable one or more locomotives, whereas a motive power depot (MPD) includes all the necessary facilities to service the locomotives. These include the obvious things like turntable, water tank, water columns and coal stage for steam locomotives, and refuelling points for diesel locomotives, together with repair facilities, enginemen's canteen, stores and offices.

A sub-shed is a small depot without most of the frills, where from one to half a dozen locomotives are stationed to work the outlying parts of a division. The locomotives used here are, however, allocated to the main MPD. Most model locomotive facilities are technically sub-sheds.

1001 What exactly is meant by scratchbuilding?

Scratchbuilding is the art of producing a model from basic raw materials and, at the most, a few basic components, as opposed to making the model from a kit. Once the norm, in both OO and HO it is becoming something of a forgotten art except in the architectural field where the diversity of the prototype makes scratchbuilding more rewarding. Indeed, one leading 4 mm scale locomotive scratchbuilder was heard to remark recently that kits were so good today that there was little point in scratchbuilding a locomotive. This is a pity since the scratchbuilder has an infinite choice of prototype and the quiet satisfaction of being able to make his own errors of scale and detail without having them forced upon him. Whilst at its most advanced levels it calls for considerable skill and not a little dogged determination, elementary scratchbuilding is actually much less bother than trying to work out exactly how a complex kit should go together.

BIBLIOGRAPHY

This list of books is confined to those which are readily available at the time of writing and which I feel should be consulted. An asterisk indicates a book which, though dealing mainly with the more advanced features of the hobby, is nevertheless of value to a relative newcomer who wishes to make the most of the hobby. I make no apology for listing my own books!

General

Model Railways on a Budget
  C.J. Freezer (Patrick Stephens
  Limited)
Modelling the Steam Age Railway
  C.J. Freezer (Patrick Stephens
  Limited)
A Home for your Railway C.J.Freezer
  (Peco)

Planning

*The PSL Book of Model Railway Track
  Plans* C.J. Freezer (Patrick
  Stephens Limited)
60 Plans for Small Locations
  C.J. Freezer (Peco)
Track Plans for Various Locations
  C.J. Freezer (Peco)
Simple Model Railway Layouts
  T.J. Booth (Patrick Stephens
  Limited)
*Model Railway Layout Design**
  Ian Rice (Wild Swan)
*Railway Layout Designs**
  Ian Rice (Wild Swan)

Buildings and Scenery

The Peco Book of Model Buildings
  Mike Gill (Peco)
Landscape Modelling Barry Norman
  (Wild Swan)
Plastic Structure Kits Ian Rice (Wild
  Swan)
*Cottage Modelling for Pendon** Chris
  Pilton (Wild Swan)

Architectural Modelling Dave Rowe
  (Wild Swan)
Industrial and Mechanised Modelling
  Dave Rowe (Wild Swan)

Electrification

The PSL Book of Model Railway Wiring
  C.J. Freezer (Patrick Stephens
  Limited)
*Model Railway Electronics** Roger
  Amos (Patrick Stephens Limited)
*Practical Electronic Projects for Model
  Railroaders+* Peter J. Thorne
  (Kalmbach)

Locomotives

*The 4 mm Engine – a scratchbuilder's
  guide** R. Guy Williams (Wild
  Swan)
White Metal Locomotives Ian Rice
  (Wild Swan)
Etched Loco Construction Ian Rice
  (Wild Swan)
Model Railway Kit Building T.J. Booth
  (Patrick Stephens Limited)

Signalling

Model Railway Signalling C.J. Freezer
  (Patrick Stephens Limited)

* Advanced
+ Published in USA

INDEX

Note The numbers refer to question numbers, not page numbers.